ADVENTURES OF A CONTINENTAL DRIFTER

Also by Elliott Hester

Plane Insanity

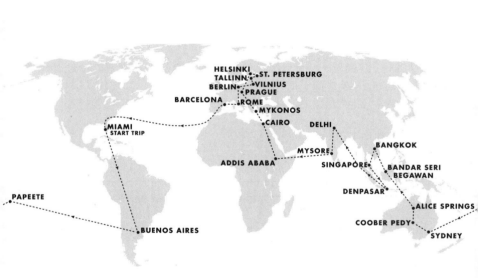

ADVENTURES OF A CONTINENTAL DRIFTER

AN AROUND-THE-WORLD EXCURSION INTO WEIRDNESS, DANGER, LUST, AND THE PERILS OF STREET FOOD

Elliott Hester

ST. MARTIN'S PRESS ≋ NEW YORK

"Don't Stare at Me, Argentina" previously appeared in different form in *National Geographic Traveler*. Portions of "Snoring in Paridise" and "Bad Night in Bangkok" previously appeared in *New York Newsday* and the *South Florida Sun-Sentinel*. "Bali by Motorbike," "The Long Camel Ride," "Snobs 'R Us," and "Hard Nipples, Limp Dicks" previously appeared in different form in the *Miami Herald, Chicago Tribune, Dallas Morning News, St. Petersburg Times, Cleveland Plain Dealer, Portland Oregonian,* and *Denver Post*.

www.stmartins.com

Library of Congress Cataloging-in-Publication Data

Hester, Elliott.
        Adventures of a continental drifter : an around-the-world excursion into
    weirdness, danger, lust, and the perils of street food / Elliott Hester.—1st ed.
        p. cm.
    ISBN 0-312-31241-5
    EAN 978-0-312-31241-1
        1. Hester, Elliott—Travel. 2. Voyages around the world. I. Title.

    G440.H545H47 2005
    910.4'1—dc 22

                                                                2005047709

First Edition: September 2005

10 9 8 7 6 5 4 3 2 1

This book is dedicated to the airline pilots, train engineers, tram operators, bus drivers, van drivers, tuk-tuk *drivers, ship skippers, ferry captains, rickshaw runners, motorcycle hacks, chauffeurs, cabbies, fuel-injected friends, and the guy in the battered Russian Lada who picked me up on Nevsky Prospekt and drove, in a post-*glasnost *fury, to the Sovetskaya Hotel.*

Thanks for getting me there in one piece.

Buckle your seat belt, Dorothy, because Kansas . . . it's going bye-bye.

—Cypher
The Matrix

CONTENTS

ACKNOWLEDGMENTS

This book began as an eighty-two-page proposal that my agent, Faith Hamlin, read with eager eyes. Intrigued by the concept of a solo trip around the planet, she messengered the proposal to my editor, Jennifer Enderlin. Editors think hard and long before bestowing a generous book advance—especially when the author plans to leave the country and write about events he or she has yet to experience. But Jennifer responded with a lightning-quick approval. For her trust, foresight, and unflustered patience, and for Faith's, I am forever grateful.

I'd like to thank Christi Phillips for giving solid writing advice when I phoned from Barcelona in a blank-page panic; Peter Blandori for hanging out with me in Russia, and for designing and maintaining my Web site; Daniel "Doc" Graham for jetting in and introducing me to Sandy Suppa (Buenos Aires) and Triinu Onton (Tallinn). They are among the world's good Samaritans, as are the following who welcomed me as a house guest: Jaime Malmad Goti (Buenos Aires); Janet Kline (Ubud); Raian Irani and family (Mysore); Michaela Vasickova (Prague); Mauri & Iina Forsblom (Helsinki); Denise Hoder and her sister Séverine (Berlin); my sister and brother-in-law, Dordie Hester & David Alcalde; and my niece, Nicole (Barcelona).

Thanks to the friends and strangers whose spare beds, air mattresses, and living room sofas provided safe havens over the years: Mateusz Sikora (Warsaw); Max Cullen (Sydney); Liddy Fleet (Sydney); the American blonde (Paris); Gilles Francfort (Paris); the two Swedish girls I met in Las Vegas (Stockholm); Tony Torres (Madrid); Jake Edgar (San Juan Bautista); Terry & Linda Bannon (Porlamar); Sonja Dumas (Port of Spain); Anthony Miner (Los Angeles); John Flinn (San Francisco); Cliff Rallins (Chicago); Raymond & Diane Pierce (Cleveland); Valerie Schields (Miami Beach); Brian Glaspy (Miami); Veronica Morrissette (Atlanta); Jay Peterson (Dallas); Michael Bennett, Anna Crankshaw, Anthony B. DePalma, Daryl Dismond, Lucien P. Redwood, and Rachel Straus (New York City—where the gutter was often my next sleeping option).

Finally, for contributions to this book, the trip, and my writing life, I'd like to express my gratitude to Ann Adelman, Ben Prost, Kim Cardascia, Cindy Cohen, Marc Levy, Shawna Ploen, Lisa Wells, Bill Albright, John Dufresne, Lynne Barrett, Elaine Petrocelli, and the annual Book Passage Travel Writer's Conference in Corte Madera, California. The struggle would have been infinitely more difficult without you.

INTRODUCTION

◀┄┄┄┄┄┄┄┄┄┄┄▶

The time had come for me to fly away.

Due in part to the September 11 terrorist attacks and the economic recession that worsened in their wake, American, United, Delta, Continental, US Airways, Northwest—virtually every major U.S. airline except no-frills goliath Southwest—suffered staggering financial losses that would force two carriers into bankruptcy and push others to the brink. Millions of passengers stopped flying. The number of scheduled flights diminished exponentially. Before the furloughs began, before thousands of airline employees were kicked to the proverbial curb, I pondered my own future on a flight from Miami to Barbados.

In those waning months of 2001, flight attendants, myself included, witnessed uncanny examples of in-flight compliance. Passengers sat quietly in their seats, eyes glued to the safety video as if Spielberg himself had directed Halle Berry in the tantalizing seat belt demonstration. Air rage had become a distant memory. Passengers and crew peacefully coexisted. People gnawed happily on chicken and beef, unaware that airplane meals would soon go the way of the Dodo. Indeed, the spirit of camaraderie was alive and well and living at thirty thousand feet. You almost expected to see passengers swaying in their seats and belting out the lyrics to *Kumbaya*. But by December 2001, when a Barbados-bound passenger pushed away her meal tray and glared at me as if I'd slapped her momma, the in-flight love fest had officially come to an end.

"I ordered a goddam vegetarian meal!"

"Excuse me?" I said.

"Meat is poison," she continued, looking up at me with a homicidal glint in her eye. "I'm a strict vegetarian."

"You mean, 'a goddam vegetarian,'" I replied. At least that's what I wanted to say. As is always the case during conflicts such as these, I stood quietly at one end of the meal cart and took the abuse like a professional. I apologized for the missing vegetarian meal, even though I was not the caterer who failed to load the meal into the goddam meal cart, or the reservationist who may or may not have included the meal on the goddam flight itinerary, or the passenger herself who may have changed flights less than twenty-four hours before departure (effectively canceling the special goddam order). After making a slew of excuses for the missing vegetarian meal, I did the only thing left to do. I re-offered the beef brisket.

In a flashback to the days of wanton air rage, the woman slammed her tray table against the seat back and gave me a nasty tongue-lashing. "You people are worthless," she said. "I've gotten better service from vending machines!"

The cabin grew silent, save for the whirring aircraft engines and an escalating hissing noise—courtesy of the cartoon steam shooting from my cartoon ears. Passengers looked up at me, their mouths hanging open as wide as my own. Veggie Woman hurled more insults. Insults that broke through the pane of professionalism and hit me where it hurts. In one of those face-saving failures we've all seen in situation comedies, my mouth began moving but no words came out. I just stood there—clad in a crisp poly-wool flight attendant uniform, an unwanted meal tray in one hand, a plastic cup of orange juice in the other—while

Veggie Woman delivered the *coup de grâce*. In a booming voice that seemed to shake the main-cabin fuselage, a voice that roared through first class, past the reinforced cockpit door, and possibly into the headset of a startled air traffic controller back at MIA, Veggie Woman told me exactly what to do. "GET AWAY!" she said, dismissing me with a flick of her wrist. "You're worthless."

This is what life had come to. Put in my place by an outraged vegetarian who'd neglected to bring a backup granola bar. In fact, a multitude of frustrations were beginning to mount on both sides of the aisle. Unprecedented cost-cutting measures eliminated main-cabin meals on many domestic and international flights. Hungry passengers went ballistic. So did flight attendants, who swallowed a 15 percent pay cut while facing a 30 percent increase in pissed-off passengers. To add insult to insufficiency, flight attendant crew meals were removed from virtually all long-haul flights at my airline—even the nine-hour trans-Atlantic routes where we continued to serve meals to passengers *and* pilots. My colleagues stalked the aisles like hungry vultures, searching for leftover food. Layovers became eight-hour pit stops allowing six hours of sleep before a fourteen-hour workday. Vacations shortened. Morale sank. A job previously touted as fun and exciting had become grueling, high-altitude factory work.

Some twenty years earlier, I took this job for the chance to travel the world. Madrid. London. Buenos Aires. Cedar Rapids. I've been fortunate enough to visit dozens of world-class cities in more than twenty countries; but due to short layovers, my exploits speak of barely being there: a view of Quito through the window of a speeding crew van; a gobbled, late-night dinner in a Tegucigalpa hotel room; a crowded Parisian nightclub seen through the fog of gin and jet lag. I longed to spend quality time at the destinations we flew to so often. I fantasized about traveling to obscure parts of the world. So, when the industry plunged into financial chaos and my airline offered leaves of absence to help offset the number of necessary furloughs, I jumped at the opportunity. Then I bought an airline ticket that would take me around the world.

Thrilled at the prospect of getting away from the job, I decided to take an extra step and get away from it all. Literally. I donated most of my clothing to a homeless shelter and gave all my books to a branch of the Miami Public Library. I opted out of my apartment lease. Sold my car, my Yamaha RX-V740 digital stereo system, every knickknack and piece of furniture accumulated over the years. The proceeds, along with meager savings, would allow me to travel for one year through perhaps twenty countries on all seven continents. Nevertheless, while standing on the southern tip of Argentina and looking across the Beagle Channel toward destination Antarctica, an icy wind came roaring from the polar cap and ripped into my flesh. Haunted by visions of clattering teeth and frostbitten testicles, Antarctica was deleted from my itinerary.

Traveling west across *six* continents, then, on a route that promised twelve months of summer and a budget of about sixty dollars per day, I hooked up with locals who led me to new lows of adventure. I became an unwitting accessory to murder in a French Polynesian cow-poaching incident, got drunk on Estonian moonshine at the maker's eightieth birthday party, was ripped off by virtual teenagers at an Internet café in Brunei, and lived with an Indian family that treated me as one of their own—even though I arrived in Mysore at the peak of the SARS epidemic plagued by a suspicious fever. After being convinced to impersonate Samuel L. Jackson at the thirty-eighth annual International Film Festival in Karlovy Vary, I dined with Ivetu Bartoŝovou, the Czech Republic's most famous (and perhaps the world's most gullible) female pop singer.

Along the way, I took thirty-four flights on fourteen different airlines. I rode in twenty-two long-distance buses, cars, and trains (including a thirty-five-hour nightmare from Delhi to Bangalore), and spent thirteen spectacular days sailing across the South Pacific on an aging cargo ship. In spite of the mileage and the mayhem and the waterborne amoeba that had me sprinting to the toilet faster than you can say "Kaopectate," in spite of the 250-pound Tahitian transvestite who tried to seduce me on a local bus, the Russian hooker who just wanted to be my "friend," the corrupt cop in Denpasar, the porno shop stalker in Berlin, slobbering Egyptian camels, man-eating Aussie flies, and the wriggling trout I clubbed to death near Tallinn, in spite of all that went wrong during my around-the-world adventure—and because of all that went so wonderfully right—I am indebted to an airborne vegetarian. "GET AWAY!" she said, on that fateful flight to Barbados. I promptly unpinned my wings and followed her goddam advice.

Argentina

DON'T STARE AT ME, ARGENTINA

The first thing I noticed were the stares.

Late one night in Buenos Aires, as summer held the city in a hot and sweaty grip, I walked through a gauntlet of outdoor cafés and was caught in the crossfire of quick sidelong glances. I was scrutinized over pizza amid the babble of Restaurante Piola, appraised by a sea of eyes beneath the thumping disco lights of Divino Buenos Aires, and at 4:30 A.M., my verve and pesos lost to the city's unrelenting nightlife, I returned to my hotel and met the conspicuous gaze of a suddenly not-so-sleepy desk clerk. The stares came not simply because I chose to wear my hat backward in a city where headgear is a definite fashion *faux pas*. The stares came because I am black—a fact that attracted attention the moment I arrived at the airport. Tired and bleary-eyed after the nine-hour all-nighter from Miami, I was confronted outside customs by a crowd of Argentineans who stared, unabashed, as if Scotty had just beamed me down from the U.S.S. *Enterprise*.

In Argentina, in contrast to other South American countries, blacks are as rare a sight as Mormons in South Central Los Angeles. As common as snow in Sydney or rain in the Sahara. Of the 37 million people who populate what is often referred to as "the Europe of South America," 97 percent are of white European origin. The remaining 3 percent are either indigenous or *mes-*

tizo (a mixed race of indigenous peoples and Europeans). Lost and officially unaccounted for are a smattering of blacks, descendants of slaves who by some accounts made up nearly 50 percent of the rural population in the late 1700s. Due to high mortality rates, migration, the decline of the slave trade after 1813, and a successful campaign aimed at "whitening" the country with European immigrants while eradicating nonwhites in the process, the black Argentinean population receded to its present state of near invisibility.

So there I was on my second night in Buenos Aires, a black North American waiting for a doorman to hail a cab in front of a spiffy hotel on Moreno Street, when two female pedestrians gave me a double dose of what I began to regard as "the Argentinean eyeball." They stopped, turned, and stared with an intensity that left me feeling as if I'd done something wrong. But theirs was not a look of repugnance, I soon realized. Not the narrow-eyed glare from narrow-minded people back in the days when I braved the wrong neighborhood in my hometown of Chicago. These were, rather, prolonged looks of fascination. Unblinking acknowledgments by curious locals who rushed over to say hello.

They spoke in rapid bursts of Spanish, posing questions that were quickly lost in a labyrinth of rolling *r*'s. Unable to decipher the language, I turned to the doorman. "*Señor*," he said. "They would like you to pose with them for a photograph." Upon hearing the translation, I laughed out loud. The two women looked at each other, hesitated, and then laughed along with me. When a camera materialized, I began to laugh even harder. These fashionably dressed ladies stared at me goo-goo-eyed as if Denzel Washington were smiling back at them instead of a wandering flight attendant. Flattering though it may have been to pose with two beautiful Argentinean women, a pessimist would raise a wary eyebrow. My ethnicity, he might say, was being singled out, mocked, carnivalized by people who live in a country where, according to my *Lonely Planet South America* guidebook, "non-Europeans have generally been unwelcome." Back home in the United States, I have been eyeballed by department store security guards, glared at by suspicious cops, and regarded on numerous occasions as though I were an alien in my own country. Had I never left the South Side of Chicago, had I not been afforded an opportunity to travel the world, to see myself apart from negative images often projected upon me at home, perhaps I may not have taken so kindly to a couple of white foreigners who stuck a camera in my face and asked for a smile. Alas, globe-trotting broadened my view of the world, which has broadened my sense of self.

I've come to realize that being different—whether you're a black among whites, a Christian among Muslims, or a bleeding-heart Liberal in a land of staunch Conservatives—is almost always cause for a double take. And in being different, one might possibly pique the ire of an unenlightened local. On at least two occasions, my skin color provoked racial slurs that were translated grudgingly by a bilingual traveling companion. But more often than not, being different has been the catalyst for acts of kindness and inclusion whenever I'm traveling abroad.

I have been coddled by paternal Italians, sheltered by benevolent Swedes, fattened by poor Indonesian families, and protected from encroaching assailants by big badass Aussies who chose to kick *arse* before taking names. Although I am often mistaken for Samuel L. Jackson due to my skin tone and predilection for Kangol hats, although presumptions are made about my prowess on the basketball court as well as on the dance floor, I've learned to surreptitiously roll my eyes while I roll with the punches. It's the acts of kinship, not the blunders, that frame my traveler's constitution.

As for the two Argentinean women who asked for a photograph, I acquiesced wholeheartedly. Poses were concocted. The camera flashed. Black-and-white images became etched onto color film. After a volley of *gracias*, a language-locked silence fell between us. We stood there on the sidewalk, staring at each other like actors who'd forgotten their lines. Three people in a city of 14 million. Two cultures unable to bridge the gap. Then suddenly, as if strafed by two Argentinean attack planes, my face was riddled with double-cheeked kisses. *"Tu eres bonito!"* they said.

Seemingly startled by the passion in her own hastily delivered smooch, one of the women giggled and stared deep into my eyes. Something passed between us. Something sweet and pure and prophetic. Something I chose not to spoil with a mundane request for her telephone number. Something . . . okay, okay. So I *did* ask for her telephone number. But what would you expect, given the circumstances? She looked exactly like Monica Bellucci who, along with lasagna and tiramisu, happens to be one of Italy's most scrumptious contributions to the world. (I can still see Monica squeezed into that tight latex dress in the restaurant scene from *The Matrix Reloaded*. Never—and I mean *never*—has a woman looked more seductive on film.)

"Sí?" she said, squinting in response to my telephone number query. Her dark eyes shimmered in the dim glow from the street light. Coiled locks cascaded against squared shoulders. She smiled slyly. It was a smile that seemed to say everything there was to say. A smile that telegraphed intent. The next thing I knew we were naked in my hotel room, moaning and groaning toward a fifth or sixth orgasm.

"Sí!" she cried, in a voice that could melt Parmesan. *"Sí, sí . . ."* She was oiled with perspiration. Her hot skin glistened in the flickering light from the television screen. Eyes shut, face contorted in a rictus of delight, her hips bucked in violent spasms, faster, faster still, lifting both our naked bodies from the sweat-soaked sheets peeling back from the corners of the quaking queen-size bed. *"Sí, sí . . ."* Hands against the headboard, she hurled her crotch against mine, swallowing me in wet pelvic slurps that sent blood rushing to my loins like fire down a trail of gasoline. "Monica! Monica! Ohhhh, MONICA!"

And then I realized we were still standing on the street.

"*Sí?*" she said, still squinting.

"Huh?"

"*Sí?*"

"Oh. Ahhh . . . Please. Give. Me. Your. Telephone. Number."
She gave me a quizzical stare instead. Either she didn't understand a single word of English, or I had actually shouted Monica Bellucci's name on the street. As it turned out, she knew at least three English words. "Bye-bye," she said, shrugging her shoulders apologetically. "No English."

"But, but . . ."

"No English," she repeated.

"No Spanish," I said, waving good-bye.

Linguistically defeated, I watched the two women move along the sidewalk, their twin shapes vanishing like ships heading out to sea. "*Tu eres bonito,*" they said in unison, blowing playful kisses over their shoulders. "*Tu eres bonito!*"

A moment later my taxi leapt onto an avenue wider and more chaotic than the Champs-Elysées. Instead of marveling at the ornate nineteenth-century buildings, the towering *oblisco,* the glassy cafés of Recoleta and the fashionably dressed patrons cloistered inside, instead of inhaling the great glittering cityscape in one trembling breath, I banged my head against the window and cursed my monolingual soul. Right then and there I swore, on an imaginary stack of *Biblias,* to enroll in a crash course at Berlitz.

THE COLOR OF FÚTBOL

◀ ·························· ▶

I went to a riot and a soccer match broke out. It happened in Buenos Aires on a warm day beneath a blue sky at Antonio Liberti Stadium. After the match ended and the first projectile had been hurled, after policemen descended upon us with their truncheons raised, after shirtless men dry humped at the enemy and Carolina tried to yank off her panties in protest, I had been converted from a nonbeliever into a raging soccer fan.

Allow me to explain.

Like many North Americans who grew up with baseball, basketball, and football, I had never attended a professional soccer match. Aside from twenty-second highlight clips on ESPN, I never watched soccer on television and could not understand why the rest of the world was captivated by a low-scoring sport that seemed best appreciated during twenty-second highlight clips on ESPN. So when Sandy Suppa invited me to the most anticipated *fútbol* match in Argentina, I went along, hoping I wouldn't nod off in my seat.

"Whatever you do, don't wear blue and gold to the stadium." Concerned for my safety, Sandy, a lovely dark-haired local, had issued the warning, which I heeded. She's a longtime friend of my buddy Daniel "Doc" Graham, a Los Angeles–based flight attendant who had flown in to see her and the match. Together with

Sandy's pal Carolina—a rabid *fútbol* fan who spoke only three words of English, "Son of bitch," and used the phrase repeatedly before, during, and after the match—we rushed toward the stadium. In our haste, we made a near-fatal mistake.

Hundreds of fans, almost all of whom were dressed in red and white, flooded down a single lane en route to what Sandy claimed would be a thrilling contest. This much-anticipated match pitted the Boca Juniors against archrival River Plate. In spite of the "championship game" atmosphere (a massive crowd, prodded with one hundred thousand volts of anticipatory excitement, surging toward the gates, chanting, screaming, waving banners), this was not a championship game. A number of teams needed to play additional games before the championship matchup could be decided. And yet for Boca and River fans all across Argentina—a country split down the middle in fanatic devotion to either red and white (River) or blue and gold (Boca)—what seemed to matter most was *this* particular contest. A pregame television interview, which aired after the match, captured the state of emotion. A news reporter asked a River fan, "Which is more important, winning this match against Boca or winning the championship?" The River fan responded without hesitation. "Beating Boca is all that matters."

Sandy and Carolina are big-time Boca fans. By association, so were Doc and I. By some quirk of fate, however, Sandy had steered us into River territory. The closer we moved toward the stadium, the more red and white jerseys surrounded us. With each increasingly tentative step, the stream of red and white grew thicker, flowed less rapidly, turned into a mob. That's when I realized we were being eyeballed from all directions. Teenage boys threw sidelong glances. Groups of men dressed in red and white looked our way and mumbled to themselves. Two guys walking in front of us spun around and glared defiantly. In a country devoid of blacks, Doc and I had attracted attention. Even if we managed to sneak away, Doc's bleached-blond hair, à la Dennis Rodman, painted a target that would be impossible to miss.

As we moved closer to the stadium the gawking became more prevalent, the mumbling more pronounced. Someone yelled at us in Spanish. Something cruel and harsh and insulting. Judging from Carolina's response, the comment must have been particularly offensive. She responded by flipping the Finger, which was followed by her favorite English phrase, "Son of bitch!" As if that wasn't enough, she put the tips of her fingers against the bottom of her jutting chin and flicked toward our assailant as if ridding herself of fleas.

Another shout. More heads turned in our direction. Without warning, Carolina jammed her thumb and forefinger beneath the waist of her blue jeans. She pinched the elastic waist of her panties and pulled up and out like a magician preparing to snatch a tablecloth from a setting of porcelain and crystal. Then she sort of jutted her butt in the direction of our assailant as if to say, "Kiss my ass," or, "Eat my shorts." Or, in this case, "panties." Blue and gold panties. Boca Juniors panties. It seems that Carolina was a Boca fan right down to her underwear. She wanted everyone in the vicinity—especially the racially intolerant heckler—to know she didn't give a shit about their opinions, ethnic or soccerwise. That's when the cold, hard hand of understanding reached out and slapped me in the face. The River fans weren't staring at me and Doc. They hadn't insulted *us*. They didn't give a damn about the color of our skin. Couldn't have cared less about the color of Doc's hair. The only color they cared about, the *colors* drawing so much resentment, had been the blue and gold of Carolina's Boca Juniors jersey. Unlike me and Doc, she had refused to heed Sandy's warning.

A five-foot, four-inch blonde weighing no more than fifty kilos, Carolina stood as the lone representative of the team River fans love to hate. And now, the unabashed Boca devotee had taken it upon herself to incite the enemy. They looked at us as if we were four malignant tumors. A gang of red and white disciples puffed up their chests in preparation for one of those infamous Argentinean ass-kickings that happen at every soccer game. Doc and I exchanged a glance that would probably be our last, thanks to Carolina's panty-pulling antics. "Come with me to the *fútbol* match," Sandy had said. "It will be much fun. But whatever you do, don't wear blue and gold." I followed directions and so did Doc. But Carolina didn't give a good goddam. As the red and white circle closed in on us, she stood there, unblinking, her tiny breasts puffing up defiantly beneath a banner of blue and gold.

Before the first punch could be thrown, an alert police officer spotted Carolina's blue and gold jersey amid the encroaching red and white aggressors. Shouting in Spanish and then shaking his head at our stupidity, he waved us over to the far side of the stadium, where we found the designated avenues for Boca fans.

Surrounded by friendly blue and gold supporters, I felt the air crackle with new energy. Groups of shirtless men danced in the street chanting, *"Bo-ca! Bo-ca! Bo-ca!"* Cheering clusters waved blue and gold banners and burst out in song. A distant roar from the stadium spurred the crowd into a sudden frenzy. We ran with the masses and were subsequently stopped at one, two, maybe three security checkpoints at which backpacks were searched, purses squeezed, intentions scrutinized. Policemen in riot gear sat atop fidgeting horses, scanning the madness with slitted eyes. Policemen stood in skirmish lines, holding German shepherds on taut leashes. I saw hundreds of policemen. Policemen clutching rifles. Policemen gripping tear gas launchers. A row of policemen with ammunition belts slung across their chests like Mexican banditos. One officer, the corners of his mouth pulled down in a formidable grimace, locked eyes with me. He slapped a truncheon repeatedly against his open hand as if eager for an opportunity to crack my skull. A police helicopter hovered above the madness, the thwacking rotors muffled by a loud systemic clamor from an irrepressible swarm of *fútbol* fans. Instead of a sporting event, we appeared to be heading for a riot.

At the entrance, everything seemed to happen at once. The crowd surged. A wall of policemen, their hands thrust forward, compelled us to stop. Carolina stumbled, caught herself. "Son of bitch." Doc's big blond Dennis Rodman head towered above the masses. Sandy. Where the hell was Sandy? Someone snatched my ticket. The heaving crowd pushed my body through a rusted turnstile. My camera? My wallet? Sandy? There she was ahead of us, being pushed into the stadium by the sheer force of the crowd.

With one great shove, several hundred bodies lurched up and into the stadium bowl. Thirty minutes before game time and the stands were already packed. Red and white banners hung across a sea of River fans on the far side. Confetti exploded overhead. Hundreds of red and white balloons shook to the rhythm of a warring drumbeat. In response, hundreds of blue and gold flags shook on the near side. Blue and gold balloons. Blue and gold pom-poms. Elaborate blue and gold signs, representing Boca-friendly barrios such as MTE. CHINGOLO, V. CARAZA, and PASO DEL REY. The two opposing fan groups were separated near the middle of the stadium by a barbed-wire fence that began at the first row of seats near the playing field and ran to the top of the bowl. As an added measure of precaution, truncheon-wielding policemen were positioned every few rows along the lengths of both fences.

The playing field had been littered with confetti to such an extent that only patches of grass were visible. Fifty thousand out-of-control fans screamed as if their lives depended upon the level of vociferousness. Judging by the celebratory cheers from both sides of the stadium, it seemed as though both sides had declared victory even before the players trotted out on the field. When we finally reached our seats at the very top of the bowl—the "safe seats," Sandy had called them, due to the proximity to escape routes—I asked about the massive police presence. "The people, they lose control," she said. "Someone here is always getting killed."

Eight months earlier, a local fourteen-year-old boy was beaten to death by rival fans at a match between Estudiantes and Gimnasia. That same day, according to *Sports Illustrated*, "pre-game violence at two [Buenos Aires] soccer matches left two men dead and twelve others injured, including six police officers." Argentinean soccer violence is directly responsible for more than 150 deaths and thousands of injuries since 1930. So prevalent are knife attacks and fistfights between opposing fans in and around Buenos Aires soccer stadiums that innovative peace promotions like the one handed to me are now distributed to ticket holders. The glossy card displayed an image of two boys, their backs to the camera. One kid wore a blue and gold Boca jersey, the other River red and white. Each slung an arm over the other's shoulder in a gesture of friendship. Bold type above their heads pleaded to the feuding masses: NO MAS VIOLENCIA!

In spite of the ominous atmosphere—or perhaps because of it—I felt a sudden pang of excitement. As the players rushed onto the playing field, fifty thousand spectators responded with a roar to end all roars. The roar of fifty thousand jumbo jets blasting off from fifty thousand runways. The powerful sound shook the stadium. Shook my very soul, in fact. Before realizing what had happened, I was jumping up and down between Carolina and Sandy, shouting right along with them: *"Bo-ca! Bo-ca! Bo-ca!"* Doc seemed to have been swept up in the moment as well. With one fist raised in the air he cheered along with us: *"Bo-ca! Bo-ca! Bo-ca!"*

When the Boca Juniors scored an early goal, I suddenly knew what it felt like to be Brad Pitt. As cheers erupted, Carolina flung her arms around my torso, pelting me with kisses and staring at me wide-eyed as if she were experiencing a heart attack. But when River Plate responded with a score of their own, Carolina's eyes filled with tears. Thousands of Boca fans fell silent.

With the score tied 1–1, the match became a defensive battle. Each time a player attempted to kick a goal, fifty thousand fans held their collective breath. The tension was not lost upon me or my bladder. Sandy pointed toward the toilets. I jogged up the stairs to the top of the stadium—past row after row of mesmerized Boca fans—hoping to find relief. I found something quite different instead.

Of the thousands of men in attendance, not a single one could be found in the men's room. It took only one second to understand why. A dim, flickering light revealed a small concrete chamber outfitted with a few doorless toilet stalls. The bathroom mirror had been fashioned from a sheet of dull aluminum. The sinks were rusted and seemingly unusable. The toilet stalls were flooded with maybe an inch of murky water. Lacking a toilet cover and flip-down seat, the naked toilet bowl bore the dark stains of neglect.

In an effort to preserve my Nikes, I put one foot on the ridge of the dirty toilet bowl, then the other foot, lifting myself above the fetid swamp. I stood there, on top of the toilet, peeing between my feet, spellbound by aim and trajectory, when an untimely shift of weight made me lose concentration as well as my balance. I slipped from the precipice. Like a fireman losing his grip on the hose, I inadvertently sprayed the walls on my way down. Miraculously, one foot splashed down on the ground. The other ended up in the pot I had just pissed in. "Shit!" Luckily, there was none in the toilet.

Wearing one dry Nike and one wet and stinky one, I wobbled back and took my place between Sandy and Carolina. Neither seemed to notice me or my Nike. They stared at the action on the field as if their lives depended on the outcome.

Shortly before time expired, Boca scored what turned out to be the winning goal. The Boca section exploded in celebration the likes of which I'd never seen. Perhaps twenty thousand voices roared in unison. Carolina damn near leapt out of her blue and gold Boca Juniors panties. Sandy threw her hands in the air. Banners shook. Shirtless men humped the air in River's direction, making suggestive hand motions with each pelvic thrust. Men kissed each other on both cheeks, dancing in circles, arms flung around one another like Allies after the fall of Berlin. Chest-thumping Boca fans—men, women, boys, girls—tossed back their heads, raised their arms, and let loose a chorus that arced high across the playing field and pierced the heart of every wilting River fan.

> *Boca no tiene marido, Boca no tiene mujer.*
> *Pero tiene un hijo bobo pue se llana River Plate.*

> (Boca has no husband, Boca has no wife.
> But it has a mentally retarded son called River Plate.)

The cruel lyrics lashed out again and again, growing louder with each repetition. Ugly lyrics. Politically incorrect lyrics. The kind of lyrics even the most depraved spectators would refuse to sing back home. Caught in a flood of blue and gold passion, I suddenly found myself chanting along with them. Lacking a Spanish tongue, my rendition sounded something like this:

> *Boca no tanny medo, Boca no tanny moho.*
> *Perry tanny a yee-ha hobo poodie River Plate.*

Unable to withstand the insults any longer, River fans began hurling objects from their side of the barbed-wire fence. Boca fans retaliated with projectiles of their own—crumpled paper cups, empty cigarette packs; someone may have thrown a smuggled rock. The brawl was about to begin. Truncheons raised, policemen rushed from their positions along the fences, attempting to herd Boca fans toward the exits. But thousands of blue and gold supporters refused to leave. And then it happened: The first skirmish broke out. Beneath the rafters, several cops grabbed a skinny teenager who had waved a blue and gold pom-pom in their faces. They pinned him to the ground and were pelted with insults from the increasingly unruly crowd.

"We have thirty minutes to get out of here," Sandy said. "That's when police unlock the exits on the River side." (In an attempt to avoid violent confrontations outside the stadium, home team fans are required to wait behind locked gates until the visiting fans have time to get away.) Following Sandy's lead, Carolina, Doc, and I tried moving toward the exit. Our progress was blocked by impenetrable hordes of revelers who broke out in song. They sang a rousing *fútbol* hymn that I could neither understand nor appreciate—at least not at first. Soon, thousands of voices joined in, filling my ears with a hypnotic chant that had me wandering among the masses and away from my friends.

In the midst of the madness I saw a man, a bug-eyed man. Beer-bellied and bursting with an emotion that could have been anger or joy, he removed his T-shirt and began to swirl it in the air. Something about me must have caught his eye because he looked up and pointed out my face in the crowd. Singing that song and swirling his shirt, the man jabbed his finger at me again and again. I don't know what came over me, don't know why I did it, but I snatched off my T-shirt, swirled it in the air, and jabbed my finger back at him. Separated by a few feet and dozens of shirt-less revelers, the two of us jabbed and swirled, jabbed and swirled—working ourselves into a frenzy that spread to one guy and then another until everyone around us seemed to be swirling their shirts and jabbing at each other. I began the familiar chant: *"Bo-ca! Bo-ca! Bo-ca!"* The pot-bellied man kept swirling the T-shirt, his eyes widening as he sang along with me. *"Bo-ca! Bo-ca! Bo-ca!"* More voices joined in—dozens, hundreds, a thousand maybe—changing the chant into a universal drumbeat that merged with the beating of my heart. *"BO-CA! BO-CA! BO-CA!"* Suddenly, I knew what it meant to be an Argentinean *fútbol* fan.

Passion is a fleeting thing, or so the saying goes. In less than twenty minutes the gates on the opposing side of the stadium would be unlocked; thirty thousand pissed-off River fans would be free to explain what it *really* means to be an Argentinean *fútbol* fan. When I realized this, my T-shirt froze in midswirl. I squeezed through the surging crowd, found my three friends, and made a beeline for the exit.

LOVE AND THE BAD EMPANADA

◄........................►

The double-decker Andesmar bus to Salta departed mid-afternoon and arrived twenty-two hours later at a depot in the dusty northwest region of Argentina. The ride was a surprisingly smooth one, not the cramped back-roads bumpathon I'd imagined it would be. My seat, one of only seven or eight on the lower deck, was as large and relaxing as a first-class throne on a small commercial aircraft. In fact, the cabin resembled the premium cabin of a McDonnell Douglas MD-80—albeit smaller and not as clean, with worn seat covers, inoperative reading lights, rattling windows, and, instead of a curtain separating the first-class cabin from tourist class, a wall dividing our cabin from the cargo compartment. Still, this was comfort. The majority of passengers had been accommodated in the lengthy upper deck, although smaller seats and a dense configuration allowed less personal space. All were served soft drinks by an unsmiling attendant and entertained by three successive movies, the last of which, *Remember the Titans*, featured my favorite actor, Denzel Washington.

I watched the first film, gazing intermittently out the window at grazing cows and dusty pueblos backlit by a slanting sun. It was the very best of bus rides. A discount traveler's dream come true. It might have been perfect if not for the tainted empanada.

The empanada is Argentina's most popular food. The farther north you travel from Buenos Aires, the more often empanadas appear on restaurant menus. Stuffed with ground beef, mine had been purchased at a greasy diner in a greasy bus depot somewhere north of Sante Fe. Even before I tasted it, I knew this particular empanada was bad. The dough crunched as my teeth sank into it. That's when I noticed the meat. Hard as pebbles, it had been fried beyond recognition. But common sense gave way to hunger. While a smirking cook eyed me from behind the counter, I sat on a stool chewing gravel-meat and washed it down with warm Coca-Cola. The fact that I was the only customer should have told me something.

Soon after boarding the bus and settling in for the second movie, my bowels became engulfed in a four-alarm fire. I sprang for the lavatory, prepared to battle the blaze. Right then and there I remembered a warning from the "Getting Around" section of my *Lonely Planet Argentina* guide. "Carry water, a healthy snack, toilet paper . . ." Toilet paper? I was smart enough to bring water, but the healthy snack had been substituted with the bad empanada. And toilet paper—the strength and quantity of which is inextricably linked to the digestion of bad meat—had been forgotten. I scanned the lavatory, hoping beyond hope . . .

Bursting from the lavatory, I poked the dangling arm of the woman sleeping in the nearest seat. She fixed me with a sluggish eye. "Excuse me," I whispered. "Do you have toilet paper I can borrow?"

The question made me roll my own eyes even before the woman frowned and said, "*¿Que?*" After using the toilet paper, was I actually planning to give it back?

"*Por favor, señora. Yo. Necesito. Papel. Muy importante!*" I stood there in the aisle, my buttocks clenching mightily beneath hastily buttoned Levi's, the volcanic eruption mere seconds away. The woman nodded sleepily. She reached into her bag, pulled out a pen, a notepad, and then—

"*No, no, no, señora. Necesito pa-pel,*" I said, stretching the word and tilting my head toward the lavatory. She shook her head, reached into her bag, and produced a flimsy roll. Instead of offering it, she snatched off a few sheets and thrust them into my trembling hand. Economy would be the spirit of the moment. I leapt into the lavatory. The fire burned. The bus rolled on and on.

Sometime later, when the fire had been doused, when passengers no longer winced and retreated to their seats after making the mistake of opening the lavatory door, a beautiful woman boarded the bus. I kid you not. Everywhere you look in Argentina, there's a beautiful woman. Eyeballing the unsuspecting tourist on a city street. Accompanying him to a soccer game. And yes, walking toward him on the Andesmar bus to Salta. During the various plane, train, and bus rides in a life defined by departure time, I have never had the privilege of sitting next to a woman as provocative as the one standing in the aisle. This trip was no exception. The tall, casually dressed Argentinean sat across the aisle from me. Too close to admire without being obvious, but not so far as to restrict conversation.

I smiled.

She said, "Hello."

"Oh, you speak English."

In the darkened cabin, lit only by the flickering of the Denzel Washington movie, I got to know Isabella Tortellini. The twenty-nine-year-old sales rep worked for a multinational textile company with offices in Buenos Aires. Of the many aspects of life she said she was thankful for, grueling long-distance bus rides were not one of them. "After the *corralito*," she said, referring to the government's recent economic meltdown, "my company, they make . . . how you say, cutback?"

"My company is doing the same thing," I said.

"Before, I fly across my territory. Now," said Isabella, shrugging her shoulders and releasing a sigh, "I must take a bus."

I felt for her. Really. And during the next hour or so, as the bus rumbled across the darkened countryside, as the conversation deepened and our eyes locked in short flirtatious interludes that we acknowledged with bashful smiles, something stirred inside me. I *felt* for her. Really. Isabella proved to be smart, beautiful, gainfully employed, and, according to her bashful confession, she was single and exceedingly available. Comparatively speaking, I was . . . well, single and exceedingly available. I leaned across the aisle and whispered something to her. She leaned across the aisle and whispered back. We were close enough to sense what appeared to be happening. Close enough to kiss. Mere inches from her moistening lips, seconds away from the most erotic bus ride of my life, I discovered Isabella's one irrepressible flaw. Bad breath. Hog's breath. Halitosis *muchas!* Hers was not simply a case of unbrushed teeth and the aftereffects of a carnivorous dinner. As Marcellus proclaimed in *Hamlet,* "Something is rotten"!

Back in Miami, there was this flight attendant named Ronnie Hamilton who always seemed to show up on my crew. Ronnie was a nice enough guy, but his breath smelled like shit. I'm not exaggerating. He'd walk up to you and say, "Hello," or, "How's it goin'?" and you'd turn away wondering if he'd licked a turd before putting on his uniform and driving to the airport. Pity the passenger who made the mistake of asking Ronnie for assistance. He liked to get right up in passengers' faces, the way stinky-breath people often do, and blabber away tangentially until the victims reached for the oxygen masks. Flight attendants disappeared whenever Ronnie approached. Pilots refused to let him into the cockpit. He must have suffered from a glandular thing, because every time I ran into him—in airport operations, on the airplane, even at an airline party in Fort Lauderdale—his breath smelled exactly the same. Like shit.

Maybe Isabella suffered from the same ailment as Ronnie Hamilton. Or maybe it was something else. Either way, her breath blast hit me like a Tyson punch. I fell back across the aisle, dazed and utterly bewildered. Try though I did to sustain a tête-à-tête from a safe distance, the sudden change in logistics forced our conversation to falter. Dialogue that once flowed as robustly as the Colorado rapids had been reduced to a trickle from a drainage ditch. Ultimately, she turned her eyes away and focused on the Denzel Washington movie I had all but forgotten about— even though he's my favorite actor.

A troubling thought occurred after she leaned away so promptly and settled into her seat. The question nibbled at my consciousness. As discreetly as possible, I cupped one hand in front of my mouth, exhaled once, twice, a third time for good measure. It was then that I realized, with no small amount of embarrassment, that my own breath—tainted by the bad empanada— smelled as skanky as a baby's day-old diaper. I stole a glance at Isabella. She stole a glance at me. Never were two people in greater need of breath mints. But the rancid winds had done irreparable damage. When Isabella disembarked an hour later in Where the Fuck Are We, Argentina, we simply waved good-bye, choosing to keep our breath to ourselves.

TRAIN TO THE CLOUDS

◄┈┈┈┈┈┈┈┈┈►

Salta's most popular tourist attraction, *el Tren a las Nubes*, departed on schedule at dawn. Belching black clouds of diesel exhaust, the Train to the Clouds chugged away from the Lerma Valley station on narrow-gauge tracks that made the faded cars seem oddly toylike. Built in the early 1900s in response to the discovery of precious minerals, the railway winds its way north through thinning atmosphere, across thirteen steel train trestles, through twenty-one tunnels, over thirty-one bridges, and along some twelve hundred twisting curves before reaching an altitude of fifteen thousand feet at Abra Corillos near the Chilean border. This is the world's fourth-highest operating railway line. An asthmatic's worst nightmare. The train returns to Salta some fifteen hours after departure, making it perhaps the world's longest-lasting day trip to hypoxia.

Through a tour operator, I had secured a coveted window seat. As the train pulled out of the station and the first shafts of sunshine lit the wooden shacks on the outskirts of town, I opened the window, stuck my head out, and let the cool wind brush against my face. In my mind's eye I saw a fast-approaching pole that made me pull in my head and sit up like an adult. From behind the open window, then, I watched the broad dusty plain stretch out to the horizon. Like an image developing on Polaroid film, the desert came alive by degrees. The dark hues of dawn turned beige, brown, and rust as the sun climbed higher and higher. The sky took on the look of faded denim. Judging by the desert landscape we could have been chugging away from Albuquerque, heading for Phoenix or Reno.

While gazing at the undulating desert, I felt a tapping on my shoulder. My seatmate spoke *Castellano* and appeared to be part of a large Spanish tour group that took up most of the seats in our car. She pointed to my seat and motioned for us to swap. I respectfully declined, having secured the window in order to take advantage of the incredible highland vistas the train is famous for. Undaunted, my seatmate conferred with a friend sitting across the aisle and tapped me again on the shoulder. Her gesticulations seemed to indicate that I was sitting in *her* seat. I shook my head. She nodded. I shook my head again. She gave me the evil eye and wiggled her index finger in that Latin way that lets you know you're wrong. Her tour leader materialized. Fifty middle-aged Spanish women turned to glare at me. When a flustered attendant joined the tour leader and began inspecting our tickets, murmurs spread throughout the cabin. Mercifully, the attendant returned the tickets and apologized to me. "I am sorry," she said. "*La señora* has the window seat. Your ticket is for 8-A, the aisle seat."

I stared at her, dumbfounded. "How can 8-A be the aisle seat?" The attendant shrugged. I glanced at the boarding stub proffered by my smirking seatmate. "How can 8-B be the window seat?" I continued. The attendant shrugged again. "As far as I know, there's no commercial plane, bus, or train with a B, A, C, D seating configuration. It's always A, B, C, D. No?" The attendant shook her head and pointed to the seat designators above the window. Sure enough, a window icon had been affixed suspiciously close to "8-B."

"But that's a mistake," I said, pointing across the aisle where the window icon had been correctly positioned next to 8-D. "It's obvious. Whoever applied the window icons on the A–B side put them in the wrong place."

The cabin attendant responded with the same kind of bureaucratic thickheadedness that contributed to the worst economic collapse in Argentina's history, the same kind of thinking that inspired the government to confiscate pensions, freeze bank accounts, and allow five successive presidents to vacate office during an unprecedented two-week period in 2002. "This is the way it is, *señor*," she said. "*Lo siento.*"

Grudgingly, I swapped seats with the Spaniard. Still, she was not satisfied. She turned from the coveted window every few seconds to trade landscape accolades with her friend across the aisle. "¿LAS MONTAÑAS ESTÁN BONITAS, no?" she shouted into my left ear as if I did not exist. Her friend responded with a blast into my right ear. "SÍ, MANUELA, ESTÁN MUY BONITAS. ME GUSTAN MUCHO!" I leapt from my seat as the two women had hoped, making my way through one crowded car after another until I found an unoccupied window seat. I looked up at the seat designators above the window. Miracle of miracles, the window icon had been correctly affixed next to "12-A."

At various points during the journey I ignored good sense and stuck my head out the window, gazing at the bluest of blue skies, the purple mountains, the reddish-brown hills, the thorny cacti standing like so many thorny sentinels in a wilderness that stretches to Bolivia. From the lowland tobacco country and across a vast Martian-like landscape, the train moved northward. We passed through Quebrada del Toro, a giant V-shaped gap carved through the mountains by an ancient river. We zigzagged up El Alisal, gaining altitude at an accelerated clip. At Los Rulos (The Curls), the train corkscrewed uphill like a dog chasing its own tail in slow motion.

The most spectacular moment came as we approached La

Polvorilla Viaduct. I had already consumed three cups of coca tea that had been sold for a dollar each by a train attendant. Plastic packets of coca leaves were for sale as well. I stuck not one but two leafy wads between my cheek and gums the way Walt Garrison used to do in the old television commercials for Skoal tobacco. The coca leaf, from which cocaine is derived, is sold legally throughout Argentina, as well as in Bolivia and Peru where the plant is harvested in abundance. Traditionalists chew it. Ladies brew it. Inca warriors were known to munch on it before going into battle (the buzz made them more eager to beat the crap out of the enemy). Locals claim that coca leaves help offset the effects of altitude sickness. Which, of course, is the only reason I loaded up on the stuff. And now, as La Polvorilla Viaduct swung into full view, South America's most popular export began doing to me what it's been doing to locals for hundreds of years.

An enormous web of steel girders rose two hundred feet above the desert canyon floor. The girders supported a massive railway bridge that stretched across the rocky chasm for more than two hundred yards. In a normal state of mind I would have sat back in my seat, ooohing and ahhhing at this marvel of human engineering and the canyon it was built to conquer. But in my present state, I gripped the seat as if riding a roller coaster without a harness. The sky grew brighter. The chilled air seemed impossibly warm. I felt light-headed. Energized. For no apparent reason I wanted to apologize to the Spanish woman for not giving up my window seat even though 8-A was actually my seat and I wanted to look out the window without leaning over her, but somehow all that no longer mattered because I was going to take her out to dinner when we returned to Salta later that evening and, in fact, I would invite the cabin attendants and the tour guide and the little old man who smiled from behind the counter each time I left the hotel.

The mammoth bridge loomed ahead like a special effect in a disaster flick. *Collapse: The True Story of La Polvorilla Viaduct Catastrophe*. The narrow bridge seemed incapable of supporting a Volkswagen Beetle, let alone a passenger train. As the high plains air grew thinner, my breath came in snatches. I looked around at the people in my car and every single one of them turned to laugh at me. Wired and perhaps a little paranoid, I nearly jumped out of my skin when the soundtrack to *Chariots of Fire* began playing in my head. At least I thought it was playing in my head. Actually, the music was part of the Train to the Clouds audio experience. In homage to the bridge we were about to cross, the music blasted from overhead loudspeakers. Hundreds of passengers reached in unison for their Camcorders and leaned out the windows on one side of the train. The sudden redistribution of weight alarmed me. I imagined the train tilting over La Polvorilla Viaduct and crashing to the canyon floor in a fiery explosion. *It's the coca leaves.* A little voice told me so. Still, I could not bring myself to look out the window until after the train crossed the trestle.

Hours later, the Train to the Clouds ground to a halt at the turnaround point more than two miles above sea level. A cracked, barren plain fanned out to forever. Snow-dusted mountains squatted on the horizon and propped up an ice-blue sky. The temperature had dropped to maybe forty-five degrees, which made the thin, swirling air even more difficult to breathe. Here in the middle of a harsh, desolate nowhere, as far from a triple-shot grande mocha latte as one can possibly get, a small group of Indian villagers had gathered to sell trinkets to disembarking passengers. Young boys held out adorable baby llamas that blinked so innocently they melted your heart. The baby llamas could be touched and photographed for a price. Young girls, some of whom were unwilling to look buyers in the eye, thrust woven bracelets high above their heads. Adults offered ponchos and gaucho sombreros, which tourists gobbled up.

I staggered through the crowd in a hypoxic daze, my eyes rattling in their sockets, lungs heaving. I was not the worst of the lot, however. Three or four unwell passengers, each surrounded by concerned companions, were at that very moment leaning against the train and puking their pitiful guts out. A local teenage boy must have noticed my condition. Dressed in a bright red poncho and jeans, he rushed over as I stumbled against the train. "*Señor, señor!*" he cried, extending a hand for support. "*¿Está bien?*" Over the years, the kid had probably seen hundreds of passengers suffer from the effects of high altitude. He must have thought I'd be okay, because he stepped directly in front of me— smack dab in front of my nozzle—and smiled a guileless smile. Then he held out his hand. In it was a plastic pouch filled with familiar greens. "*¿Coca?*" he said, nodding his head.

I shook my head ferociously and immediately wished I had been less expressive. A wave of dizziness—the likes of which I hadn't experienced since toking on a homemade bong in 1979— sent me sprawling in the dust.

Coca leaves do not offset the effects of high altitude. I repeat: Coca leaves do not offset the effects of high altitude. Chewed, brewed, or otherwise ingested, the little green plants only take you higher.

BODILY FLUID

Suffering from a nasty flu virus, I dropped my bag at the check-in counter and staggered into the men's room at the Buenos Aires International Airport. I was sick, all right. Deathly sick. The prospect of a nine-hour flight to Miami followed by a cross-country jaunt to Los Angeles and an eight-hour flight to Tahiti didn't make me feel any better. Trousers piled around my ankles, head cupped in my hands, I sat on the toilet in a men's room stall, unable to think or care. Cymbals crashed rhythmically inside my head, forcing my eyelids to clench. My muscles ached. Heat emanated from my neck and forehead as if I had been plugged into an electrical outlet. Worst of all was the pain in my throat. Every time I swallowed, a jagged razor ripped into my esophagus. So, I tried not to swallow. This of course brought the act of swallowing to the forefront of my consciousness and had me swallowing with Pavlovian regularity.

After regaining consciousness on the toilet, I opened my eyes and noticed, for the first time, a pool of yellowish liquid around my heels. My predecessor had no doubt demonstrated piss-poor aim. Or so I thought. When my eyes regained focus, I noticed that the pool of liquid was *spreading*. Not rapidly, but fast enough to indicate a spill. I looked more closely and realized, to my horror, that the guy with piss-poor aim was, in fact, yours truly. The floor was not my only wayward target. The crotch and seat of my pants, as well as my brand-new Calvin Kleins, had been drenched in my own malodorous juices.

I freaked. What else would a grown man do when his flight departs in fifty-five minutes and his trousers, the only pair in his possession, are soaked in urine? He freaks, that's what he does. His mind races. He grits his teeth. He sighs, stomps his foot, and grits his teeth again after realizing his pant leg has now been splattered. From a toilet stall in a spanking new airport terminal near Buenos Aires, Argentina, he throws back his head and manages to stifle a scream. He freaks. Yes, ladies and gentlemen. That's what happens to a traveling man who suffers the ultimate humiliation. And then he stoops to new lows of daring and intrigue.

I opened the stall door wide enough for my head to poke out. Looked right, left, right again. Miraculously, the men's room was vacant. I shuffled toward a wash basin, restrained by the soggy corduroys bunched around my ankles. The pants came off. I tossed the tainted Calvins into a rubbish bin. Naked from the waist down, I stood before the sink, holding my corduroys beneath a stream of warm water, squirting soap on contaminated areas, rubbing it in, sniffing, squirting, rubbing again, rinsing, and then twist-drying the fabric. After donning the pants, I looked in the mirror. The seat, crotch, and upper-thigh areas had become dark wet patches of embarrassment. Hunched and increasingly jittery, I looked like a geezer suffering from torrential incontinence. A toddler, ready to be potty trained. Despite my best cleaning efforts, the pants reeked of piss. The flight attendants would surely boot me off the plane. Airline regulations allow for the removal of any passenger emitting a stench. I know this from personal experience. On more than one occasion while working a flight, I've had to eject horrendous stink mongers before takeoff. Now it was time for karmic payback.

My head ached. Razors tore at my throat. Think, dammit. *Think!*

Unable to come up with a better plan, I went over to the electric hand dryer, punched the silver button, and twisted the vent to direct a stream of warm air downward. But the vent was broken, or questionably designed. The only way to keep the airflow moving at a constant downward angle was to hold the vent in place. And the only way to hold the vent in place would be to turn around, push my butt against the vent, grab the vent, and bend over.

Facing the entrance to the men's room, my backside beneath the whirring dryer, I reached behind my thrusted butt as if auditioning for a role in a gay porno flick. If there really is a God, He or She would have prevented anyone from entering the men's room until my pants had dried. As it turns out, God does not exist. Just as I began wiggling my ass in an attempt to expedite the pants-drying process, two Argentinean men in business suits strolled in. They took one look at me and froze. I straightened, shook my head, and grinned the shameful grin of one who has been caught in a compromising situation that can never, ever be properly explained—even when a language barrier does not exist. The two men exchanged a look and fled. My future flashed before my eyes. Airport security. Detention. International headlines:

North American Pervert Arrested in South American Toilet

Attempting to blow heat up his own ass,
the suspect, a vacationing *flight attendant* . . .

The clock was ticking. The boarding announcement had probably been made. I still needed to clear immigration and security before boarding the flight. Trying not to panic, I snatched off my turtleneck, tied it around my waist, and rushed toward the departure gate wearing an undershirt and wet corduroys. Immigration proved to be a cinch. While passing through the security checkpoint, however, an inspector waved the magnetometer wand across my chest. He stopped abruptly, took one whiff, and cocked his head backward in disgust. He gestured for me to move on even though the security check had yet to be completed. (To guarantee an unfettered passage through airport security, be sure to pee on yourself before getting there. It worked for me.)

Once aboard the aircraft, I inched down the aisle, leaving a vapor trail that turned heads in the first-class, business, and economy sections. I stared ahead, stoically, hoping to avoid anyone I knew. After all, this particular airline happened to be the same one that had employed me for nearly two decades. The flight attendants were Miami-based, as were the pilots. Of the eleven crew members on board, I'd probably flown with at least one.

The moment I sat down in my assigned aisle seat, the precise instant, in fact, my seatmate turned her head and stared out the window. She would remain that way for the duration of what must have been the longest flight of her life. It was certainly the longest flight of mine. Prior to takeoff, the unthinkable happened.

"Hey, you!" A familiar voice. A woman's voice. I felt my head pivot in slow motion as if operating on hydraulics. A flight attendant stood in the aisle, fists on her hips, a warm smile spreading on her face. "Elliott Hester! I haven't flown with you in ages. Where the hell have you been?"

I shrugged. Tried to smile.

She crouched down in the aisle beside me. Placed a gentle hand on my arm. "So, what have you been up to all this time?"

I shrugged. Tried to smile.

"I heard about that Caracas thing." She shook her head and chuckled. "You know, you really need to . . ."

Her voice trailed off. She stood up, abruptly. "I just remembered something," she said. "I'll come back to chat after takeoff." But she never did.

I sat motionless for hours—not drinking, not eating, not even daring to reach for the plastic headphones to get audio for the in-flight movie—fearful that the slightest shift in position would release more of a stench and send me to new heights of guilt and embarrassment. My head pounded. The fever turned up a notch. Each time I swallowed, the razor ripped me raw. I closed my eyes and drifted to the edge of something that resembled sleep. Moments later, I woke in a cold sweat. In my dream, the plane landed safely in Tahiti. But while attempting to deplane, I was snatched by a team of hooded health officials and tossed ceremoniously into quarantine.

French Polynesia

LE FREAKS COME OUT AT NIGHT

◄·······················►

Unlike Moorea and Bora Bora, otherworldly islands that offer paradise on earth, Tahiti—French Polynesia's most identifiable island—inspires a rapid departure. The capital, Papeete, is a hot and oily port town. French-colonial buildings, warped by the sun and sullied by diesel fumes, line the congested boulevard that curls along the congested bay. There are no white sand beaches here. No turquoise waters in which to frolic. The small, crowded sidewalks move to a big-city beat. A four-dollar Coke at Café Le Rétro cannot quench a smog-induced thirst. An overpriced room at the Hotel Prince Hinoi imparts the charm and spaciousness of Dracula's coffin, which is why I walked the streets aimlessly during my first and only night on the island, and ended up a prisoner on *le truck*.

Loud, gargantuan, flaunting the brash disposition of a fourteen-wheeler, *le truck* is a local term for a Tahitian public bus. Following this line of reasoning, one might assume that actual trucks, in all their various forms, are referred to as *le buses*. Alas, this is not the Polynesian way. *Le trucks* roar along Papeete's major streets, screeching to precarious halts at official blue and white bus stops—or anywhere along the road when flagged down by a hopeful pedestrian.

Having spent most of the twenty-four-hour layover nursing a cold in that tiny hotel room, I hit the streets with little money and even less time to check out the island. Like a beast let loose upon the masses, *le truck* came barreling down Boulevard Pomare. With nothing better to do, I raised my hand, hoping for a late-night glimpse of Papeete. *Le truck* rattled to a halt. I stepped onto the vehicle and was taken on the ride of my life.

Music blasted through the doorway to greet me. From a three-foot-high loudspeaker bolted to the floor where the fare box should have been, Michael Jackson sang defiantly, claiming that Billie Jean is not his lover. *Hee, hee, hee . . . Ooo!* The bass boomed at a volume that rattled my bones. Michael screamed in my ears. *Hee, hee, hee . . . Ooo!* A woman who might have been the driver's assistant, girlfriend, or both sat dutifully beside him in a spacious enclosure. From behind the Plexiglas window, she turned without looking and pushed an open hand through the collection slot.

Now that an outsider had crashed the private party, I assumed the music would drop to a more reasonable volume. As I took a seat on one of two long wooden benches running the length of the vehicle, however, Michael's voice actually went up a notch. The world-famous song—with its pure, rich, irresistible beat that over two decades has jiggled perhaps 5 billion booties—now rattled the timber beneath my own. But that's not all. Vines of blinking Christmas lights ran along the ceiling and down the back of the bus. Vivid bursts of green, red, and yellow lit up the cabin, evoking the thrill of a carnival ride. *Hee, hee, hee . . . Ooo!* It had taken a minute to adjust to the volume, but now I was singing along with Mike. "'She said I am the one, but—'"

Le truck stopped suddenly to pick up a Polynesian gentleman. Advanced in age and using a walking cane for leverage, the frail old man hobbled to the rear of the blinking bus and sat. In spite of Michael Jackson's deafening protestations and seemingly oblivious to the booming bass line, the old man folded his hands atop the cane, closed his eyes, and appeared to fall asleep.

Once we reached the outskirts of Papeete, the bus rolled into a gas station and parked in front of the pump. The driver walked inside the mini-mart, returning a moment later with a brown paper bag that was promptly handed over to his "assistant." Curiously enough, the bus drove off without the benefit of pumped gas. I watched the woman pull out of the bag a two-liter bottle of 7 UP. She took a swig, passed it to the driver. He drank from the bottle and passed it back. This seemed like odd behavior for the operator of a public bus, but not as odd as what happened next. The woman lit a cigarette and took two suspiciously long hits before handing it over to the driver. He took a couple of hits and passed it back. The familiar aroma took only a few seconds to drift from the enclosure. The bus driver and his friend had sparked a spliff.

Initially, I chuckled. Here I was in the middle of the South Pacific on a blinking bus driven by a pot-smoking local who had brought his girlfriend and Michael Jackson along for company. But weirdness gave way to worry as *le truck* careened down the road and plunged into deepening darkness. The bus swerved, straightened, swerved again. It lurched forward during a ragged shift in gears. When we stopped moments later, my first impulse was to get off. But how long until the next bus came by? What lurked out there in the darkness behind the coconut palms? I found out a moment later when five female passengers climbed aboard.

At first, I could only make out that the women were large. Not fat. Not chubby. Large, as in strong and sturdy. They were 250-pounders, each and every one of them. Feet clomping like hooves, miniskirts stretched to the ripping point across five gargantuan butts, they lumbered one by one onto *le truck*. The floor groaned. A booming Kool & the Gang bass line skipped a beat.

Although the bus was nearly empty, the group decided to plop down on the bench directly across from me. That's when the nightmare began.

The blinking lights froze their faces in stroboscopic frames of horror. With each split-second burst of color, I was able to make out more details. The women had been spackled with heavy makeup. Lips gleamed in glossy shades of crimson. Eyelids fluttered in neon blue. Blush, eyeliner, and something that might have been perfume—all had been applied in stultifying excess. Towering above the clownish faces were five beehive wigs.

In an act of pure audaciousness, the largest of the group looked into my eyes and blew a kiss. It sounded like the cork in a wine bottle being slowly turned and then yanked out for effect. She smiled sardonically, revealing a gap in her teeth through which a fat pink tongue darted out. *"Bonsoir, Monsieur,"* the woman said, her voice as deep as Barry White's. *"Comment ça va?"*

Big hair. Bad makeup. Baritone voice. The three Bs could mean only one thing: The hefty Polynesian laid no claim to womanhood. Neither did her traveling companions. They were transvestites. Big, bold, blatant transvestites—a freaky-deaky posse that only a cross-dressing Sumo wrestler could love.

Unsure of what might happen next, I looked to the driver, who was all but lost in a swirling cloud of cannabis. I turned to the old man, who continued to sleep through the riot of music and blinking lights. Averting the eyes that beamed at me from across the aisle, I looked down and wished I hadn't. Five pairs of thick, muscular legs protruded from a Rockette row of high-heeled pumps. Was this Tahiti or the Twilight Zone? I thought transvestitism was a mainland thing. Then I remembered. According to my trusty guidebook, a local joint known as Piano Bar hosted a drag show at 1:00 A.M. on Fridays and Saturdays. The infamous club attracted a hodgepodge of patrons not to be found at your typical island bar. On any weekend night there might be straight and gay hookers, locals with a thing for men in skirts, lonely expatriates, wobbling drunks, and sex-starved sailors ready to screw anything that moved—including wayward tourists.

Lips licked, bras stuffed, biceps flexing from across the aisle, the five transvestites whispered among themselves and stared at me lasciviously. The big one spoke up again. *"Je ne parle pas Français,"* I said, my response delayed by trepidation. By saying, "I don't speak French" in French, however, he must have assumed that I spoke French. Biggie's eyes lit up. He smiled, revealing once again the gaping black hole between his teeth. He began *voulez-vous*-ing away in a thunderous voice that made me increasingly nervous. After realizing communication was fruitless (no pun intended), Biggie stood up, lunged across the aisle, and plunked his big ass next to mine. I scooted away. He scooted closer. I slid to the far end of the bench, near the driver. But the big man in the little skirt slid even closer. So close, in fact, his naked thigh pressed against mine. The pursuit was not lost upon his four beefy accomplices, who laughed like epileptics at a comedy show.

With a suddenness that startled even me, I jumped up and tapped hard on the driver's Plexiglas window. The female "assistant" slid open one of the panels. Smoke poured out. Sensimilla. Damn near gave me a contact high. "I think I've missed my stop," I said, shouting above Hootie and the Blowfish. She squinted and shook her head, unable to hear my voice above the screaming music. "I think I've missed my stop," I repeated. She jutted her chin at the driver, who took a massive toke from the spliff, oblivious to me and my predicament. *"I think I've missed my stop!"* The driver shrugged his shoulders. Twin streams of marijuana mist gushed from his nostrils, "Who Gives a Fuck?" written in his eyes. "CAN I CATCH ANOTHER BUS BACK TO PAPEETE ON THIS ROAD?" By some quirk of fate, the driver managed a sluggish nod. A moment later, *le truck* swerved to the side of the road. Even before the wheels stopped rolling, I rushed through the doorway and jumped off.

But what would happen if all five transvestites followed me out here on this deserted island road? Each man stood over six feet tall and outweighed me by fifty or sixty pounds. There were no witnesses to see them dispatch me. No buildings into which I could run. Only a dark road lined with thick tropical foliage through which wind began to whisper. I looked up nervously, a rustling jungle wall behind me, a forest of coconut palms on the other side of the desolate road. The bus idled, as if unwilling to run the leafy gauntlet. From behind the window, Biggie stood up and blew the nasty kiss I'd grown to know so well. He lumbered toward the doorway, bending to speak with his companions. The seconds ticked by like hours. Crickets sang with demonic rectitude. The bus continued to idle—lights blinking, music blaring, the old man sleeping in the back—allowing ample time for the men to disembark, if that had been their plan.

And yet a wave of relief washed over me even before the pot-smoking driver shifted into gear and *le truck*, with its strange cargo, disappeared into the Tahitian darkness. The five hulking cross-dressers were wearing high-heeled pumps after all. I wore cross-training Nikes.

SNORING IN PARADISE

My first day at Club Med Moorea, I had problems. Back bruised and aching, skin lightly broiled from the South Pacific sun, I hobbled to my bungalow after a waterskiing mishap sent me cartwheeling across the water in front of horrified vacationers. Slowly, achingly, I sat next to the big blue Samsonite laying open on my bed. Because I was traveling alone and didn't own a big blue Samsonite, the air grew thick with suspicion.

A shuffling Quasimodo, I searched the place for more signs of the intruder. In the bathroom, I found a toothbrush with flattened bristles and a family-size bottle of Scope. Beneath the other bed, a pair of scuffed size-fourteen brogans. In the closet, a trio of Hawaiian shirts that screamed in electric colors and flower motifs. Baffled, I made my way across the complex and into the lobby, where a stiff, humorless French G.O. (Group Organizer: a Club Med employee) eyed me from behind the check-in desk. Despite wincing in pain during pauses in my story, I pleaded my case with verbal adroitness that would make Johnnie Cochran proud. The G.O. looked at me with unblinking eyes. With the casual indifference of a weary Parisian waiter, she said "zingal"-room status allowed for guest pairing.

"That doesn't make sense," I said. "A single room at any other hotel usually indicates occupation by one individual." She shrugged her shoulders, leaned her head to one side, and hissed between her teeth. *C'est la vie.* The G.O. told me I must not have read ze fine print in ze goddam contract. The contract materialized. I read ze fine print. As it turned out, she was right. Reluctantly, and not without a few muffled English words, I hobbled back to the beach.

Club Med Moorea sits on a carpet of sugar-white sand that disappears beneath turquoise water that is far too beautiful for words. A crowd of guests, mostly Japanese and Australian, mingled in the open-air lobby and lounged at the pool. I slunk through the sprawling complex and out to the beach. Staring out to sea, nudged by a gentle breeze that sneaked between twin coconut palms, I pouted like a four-year-old.

Upon entering the bungalow later that evening, I was greeted by George Langley, a plump Canadian schoolteacher who laughed with the gusto of a department store Santa Claus. He extended his hand and offered an apology that seemed as sincere as his smile. The front-desk G.O. had given him the "zingal"-room lecture as well.

George turned out to be a nice guy. We hobnobbed throughout the all-you-can-eat dinner buffet, yawned through the campy Club Med cabaret show, and later at the discothèque—pounded by bubble-gum dance music and untold quantities of beer—we spoke of home and the pleasures of being away. We clicked. We bonded. But in a fraction of the time it took to become friends, our bond came unglued.

George dozed off in his twin bed. I read a Stephen King thriller in mine. The protagonist had just stumbled over the tip of a buried alien spacecraft when my eyelids grew heavy. I flicked off the light and settled in for a good night's sleep when, suddenly, I heard *the sound*. My eyelids flew open like window shades. I prayed that my ears had deceived me. They had not. Mr. George Langley, my illustrious Canadian roommate, snored with the vigor of a drunken wildebeest.

The snoring lightened up for a minute. George whirred spasmodically in short, raspy hitches like an economy car engine that won't catch. But soon the snoring deepened, shifting into long, gargling reverberations that thundered in my ears as if native drums were being pounded at a virgin sacrifice. Finding it impossible to sleep through the uproar, I was overtaken by an urge to strangle my new roommate until every last gust of Canadian wind had been exorcised back to the provinces. I settled, instead, on a more civilized plan of action.

First, I buried my head in a pillow. When that didn't work, I stumbled to the bathroom in the darkness and stuffed bits of toilet paper in my ears. The primitive earplugs not only didn't work, but it took fifteen minutes with a pair of tweezers to remove stubborn shreds. As a last resort, I limped over to my bed, donned my Walkman headphones, and cranked up an Anita Baker tape to a volume sleep could withstand. That worked for a while, but George's relentless howling drifted in and out of the music like a backup singer from hell.

Enough was enough. I raised myself on one elbow and in a hushed voice called out, "Hey, George."

No response.

"George!"

Still nothing.

"Dammit, George!" But the howling Canadian hurricane simply shifted to a position from which more damaging winds were unleashed. "GEOOOOOOOORGE!" This time it worked. George's snoring broke up into a succession of snorts that sounded like a bush pig achieving orgasm. Finally there was silence. Beautiful silence. I shut my eyes, hoping to drift unmolested toward a good night's sleep. But before long, old George's engine kicked over again, coughing and sputtering until daybreak.

Through swollen bloodshot slits, I watched my roommate wake to a glorious day that had been ruined for me. He yawned for nearly thirty seconds and leapt to his feet like a kid on Christmas morning. He whistled on his way to the bathroom. So vivid was his rendition of the *Hawaii Five-O* theme, I had flashbacks of the episode in which McGarrett and Danno foiled the assassination of Don Ho. When the whistling ended, George gargled with a fervor only a dentist could love. His flip-flops slapped violently against the floor during the triangular trek between bathroom, closet, and dresser. Irrevocably dressed in Bermuda shorts and one of those fucked-up Hawaiian shirts, George donned mirrored aerodynamic sunglasses and left the room, snapping his fingers to an LL Cool J rap emanating from a handheld boom box.

That night I found myself curled up in bed, poring over the same Stephen King novel. Frightened by the murderous glare in my good eye, the front-desk G.O. had given me the key to my own private room. I flicked off the lamp, stretched out in bed, and listened to the faint musical chirping of sleepy island crickets. Moonlight crept between the slats of the shutters. The ceiling fan blew languid good-night kisses. Just before drifting off, I heard a whisper from the adjoining room. The whisper grew into a noise. The noise became an apocalyptic roar, rising, falling, rising again—the song of a Canadian snoremonger.

Even before realizing I had done so, I jumped out of bed and pressed one ear against the wall. Gurgle, snort, wheeze. Gurgle, snort, wheeze. Gurgle, snort, snort, wheeze. So recognizable was the snoring pattern, so familiar was the miserable melody, I found myself pounding the wall to the rhythm of my own screeching voice. "George! George! Damn you, George!" The bush pig orgasmed. The snoring stopped. A moment later, it started up again.

Had George followed me to a new bungalow with the intent of ruining my stay? Had the front-desk G.O. orchestrated a vengeful prank? Would paradisiacal Moorea bear witness to not one but two grisly murders in the very same night? As the snore winds grew to hurricane strength, I started banging the wall again. Suddenly, there was a new voice, a woman's voice. Then a muffled exchange with a man. I pressed my ear to the wall and was nearly knocked to the floor by ferocious pounding from the other side. "Bloody wanker . . . I'll knock yer bloody block off!" The voice was gruff, inconsolable, unmistakably Australian.

I lay in bed that night and the next, eyes wide, mouth shut, listening to the gurgulations from Down Under.

SLOW BOAT TO NAUSEA AND OTHER EXOTIC PORTS

————◆·······················▶————

Its powerful engine rumbling, the 340-foot freighter eased away from the wharf, cruising past a maze of pleasure boats and splashing through swells as the harbor gave way to the sea. I stood on the promenade deck with a smattering of passengers, my eyes drawn to the twinkling lights of Papeete. As the vestiges of sunlight drained from the sky and the stars began twinkling by degrees, I stretched out on a plastic lounge chair, took a deep breath, and fell into rhythm with the universe. Stroked by great Pacific rollers and a stiffening breeze, the *Aranui* chugged across an open sea that seemed as black and endless as the cosmos. With no discernable horizon from which to gain perspective and not a single vessel in sight, we plunged through charted waters, ninety disparate passengers and thirty-two crew on a cargo ship guided by stars.

As the constellations began to blur, and the motion of the ocean began to have its way with me, I retired to my tiny cabin above the engine room. Waves and the rumbling machinery denied the womblike sleep I had hoped for. In fact, sleep was the last thing on my mind. The ship lunged across increasingly rough breakers, which triggered in my stomach a different kind of rumble that had me stumbling from my cabin and into the hallway. I snatched open the lavatory door. Unable to gain my sea legs in the wobbling chamber, unable to stop the lurching in my gut, I dropped to my knees and prayed—not to a ceramic throne, but to a metal one. Rarely has an embrace been as passionate. Never has a man puked so much.

Throughout that long sleepless first night, I rode the *Aranui* as if it were a bronco. I sat on my fold-out cot with my back against the wall, clutching the frame with both hands, watching with crisscrossed eyes as my cabin and the three objects squeezed into it—an anchored armoire, a night table, my duffel bag—swayed like visions in an acid trip. I had no Dramamine, Antivert, or Benadryl to quell my queasy stomach. Until now, I hadn't needed pharmaceuticals. Never suffered from motion sickness of any kind, not in trains, planes, automobiles, even boats. And this was a *ship*. My first voyage in an oceangoing vessel, in fact. Like a wide-body passenger jet compared to a twin-engine prop, a large ship is supposed to provide a more stable ride. When properly motivated by the sea, however, a ship can be as turbulent as a Cessna in a thunderstorm. As if to prove this point, the *Aranui* bucked again. Not enough to throw me to the floor, but enough for me to realize that the floor was the safest place to be.

I crawled into the lavatory and snuggled with the toilet until daybreak. By then, all my cookies had been tossed.

That day was spent out at sea. I sat on the promenade deck, chatting with passengers who, judging by poise and demeanor, had arrived long ago. There was an effeminate British barrister who told jokes at his girlfriend's expense, an elderly California couple who bragged incessantly about how often and widely they travel, and an eccentric widow who had come all the way from Brussels to visit Jacques Brel, the famous Belgian singer who lies buried on Hiva Oa. I shook hands with a retired French anesthesiologist, a Norwegian anthropologist, a Swiss ophthalmologist, and a German proctologist (just kidding; I believe the self-righteous asshole was a plastic surgeon). The most peculiar passenger, an eighty-five-year-old woman from Arkansas, was part of an Elderhostel tour group. She could be seen wandering the ship at various times during the voyage, dressed in cotton pajamas and a baseball cap, and swinging her cane at anyone foolish enough to stand in her way.

These people, many of whom you'd expect to see lounging on a chaise in St. Moritz, had chosen to spend their time on a working cargo ship. The *Aranui* boasted no glitzy shops. There was no on-board concierge, no spa or discothèque. Meals were basic, entertainment virtually nonexistent. The ninety passengers slept in utilitarian cabins or in hammocks strung up in a crowded dormitory. Crew members wore grungy T-shirts and hard hats rather than the spiffy white uniforms you'll remember from *The Love Boat*. Arguably the world's most spartan ocean cruise, the *Aranui* has an allure that is summed up in one sentence from an eight-page color brochure. "The *Aranui*'s down-to-earth essence remains the same—that of an inter-island trading ship bringing life's necessities, from beer to cement mixers, to communities largely cut off from the twentieth century."

Positioned more than three thousand miles east of Australia and four thousand miles west of Chile, the Marquesas are definitely "cut off." In fact, the twelve isolated jewels lie farther from continental landfall than any other island group on earth. This makes the *Aranui*'s mission both worthy and wonderful. Islanders receive much-needed provisions, while passengers feast their eyes on some of the world's loveliest islands.

From my perspective, there was one major problem. Boredom. The sixteen-hundred-mile round-trip voyage to the Marquesas and back lasted sixteen days. If there had been an on-board disco, I might have been forced to do the Electric Slide with French-speaking septuagenarian widows. Instead, I spent much of my time lounging on the promenade deck, watching sunblock being applied to the doughy limbs of French-speaking septuagenarian widows.

When we anchored the next morning at Takapoto, our first port of call, passengers descended the metal stairs on the port side of the ship and stepped one by one into a wobbling whaleboat. Imagine, if you will, some twenty-five or thirty passengers, many of advanced age and limited dexterity. Now imagine them squeezed onto narrow planks stretching across the width of a whaleboat. Imagine the sun beating down with a vengeance. Two dozen sweat-soaked brows. Now imagine an eighty-five-year-old woman being lowered aboard. Even the seventy-year-olds watched in wide-eyed wonder. Assisted by two crewmen, the Pajama Lady stepped off the bottom rung, lips quivering, her cane slicing savagely through the hot and humid air. She sat at the bow as we motored toward Takapoto. Believe it or not, she held up just fine. (A middle-aged Frenchwoman did not. On the return trip to the ship, the medical emergency would leave passengers stunned and silent.)

The brief Takapoto itinerary, outlined in a pamphlet and reiterated by the *Aranui* guides, went exactly like this:

(10:30 A.M.) We walk through the village, then we will take a canoe through the lagoon to a pearl farm. There we will have a lecture about black pearls (possibility to buy some) and also have time to enjoy the lagoon, by swimming and snorkeling. (11:30 A.M.) We will have a picnic on this wonderful site. (1:00 P.M.) Back to the village by canoe or 40 min. walk through coconut plantation. (2:00 P.M.) Back on board the *Aranui*. Notice: Wear strong sun protection, sunglasses and a hat.

We spent less than three and a half hours on Takapoto. Like I said, the itinerary was brief. Slathered in sunblock and covered in headgear—everyone except the middle-aged Frenchwoman (you're beginning to understand why she had a medical emergency)—the more mobile among us opted to walk. We marched from the edge of the water where a few islanders had gathered to receive long-awaited goods. Eyes squinting in the sun, they smiled shyly, waiting for the first load to arrive by whaleboat.

It took twelve seconds to walk through the village, which consisted of a few low buildings hugging a paved road. For almost forty minutes we navigated the wide lanes of a coconut plantation where *copra* (dried coconut) is harvested and hauled back to Tahiti to be converted into coconut oil. Beyond the plantation lay an utterly spectacular sight: A ring of bright white sand traced the circumference of a turquoise lagoon. It looked more like a lake, really. One of those picturesque glacial lakes you'll find in Canada and western Argentina. But this one was surrounded by coconut palms, some of which jutted horizontally over the water like gigantic fishing poles.

Unable to restrain myself, I stripped to my swim trunks and jumped in. The water was as tepid as a baby's bath. Giggling children, their skin as brown as my own, frolicked in the turquoise water. White clouds dotted a powder-blue sky. Paradise isn't a fantasy after all. But the clock kept ticking. The *Aranui* had a schedule to keep. After maybe a half hour of beach time we ate steamed fish with our fingers in the shade of a makeshift tent. Most passengers then headed for the pearl farm. A splinter group, of which I was a member, spent the last precious moments on the beach. Then it was back through the coconut plantation and into the whaleboat.

The Frenchwoman climbed in and sat beside me. Her husband sat between her and the port side. The sun hammered even more brutally than before. Like everyone else aboard the crowded whaleboat, the Frenchwoman sweat profusely. Perhaps even more so because she wore no hat. Tufts of thick, dark hair clung to her forehead. She began snatching at the neck of her soggy T-shirt. She wiggled uncomfortably on the crowded plank. Shook her head sluggishly and moaned as if having a bad dream. I didn't realize she was in trouble until a moment later. Apparently, neither did her husband. He leaned over the side of the boat, staring at the sea, even as his wife's spasms began. Without warning, she fell backward against a row of startled seniors and threw her arms open as if filled with the spirit of the Holy Ghost. Her head flopped drunkenly against my shoulder. She grabbed at her shorts. She mumbled in an ethereal voice that even a boatful of Frenchmen could not understand. Forget about a doctor. The woman needed le Exorcist.

While everyone else stared in disbelief, the husband looked on as if watching a Cousteau documentary. He offered no assistance. Showed no concern. It was almost as if he didn't know his wife at all. The woman began to wail. She was Helen of Troy after the abduction. Mother Teresa at an unmarked grave. Someone needed to do something. Someone needed to do something fast. As if on cue, Tino, the *Aranui*'s foreman, threw a bucket of water in her face. "Sunstroke," he said, matter-of-factly. Tino was clearly a man of action, not words. Up until this point, I had yet to hear him speak. "Sunstroke," he repeated. "No hat."

That night at dinner, the Frenchwoman and her husband strolled into the tiny dining room as if nothing had happened. As stiff and proper as bankers, they sat quietly at a table for two, staring into their plates as they chewed, not talking, not smiling, communicating with only the most subtle of gestures—exactly as they had done the night before the sunstroke incident and all the nights thereafter. Takapoto was soon forgotten. The *Aranui* sailed on.

Gossip about the French couple became the No. 1 on-board activity. Pajama Lady chitchat came in a close second. Reading was without a doubt the third most popular pastime. At any given time you might find five or six ladies lost in a paperback on the promenade deck, their plump legs slathered in sunblock and crisscrossed with varicose veins. As the ship plowed toward the first of six Marquesas stops, I lay among the lounging ladies, reading Herman Melville and dreaming of escape.

Over the course of the next week or so, we anchored at Ua Pou, Nuku Hiva, Tahuata, Fatu Hiva, Hiva Oa, and Ua Huka. Each morning passengers woke to the sight of a lush volcanic island rising from the open sea. Each morning the *Aranui* carried out its primary function. With the skin of the ship peeled back, exposing the multilevel hold jammed with two thousand tons of cargo, the crew performed the off-loading ballet. The crane operator, Kadafi—as fitting in the cockpit of the ship's towering crane as in the pages of *Moby-Dick*—acted as conductor. Sporting a large hoop earring and boar-tooth necklace, he stuck his bald tattooed head out the tower window. After shouting instructions in a language we could not understand, he sat back in his seat and lowered the giant mechanical arm into the hold. Back and forth went the crane, hoisting crates of food, drums of petrol, pallets stacked with sacks of cement. Men in hard hats ducked beneath the dangling loads. Chains rattled. Steel screeched. The cargo was expertly lowered onto a barge and motored to the island. Afterward, so were the passengers.

Of all the Marquesas Islands, Fatu Hiva was really something to behold. The morning we anchored there, I climbed from the belly of the ship and stared into a James Michener dream. Beyond the surf, sheer cliffs shot upward, leading to a wall of dancing palms at the base of a volcanic mountain. Carved with deep gorges and narrow ravines, the mountain was blanketed by thick green foliage and topped by at least four rock chimneys that disappeared into an unremitting layer of mist. Six hundred people live on the island. From our point of view, however, a broad white building at the edge of the beach was the only sign of life.

The shore excursions were a step above what you might expect on a standard cruise. Our herd roamed through one quaint village after another, smiling at locals who seemed genuinely pleased to see outsiders. We listened to archaeological lectures at overgrown tiki ruins, watched grass-skirted dancers and purchased cow-bone pendants and rings made of coconut shells. On the island of Tahuata (pop. 800), I attended morning Mass in the tiny village of Hapatoni. Inside a small white church across the road from the crashing surf, most of the eighty villagers had assembled. A four-piece band, complete with a ukulele strummer, played uplifting melodies during pauses in the sermon. The Marquesan congregation sang along in sweet, flowery bursts that my foreign ear could not decipher. But when I closed my eyes and locked arms with a stranger, the message came in loud and clear.

On Ua Huka my horse trotted down a hot asphalt road instead of galloping along the edge of a frothing beach the way I'd always seen in movies. On Hiva Oa, the Belgian woman fought back tears at the hillside grave of Jacques Brel. We dined on *poisson cru* (raw fish) at Rosalie's Restaurant on Ua Pou, watched giant manta rays perform an aquatic ballet off the coast of Ua Huka, and after returning to the ship each afternoon with my geriatric friends, I ate hearty dinners, drank goblets of wine, and gossiped about the French couple and the Pajama Lady while the *Aranui* sailed into the night.

THE MARQUESAS COW-POACHING FIASCO

With no hotel reservations, no real plan, and only a "novel" idea as to where the *Aranui* had anchored, I jumped ship at Nuku Hiva, compelled by the fact that Herman Melville committed the same rash act here in 1842. Two weeks aboard a cargo ship had me craving a bed that would not sway all night. Melville's reasons for abandoning ship were more urgent. Weary from eighteen months aboard the *Acushnet*, he wanted no more of the sea. With a vague idea in his head and a couple of stale biscuits in his pocket, the thrill-seeking New Yorker snuck away from his ship and disappeared. Pursued by an armed search party, he scampered inland through the tropical forest and across the mountains. He staved off hunger, the elements, and a shitload of second thoughts, until ultimately finding solace among the cannibals of the ancient Taipi tribe.

For nearly a month, Melville and the Taipi peacefully coexisted. But cannibalistic tummies soon began to growl. Unwilling to be served up as white meat, he escaped on an Australian merchant ship. Based on the experience, which afforded him a brief stay in a Papeete prison, Melville wrote *Typee: A Peep at Polynesian Life*, the first of five novels that preceded his masterpiece, *Moby-Dick*.

Dragging my duffel down the desolate main road that curves around Tahioae Bay, I tried to imagine the hardships Melville endured on this very island. During those first frantic nights, the would-be literary legend slept outside—battling hunger and drinking rainwater caught in the fold of a plant leaf—until stumbling upon the Taipi. How thrilling it must have been to embark on such an adventure. What a great tale to parlay into a novel. If I had had even an inkling of the Melvillean adventure awaiting me in less than forty-eight hours, however, I would have kept my butt on the ship.

It began with Filimoeika Kopeni. He appeared along the side of the road as if by magic. "Where you come from?" he said, stepping from behind a palm tree with a suddenness that made me jump. He stared at me, his dark eyes squinting in the sun. I stared back, stunned by his appearance. The unsmiling Marquesan stood eye to eye with me, but boasted a powerful chest and Popeye forearms upon which crude tattoos had been scrawled. What stood out most was Filimoeika's head. It had been shaved clean like mine, but was covered in tattoos that formed a maze of Polynesian symbols.

I stared at Filimoeika's head for what seemed like a day before I answered.

"I come from Miami Beach."

"Ahhh," he said, nodding his decorated noggin. "*Miami Vice.* Don Johnson!" When he learned I had just arrived on the *Aranui* and was looking for a place to stay, he gazed at the ship that lay tethered to the wharf at the far end of the bay. His eyes shifted to my dusty duffel and then to my Nikes. Filimoeika nodded approvingly. "I fighting man," he said, tapping his chest with one hand and reaching into his pocket with the other. The photograph he presented showed himself as a much younger man. A man with cropped hair and no cranial tattoos. Appearing with him in the photo were several white men wearing crew cuts and army fatigues. The photo, Filimoeika claimed, had been taken in France. "Commando!" he said, tapping his chest again. "I fight with French Foreign Legion." He said this with a measure of pride. "You need room?"

"You mean, hotel room?"

"I have friend," he said. "He give you good price."

Filimoeika grabbed my bag with only one hand and carried it over to his Jeep. Less than fifteen minutes on the island and I had already found a hotel room and a friend. This was going to be a great three-day stay. I could sense it.

We drove down the main road alongside the bay, turned onto a residential lane, and pulled into the driveway of Pension Paahatea Nui. Before introducing me to the owner and helping me with my bag, Filimoeika extended a warm invitation. "Tomorrow you come my house."

The next morning, I waited for Filimoeika but he never showed. Disappointed, I ambled down the main road, wondering what to do with the day. I passed a ramshackle graveyard, a group of tiki statues staring out to sea, a concrete basketball court with a ragged volleyball net stretched across the middle, the surprisingly modern Banque Socredo, which must have been closed for an early lunch, and a sagging wooden inn called Chez something or other. The village seemed utterly deserted. An indigent man was the only human being in sight. Eyes shut, his back propped against a wall, he sat quietly near the entrance to the general store. I sidestepped his outstretched feet and walked inside.

The shelves were stocked with all the basic necessities. Because 85 percent of French Polynesia's products are imported, however, tariffs, taxes, and transportation fees bump up the prices a tad. A box of Kellogg's Froot Loops goes for $6.63 U.S. A 500-ml. bottle of Palmolive dishwashing liquid, $6.54. A 200-ml. tube of Garnier Laboratories sunblock (imported from Paris) costs $18.05. Such inflated prices could drive locals to drink. If they could afford it. Seven hundred fifty-ml. bottles of Tanqueray, Bailey's, and Cointreau sell for about $40 each. But wait, it gets better.

Perched on a shelf directly above the liquor bottles were three spanking new Alpina professional chain saws: the PR-350, the P-460, and the strapping twenty-four-inch P-760. Liquor and chain saws, they go so well together. *Sweetheart, would you be a dear and pick up a couple bottles of Smirnoff? And while you're at it, grab one of those Alpina P-760s. I'm feeling woodsy tonight.* Such random product placement could inspire a rash of Marquesan chain saw murders. Thankfully, the machines were overpriced.

Just as I left the store, a familiar Jeep nosed up to the door. Filimoeika Kopeni stepped out into the sunshine. After I politely mentioned that he'd forgotten to meet me at the Paahatea Nui, Filimoeika's face lit up.

"Oh. Change program," he said, his eyes flicking uneasily. "We go home now."

"Now?"

"Yes, yes. Change program. We go now."

Because I had mispronounced his name every time I'd used it, Filimoeika suggested I call him "Fili."

He told me to wait in the Jeep while he picked up something from the general store. I followed orders, wondering if he would return with a bottle of Cointreau in one hand and an Alpina P-760 in the other. As soon as I sat in the passenger seat and closed the door, the indigent man struggled to his feet and began inching ever so slowly toward the Jeep. With the help of a rickety cane, he placed a bony hand on the rear door handle and began to pull.

"Uhhh . . . excuse me," I said. But the old man didn't seem to hear. He pulled at the handle even harder. "I think you've made a mistake," I continued. Frustrated by his inability to open the door, yet acting as if I did not exist, he pushed his cane through the open window. It landed lengthwise on the backseat. With one great grunting effort, the old man yanked open the door and crawled inside. He laid the cane across his thighs and sat there, trembling. I thought he was about to have a heart attack.

Unsure what to do, I sat quietly in the passenger seat, waiting for Fili to return. A moment later, he hopped in and started the engine, failing to acknowledge the old man. Instead, Fili launched into a tirade about the lack of meat on the island. "Fish, fish, every day eat fish." He shook his head, threw the Jeep into reverse. Despite Fili's agitated state, he must have noticed our new passenger. But the old man and Fili never exchanged a word, never even exchanged a glance. Like a stuntman in *The Dukes of Hazzard*, he whipped the Jeep around, and we went flying up the main road in a cloud of dust.

After a lengthy silence, I felt compelled to speak up. "Do you know this man?" I whispered.

"Yes, yes. He live near my house."

And so we drove the five-minute distance to Fili Kopeni's house. "Fish, fish," he repeated, shaking his head again and again. According to Fili, he and his family ate fish three times every day.

We turned up a dirt road and stopped to let the old man out near Fili's house. It looked more like the beginnings of a house, really. Perched on a lumpy hillside, the frail wooden frame rested on cinder blocks that had been positioned on the corners and in the middle. A doorway had been carved out, but there was no door. More cinder blocks had been stacked in front of the doorway to create crude front porch steps.

The interior looked as if a cyclone had struck. Clothing was strewn on the floor and piled high in plastic baskets. Damp clothes hung from a line that stretched across the kitchen area. The kitchen table was littered with all sorts of things: buckets, knives, pots, jars of dark liquid, plastic bags filled with unimaginable things. A sheet hung from the doorway of the tiny bedroom Fili shared with his wife. The other room belonged to their twelve-year-old daughter. All this was covered with a corrugated metal roof. With the sun pounding relentlessly upon it, the heat was almost unbearable.

Fili's daughter sat on a stained mattress in front of the television. Hypnotized by televised images, like twelve-year-olds all over the world, she turned to look at me and smiled shyly when she did. "Sit, sit," Fili said. Unable to find anything to sit on, I cleared a space near his daughter. Together, we watched an *X-Files* episode dubbed in French. Mulder and Scully were in the middle of a car chase. *"Aller, aller!"* cried Mulder, as Scully gunned the engine. *"Voulez vous froie gras en le poo poo avec moi?"*

When Fili called my name from the backyard, I had to yank myself away from the provocative TV dialogue. There I found him, standing inside a dilapidated pigpen with two grimy oinkers, one of which he held by its hind legs. The pig squealed as if it were being murdered, which, considering what happened moments later, seemed like an appropriate response.

Holding the animal with both hands, Fili tried to step over the fence. Alas, the fence was too high. Consequently, he held the pig over the fence and motioned for me to grab it. As much as I wanted to help, a life weaned in the city had severed my connection with nature. (I grew up believing bacon was created, like Corn Flakes, in a food factory.) Holding a wriggling pig in my hands—a screaming one at that—was too much to ask.

Fili rolled his eyes. Grabbing the screaming pig by one leg, he used his free hand for balance and swung his body up and over the sagging fence. He carried the pig to the front of the house, tied one end of a rope to one hind leg, tossed the other end over a low-hanging branch, and hung the screaming animal upside down beneath a giant banyan tree. More intense than a scream, really, the pig let loose a piercing wail of horror. There were no pauses in the sound, just one long continuous screech that seemed to require no breath or energy.

Fili positioned a bucket directly beneath the wiggling swine. He walked over to a warped picnic table upon which lay an assortment of torture-chamber instruments: a corroded handsaw, a hammer claw, meat hooks, soiled ropes, the rusting carcass of a chain saw (he could use that new Alpina P-760). Among the cruel utensils lay a shiny, six-inch hunting knife. Fili picked it up. He walked over to the screaming pig. With one hand he clamped its snout shut. Waving the knife in his other hand like a magician about to perform a clever trick, Fili looked at me and grinned. He obviously enjoyed this sort of work. The pig did not. He pressed the tip of the blade against Little Piggy's throat, making a dimple there. The animal's eyes seemed to grow larger as the gravity of the situation sank in. Fili moved the blade, dimpling one area of the neck, then another, much like a doctor might move a stethoscope. Having finally found just the right place, Fili slid the blade in, slowly, almost lovingly, shoving it deeper as blood splashed noisily into the bucket. The pig's muted screams turned into gurgling whispers. Four little pink legs squiggled no more.

"Commando!" Fili said, letting the word hang victoriously in the air. A moment later we were in the Jeep, reversing down the rutted slope. I sat quietly in the passenger seat, fighting an urge to regurgitate, not knowing where we were headed. I had never seen an animal slaughtered. Never watched skin being separated from flesh, never seen blood squirting, guts being ripped out. Never saw limbs being hacked off a creature from a beloved nursery rhyme. *This little piggy went to market. This little piggy stayed home. This little piggy is a pork chop* . . . So gory was the killing, I found myself contemplating a life of vegetarianism. But by the time we pulled up to the German's home, I was already dreaming of a double Whopper with cheese.

After exchanging whispers with Fili, the German climbed inside and shook my hand. That seemed odd, the whispering. But when Dieter Grosz introduced himself, I thought no more if it. Tired of the bourgeois life in Düsseldorf, he gave up a thriving accounting practice and came here several years ago to live a simple island life. Wearing wraparound sunglasses and a bandanna around his neck, Dieter slid something long and heavy beneath his seat. Whatever it was, it had been wrapped in an oilcloth. When I inquired about the contents, Fili turned and looked at me. "Shhhhh . . . ," he said, putting his index finger to his lips. "It not legal."

The road that winds up Mount Muake was a bumpy dirt track just a few weeks earlier. But now that the road had been paved, many islanders, especially the younger ones, were speeding around the turns at breakneck speed. As we lurched toward yet another sharp curve, Fili pointed to fresh skid marks and told of a car that had driven off the cliff a few days earlier. Two men were dead. Progress has its disadvantages.

We climbed farther up the mountain, rounding the curves, plowing through the straightaways, climbing higher, turning some more, feeling cool air rush through the open windows. The drive up Mount Muake was breathtaking, and not only because of Fili's kamikaze driving. From here the view of Tahioae Bay is spectacular. Framed by fertile green hills, the bay stretches outward in a dramatic sweep of blue. Gentle rollers, caught one after the other in brilliant streaks of sunlight, pushed ever so slightly toward the shore. A lone white bird, silent and free, swooped down into the valley and disappeared. When we pulled to the side of the road to appreciate yet another picture-postcard view, I couldn't get over the silence. There was absolutely no sound. No screeching tires. No roaring jet engines. No voices, and no ringing cellular phones. The only place I'd experienced quiet like this was in the skies above southern Florida, during my one and only skydiving attempt. When my parachute opened, I sailed through the clouds in beautiful, blissful silence. You can live a hundred years and never experience a truly silent moment. Having had the opportunity twice in my life, I considered myself a lucky man.

When our Jeep finally rolled to a halt among the eucalyptus trees, I thought Fili had stopped to show off yet another of Nuku Hiva's spectacular views. But when he and Dieter leapt from the vehicle, I realized we had come for something else. Fili tied a camouflage bandanna around his head. He strapped a hunting knife to one leg, and unwrapped one of two rifles that had been wrapped in the oilcloth. He inserted a cartridge. Dieter followed suit. I heard the clicking of metal, the clipping of belts. The sound of macho warfare. Dressed in army fatigues and boots, rifles clutched against their chests, Fili and Dieter had gone Rambo. I stood there in a T-shirt and dirty Nikes, wondering why they had brought me here. Fili handed me a pink plastic bag containing two water jugs. I looked inside, saw the containers, and understood my mission. We had embarked on an illegal hunting expedition; I was the designated water boy.

Without a word, without giving me instructions, the two commandos exchanged a nod and darted into the bushes. For a moment, I stood alone beneath the canopy of trees, feeling like an abandoned child. Then I bolted after Fili and Dieter, a camera in my left hand, the pink plastic bag in the right.

Through the low prickly bushes I went, following the sound of crackling branches. The two men moved expertly along the crest of a primordial valley. Blanketed with green shrubs, the gorge descended precipitously toward a monumental V that led to the hazy blue sea. From there I could actually see the shimmering curve of the planet. No time to dwell on Mother Nature, however. I had to keep up with Fili and Dieter. Every minute or so I'd catch glimpses of movement between the bushes. Silence. The echo of a baying goat. A shout. Then a gunshot. I ran toward the sound, realizing almost instantly the futility of my path. An echo can play tricks on the uninitiated. The gunshot had seemingly come from every corner of the valley. Suddenly, there was movement up ahead. I ran over to investigate, and saw Dieter. He walked down the slope and stood over a wounded goat. The poor animal lay in the grass, gasping, its tongue hanging limply from its maw. The German reached down with his hunting knife and with one fluid motion he slit the creature's throat. For the second time that day, the second time in my life, I watched the killing and disembowelment of an animal.

At one point Dieter ripped out the neat white sack of innards and tossed it into the grass. "Tomorrow in ze morning, zis vill be gone," he said, pointing his bloody knife toward the sack of guts. "Ze vild pigs, zey come out at night. Zey vill eat it."

By the time both water jugs had been emptied, sunset had come upon us. The air cooled. In an hour or so, ze vild pigs would be burrowing through ze darkness, munching on goat innards and God knows what else. When Fili finally showed up and saw Dieter's kill, the Marquesan became visibly upset. "Fish, fish, everyday eat fish," he muttered, as we stomped through the bushes on the way to the Jeep. We walked for what seemed like a long time. Uphill. Downhill. Around in circles. As we stumbled through the woods, my pink plastic bag—which now contained the bloody goat skin—got snagged on the prickly branches of low-lying bushes. Holes appeared in the plastic. To prevent the bag from being literally ripped to shreds, I tossed it over one shoulder. (Not until later would I realize that goat blood had seeped through the holes in the bag and onto the back of my T-shirt.)

After a while, it became apparent that we were lost. Fili assured me we weren't. Dieter did not seem convinced. His head swiveled among the bushes, scanning the valley in the most helter-skelter manner. We walked. The sky darkened yet another notch. Fili joked about having to sleep outside that night. Wild pigs. *Zey come out at night.* I did not find this funny. Just when I cursed myself for abandoning the *Aranui*, we walked into a clearing and sprinted when we saw the Jeep.

We drove toward town. I sat in the backseat, slobbering gleefully in a state of semiconsciousness. Before the lights went out completely, I noticed Dieter. He sat in the passenger seat with his rifle leaning against the inside of his left leg. The barrel angled back and pointed directly at my face. At first I didn't say anything.

But as we rolled over a bump in the road, a scene from *Pulp Fiction* came to mind. Samuel L. Jackson was driving the car. John Travolta sat in the passenger seat, his handgun pointed carelessly at a guy called Marvin in the backseat. When their car rolled over a bump in the road, Travolta's gun went off accidentally. "Oh shit," Travolta said, after he and Samuel L. had been splattered with blood and brains. "I just shot Marvin in the face."

The unforgettable scene set my mouth in motion. "Excuse me," I said, hoping not to startle the German commando. "But your rifle is pointing at my face."

"Oh. Don't worry," Dieter said. "We are very safe." He leaned the rifle against the other thigh. "If you were safe," I wanted to say, "you wouldn't have had a goddam rifle pointed at my goddam face!"

When I woke up perhaps thirty minutes later, the Jeep had pulled to the side of the road. Fili and Dieter were whispering. Outside, I saw the dark outline of a mountain against a background of stars. Then I saw the cows. Maybe a dozen of them. They marched down the middle of the road, nudging each other as if in conversation. Dieter rolled down his window, pointed the rifle, and squeezed off the first shot.

You'd be surprised how fast a cow can run when it's being shot at. Caught in the flicker of headlights, its massive belly swinging from side to side, the elusive bovine galloped around a bend in the road the way Seabiscuit charged the turn at Churchill Downs. Along the dark island path it went—fleet of hoof, wide of rump, running from our Jeep and for its life.

Fili leaned over the steering wheel with an eagerness that begged to send his face crashing through the dusty windshield. Despite the fact that cow poaching is illegal just about everywhere on the planet—including the island of Nuku Hiva—Fili's hunched body wriggled in anticipation of the kill. He traded a conspirator's grin with Dieter, who sat vigilantly in the passenger's seat. Dieter drew the stock of the rifle across his own chest; the barrel angled out the open window. He glanced again at Fili, then tossed a look over one shoulder and grinned at me. I tried to smile, but couldn't. Wanted to say something, but knew I shouldn't. Like it or not, I was about to become an accessory to murder.

"*Arrêtez, arrêtez*," Dieter whispered seconds later, speaking French rather than German. The cow had come to a precarious halt perhaps forty yards ahead. It stood sideways, panting, the length of its fattened body blocking the road as if by design. Fili braked. The Jeep squealed and stopped. Lips moist with drivel, head angled upward as if contemplating a philosophical question, the animal stared into the blinding headlights and appeared to wink at us. These eerie human qualities, not to mention the illegal weaponry (hunting on Nuku Hiva, according to Fili, is permitted using bow and arrow only), made our impromptu attack even more atrocious. Where was the sense of gamesmanship? As the cow began to ruminate, Dieter leaned out the window and leveled the rifle. I looked away. Fili whispered, "Now . . . NOW!" One second. Two. A single shot crackled across the inky countryside and echoed beneath a ceiling of shimmering stars. The echo died. Unlike the crafty cow. Dieter could no longer contain himself. "*Merde! Putain de merde!*" Having eluded a bullet for the third time in as many minutes, the four-legged target turned tail. It sprinted boldly past our Jeep and down the road again.

Fili hit the gas. The Jeep swung around in a screechless fishtail. Like the bad guy in a good action flick, Dieter leaned out the window of our speeding vehicle and squeezed off another round. "*Merde!*" Here on the tropical island of Nuku Hiva, the same remote location of the fourth *Survivor* television series, same place where Herman Melville lived among cannibals after jumping ship in 1842, home to three thousand latter-day Marquesans who have since lost their appetite for human flesh, land of wild white sand beaches, centuries-old archaeological sites, and Vaipo waterfall, one of the world's highest and most beautiful, here, in this unspoiled paradise, beneath a crescent moon veiled by drifting clouds, three potential felons—one Marquesan, one German, and me, the hapless American—pursued a fat farm animal that dodged bullets like the hero in *The Matrix*.

Unable to keep my mouth shut any longer, I sat upright in the backseat. "I don't mean to spoil anything. But that cow . . . doesn't it belong to somebody?"

Fili's tattooed head swiveled around as if mounted on ball bearings. He threw a look that made me lean back in my seat. "Shut up," he said, without having to open his mouth. "You're just a fucking tourist. . . ."

Fili's failure to bag a goat had apparently encouraged a cow poaching. Separated from the herd, the target galloped around the bend and stopped. Dieter fired. Missed again. We chased the cow in the opposite direction. At some point, it darted from the road and into the pasture, which was separated from the road by a barbed-wire fence.

Fili stopped the Jeep. He put on a miner's helmet with a flashlight strapped onto it. Intent on finishing the job Dieter had started, Fili snatched the rifle and took off running. From my position on the road about fifty yards away, I watched the drama unfold. The cow stopped cold, illuminated by the swath of light cutting through the darkness. The poor creature stood there in the pasture, panting, lit up like a prop in a Broadway play. Filimoeika, which in Polynesian means "enemy of sharks," quickly became "enemy of cows." He aimed the rifle. Fired. The cow jumped almost comically, its hooves kicking in the air like Wylie Coyote before the anvil falls. Then it fell to the ground in a heap.

Dieter joined Fili at the crime scene. I heard whispers. Someone called my name. It was Fili. He and Dieter needed help. "Come, come," he shouted.

"No," I replied, between clenched lips. I wasn't about to drag a dead cow across the pasture.

"Come, come. Hurry!"

What were my options? Refuse, and run the risk of being left in the middle of nowhere? Or bathe in cow blood? Reluctantly, I walked over to the barbed-wire fence. I'd often wondered about the restrictive nature of barbed-wire fences. Perhaps they could keep a herd from disappearing, but it seemed easy enough for a human to slip through the gaps between wires. "Seemed," was the operative word. I did not slide neatly between the barbed wires. The barbs caught the front of my T-shirt. While attempting to pull loose, my pants got caught. The back of my T-shirt, too. I hung there like a fly in a spiderweb until Fili rushed over and pulled me loose.

I followed Fili across the grass. We soon joined Dieter, who was bending over the dead cow and staring with morbid fascination. Fili whispered in the darkness. "Okay, grab leg." Dieter shook out of his trance and grabbed one leg. Fili grabbed another. They looked up sharply, waiting for me to become an accessory after the fact. Against my better judgment, I took hold of a bristly leg and pulled. Beneath the crescent moon, we dragged the body across the pasture, loaded it into the back of the Jeep, and drove away. Dieter and Fili giggled like teenage boys in a topless bar. Speaking excitedly in French, and no doubt dreaming of filet mignon, Fili guided the Jeep along the darkened road.

Meanwhile, I sat in the backseat, closer to the deceased. The cow stank of manure and animal sweat. Its four legs stuck straight in the air. Fili must have noticed too because he asked me to climb back there and push down the legs.

"No," I said, shaking my head. "I am not climbing on top of a dead cow."

"We need move legs," he said. "The people, they see through window when drive through village."

"Nope."

"Come, come. Please?" Then a low blow. "I took you to good tourism, no? I save you from barbwire fence."

With that, I crawled over the backseat into the cargo compartment and straddled the dead cow. My knees sank into the soft flesh of its belly. My hands pushed into the hot, sweaty skin. The stench of cow shit—the animal's final, defiant act—filled my nostrils. I grabbed a bristly cow leg and pushed down. The leg popped up. I pushed down again. The leg popped up again. This wasn't going to work. I told Fili so. "Okay, okay, change program," he said. Instead of driving straight to his house along the main road, we took a back road and sneaked up Fili's rutted driveway without detection.

In the backyard of Filimoeika Kopeni's house, aided by flashlights and two accomplices, the deft Marquesan butchered the cow using only a hunting knife. It was a forty-five-minute surgical spectacle that began with an incision along the belly and ended with a bony carcass. Each time Fili severed a flank, he cut crude handholds into which I slid my hands. I carried the bloody body parts and hung them from meat hooks that dangled from the same tree limb the pig had dangled from earlier. After the grisly task had been completed, Fili waved goodbye and disappeared into the house. Instead of "fish, fish," there would be steak for the Kopenis tonight.

Dieter drove in silence, delivering me to the Pension Paahatea Nui five minutes later. When I closed the car door, he stuck his head out the window.

"I am sorry you must zee zis," he said. "It is not what you expect on zis beautiful island, no?" Truer words were never spoken.

I staggered into the bathroom and stared at the gaunt face in the mirror. Writer. Flight attendant. International cow poacher. But something more than guilt had altered the vision of myself. Turning one cheek to the mirror, I suddenly realized what it was. Splattum. Cow gore. Clinging to the skin below my left eye was a pale, gelatinous clump of matter that looked like something a baby might cough up. As I flicked it from my face, my stomach began to rumble uncontrollably. I shut my eyes. On the dark screens of my inner eyelids flashed a graphic triple feature. First up, the grossly entertaining pig-butchering scene, complete with squealing audio. This was followed by a dead goat highlight film. *Tomorrow, zis vill be gone.* Next came the feature attraction: Poached Cow. The poor defenseless animal shot at point-blank range by a meat-deprived Marquesan and then sat upon by a whining American. The cow's flanks hacked off. Its belly slit. Guts removed. Warm blood seeping from the carcass into the moist black earth in back of Filimoeika Kopeni's hillside shack. (Herman Melville lived with cannibals for nearly a month and I bet he never saw this much blood.) Eyes shut, hands gripping the sink in an effort to brace for the inevitable, I lowered my face in time for the first convulsion.

Australia

SEX(?) ON THE BEACH

◄┈┈┈┈┈┈┈┈┈┈►

After a two-hour flight from Nuku Hiva to Tahiti, a six-hour wait at the airport, and an eight-hour connecting flight to Sydney, Australia, I checked into the Bernly Hotel and emerged the next morning to find a prostitute with her skirt hiked up, squatting—not ten feet outside the lobby door—in the midst of an urgent bladder purge. She actually looked up and winked at me without interrupting the flow. Was I supposed to stop mid-stride, overlook the tattoo dragon slithering up her pasty arm, ignore the matted hair, the piercings, the bloodshot eyes, the yellowish fluid pooling between her scuffed stilettos, and the sudden sickening realization that her panties were as grimy as a car mechanic's hand towel? Was I supposed to ignore all this, wink back, and say, "Oh yeah, baby . . . you are *soooo* hot"? Steering clear of the runoff, I hurried past the squatter en route to the subway and salvation.

The previous night, this very same sidewalk had been packed with men. An endless parade of men. Eyes wide, faces lit with glee and expectation, they seemed hypnotized by the neon lights of Darlinghurst Road—specifically, the neon lights outside the strip clubs. Some of these men were lured into the clubs by huskers wearing dingy white dress shirts and black ties. "Aw, come on, mate . . . have a look. Plenty of sheilas inside."

Two men—they may have looked a bit too long that night—lay unconscious on the sidewalk. Sidestepping the drying splats no doubt attributable to both of them, I descended the steps to King's Cross Station and asked the metro employee for a ticket to Bondi Beach. "Not *Bon-dee*," he said, mocking my accent through the window vent. He slid a round-trip ticket underneath the window and pronounced the word properly. "It's *Bon-dye*, mate. *Bon-dye*." Named for the Aboriginal word that means "water breaking over rocks," Bondi, Sydney's preeminent beach, would be a sight for very sore eyes.

The beach was packed by the time I got there. Surfers paddled away from shore, hoping that at least one of the gentle waves would turn into a monster. Topless women lay sprawled across the sand like survivors from a shipwreck. Trying not to look and failing miserably, I jogged from one end of the rambling beach to the other. Back and forth I went, smiling, trotting, looking, but not really, until overcome by the need to go barefoot. After removing my Nikes, I ran wind sprints in the sand. This was a mistake, of course. During the third or fourth sprint, I stepped on a rock. An explosion of pain sent me tumbling to the wet sand. There were chuckles from several onlookers, but a couple of concerned guys ran over to see if I was okay. I wasn't. My ankle inflated like a cheap inner tube, right before our eyes. Sometime later I found myself in the emergency room at Sydney Hospital.

X rays were taken. A specialist consulted. A hospital cash register went *cha-ching* inside my head. The doctor analyzed the X rays and said nothing was broken. It was only a severe ankle sprain. He told me to keep the foot elevated, apply ice, and fill the prescription for painkillers that he handed over after slapping me on the shoulder and saying, "Gooday."

I sat on the examination table, expecting someone to direct me to the bill payment queue. But no such direction was given. Five minutes went by. Ten. Had the system broken down? Did hospital bean counters allow me to slip through the cracks? As fast as my injured foot would carry me, I limped out of Sydney Hospital, worried that at any moment a health care professional would come charging down McQuarie Street with an unpaid bill jutting from her outstretched hand. Then I remembered. This was Australia, not the United States. Unlike the situation back home, the Australian government views basic health care as a birthright. X rays, treatment, and consultation had been 100 percent free. God bless Australia. Maybe I'll retire there one day.

After two days of therapeutic television in my room at the Bernly Hotel, I returned to Bondi Beach. Instead of jogging, however, I hobbled to a spot in the sand and collapsed on a beach towel. My injury turned out to be a terrific icebreaker. The woman lying near me—yes, she just happened to be topless— volunteered to watch my bag as I struggled to my feet and limped toward the water. When I returned, refreshed by a frigid ninety-second dip, the woman introduced herself as Tanya (*Tan-ya*, not *Tahn-ya*). Although her parents hailed from Malta, she was Australian through and through. Bronze skin glowing in the hot summer sun, her head topped with luxurious coils, Tanya turned out to be the epitome of Aussie friendliness. Her parents had immigrated to Australia some twenty-five years earlier. Like the Lebanese, Greeks, Italians, and countless others, Maltese began flocking to Australia in droves after the government opened the immigration floodgates in the 1950s.

John Pilger's *A Secret Country* tells how the Australian government dispatched immigration officers to Europe in an effort to recruit citizens for its population-starved country. Thousands of men and women from Naples to Istanbul hoped to qualify for passage on the voyage Down Under. One determining factor was skin color. If an applicant's skin was too dark, according to a retired immigration officer interviewed in Pilger's book, he or she was simply not invited. Tanya's parents had apparently passed the test. Ironically, a couple of decades of Australian sunshine had darkened their daughter's skin considerably. If latter-day

Tanya had stood in the same immigration line with her parents years ago, she might have been forced to stay behind.

Tanya was between jobs. She eked out a living on the government dole and spent her days much like this one—lying on a towel at Bondi Beach. According to the voluptuous sun worshipper, the Australian government allowed a liberal dispersal of welfare benefits. Rumor had it that some high school graduates applied for the dole soon after graduation day. How tempting would this be for a teenage hedonist? *Hmmm . . . let's see. Should I get a job and work my butt off, enroll at a university and study my butt off, or lie on a beach towel all day long at Bondi?* In the Australian TV documentary series *Tales from a Suitcase,* an aging Estonian immigrant was asked about the best aspect of being Australian. "You don't have to do nothing if you don't want," he said, his voice laden with a Baltic accent. "The government, it takes care of you."

Thirty minutes into the conversation, I mentioned to Tanya how nice it would be to live here. To lie on a beach towel all day and feel the Bondi breeze at night. Tanya raised her Jackie-O sunglasses and measured my eyes with her own. "You can move into my apartment if you want."

You're probably beginning to question the veracity of my story. The ease with which Tanya (*Tan-ya,* not *Tahn-ya*) invited me into her home is something worth considering. But it's true, every word of it. There's only one way to explain my good fortune. Serendipity. Plain and simple. I'm certainly not the kind of guy who makes women weak in the knees. In fact, *my* knees are weak. Weak and bony and attached to legs as thin as No. 2 pencils—at least that's how they were described back in high school. And sometimes, when in the company of an attractive woman, I stutter. Even when she's carefree and responsive and lying topless on Bondi Beach—*especially* when she's carefree and responsive and lying topless on Bondi Beach.

"M-m-move into your apartment?"

"Yeah. I'll charge you . . . hmmm," she tapped her chin thought-fully and squinted in the sun. "How's ninety dollars a week?"

We rolled up our towels, crossed Campbell Parade, and en-tered a minuscule apartment that boasted one small well-furnished bedroom and a smaller one outfitted with a chair and twin bed. The view from the small room was astounding. A tiny window overlooked a swath of Bondi Beach and the deep blue ocean beyond.

Back to King's Cross I limped to gather my things. The follow-ing day, I knocked on Tanya's door with my rolling duffel in tow. "Come in," she said, her voice far away. "The door is open." Once inside, I parked my duffel and nearly had a heart attack. The Maltese-Australian beauty with the caramel-candy body was standing behind an ironing board in the middle of the living room. She wore a big smile, a pair of thong-bikini panties, and nothing else. "You gonna' stand there with the door open?" she said.

I closed my mouth.

"The door?"

I followed orders, staring, and yet trying not to stare at Tanya's naked breasts.

"Look," she said, holding the steaming iron in my direction as if threatening to singe my bulging eyes. "You've seen me like this on the beach, right?"

"Ahhh . . . yeah."

"It's no different here in the flat."

"But do y-you think this is appropriate?" I said, feebly.

"Appropriate?"

"You know . . . us being alone and all."

"Yanks," Tanya replied, shaking her head and pressing the steaming iron against a blouse she donned a moment later. "You're all so . . . American."

Later that evening, when I returned to the apartment after crisscrossing Sydney Harbor (*Ha-bah*, not *Har-ber*) on a succes-sion of ferries, I passed Tanya's bedroom door, which was closed.

I showered, dressed, and prepared to hit Campbell Parade in search of fish & chips. But after leaving my room, I noticed Tanya's door was suddenly wide open. She lay in bed—dressed in a flannel nightgown that deemphasized her curves—chewing an apple and reading a dictionary by candlelight.

Tanya asked about my day. I leaned against the doorjamb and inquired about hers, which, to no surprise, had been spent on a beach towel at Bondi. As she spoke, I noticed that the quality of her voice had changed. It sounded deeper. More resonant. Her voice was soon lost to the shadows, however. It was the apple that did it. The way she bit into it so viciously after sliding the dictionary beneath the bed. The loud crunching sound it made, bite after ravenous bite. I couldn't stop staring at . . . the apple.

As if on cue, a languid breeze rustled the curtains behind Tanya's gorgeous hair. She propped herself up against the pillows—an actress preparing to film the love scene in a music video, a Victoria's Secret model flaunting the latest in flannel loungewear. Silence, broken only by the prodigious chomping of fruit, stretched between us. I felt my heart hammering against my chest. A sudden tingling in the testes. Without warning, Tanya thrust the apple forward and held it up at a provocative angle. In a voice as sweet and hypnotizing as the big brown eyes that held me in a blinkless gaze, she said: "Would you like a bite?"

Tanya turned out to be a freak. A board-game freak. The morning after sharing the first of what I thought would be many apples, she leapt out of bed, reached into the closet, and tossed upon the tangled sheets a Deluxe Edition Scrabble game by Milton Bradley.

"You play?" she said, her voice brash and cocksure.

"Uh, yeah," I replied, shielding my eyes from sunlight slicing through the open window. "But usually when I'm awake."

"Wake up, then. Let's play."

Interested in playing a different kind of game, I moved a stealthy hand toward Tanya's naked thigh. She smacked it away. "Don't hassle me," she said. "Let's play."

"Scrabble?"

"What else?"

"First thing in the morning?"

"That's when the mind is at its best, mate." Without waiting for a response, Tanya rubbed her hands together. She opened the Scrabble board and dumped the pouch of letter squares. Perhaps this was an early morning custom in Australia. In Vietnam thousands of locals rise at dawn, not to work the rice fields or factories, but rather to play badminton. It's the country's national pastime. Maybe Scrabble had a similar hold on the Australians.

During the first moments of board-game competition, Tanya showed glimpses of what proved to be a superior vocabulary. After each of three successful turns in which she spelled words I'd never heard of, I reached for the *Oxford Unabridged English Dictionary* she kept beneath her bed. We had agreed to accept both the *Oxford* and *American Heritage* spellings, seeing as how we were accustomed to conflicting lexicons. Both "color" and "colour" would therefore be accepted, as would "aluminum" and "aluminium." But when she spelled GNUS, I had to stifle a laugh before reaching for the dictionary to challenge the word. "Gnus? I think you blew this one, my dear. What in the world is gnus?"

Tanya cleared her throat and spoke in the voice of a pompous schoolmarm, a voice that strangely enough seemed to suit her. "First of all, the word is pronounced *noos*, not *ga-nuss*." She rolled her eyes. "Because 'gnus' happens to be the plural of 'gnu,'" she continued pompously, "the proper question would then be, 'What in the world *are* gnus?'"

"Okay, okay, so what are gnus?"

"Antelope. Very large African antelope with heads like oxen. They have downward-curving horns and a beard."

I looked it up in the *Oxford*. Damned if she wasn't on the money. Right down to the part about the beard. GNUS. With those same four letters I probably would have spelled a lowbrow word like SNUG or SUNG, which were no doubt considerations for Tanya as well. GNUS was her way of showing off. That smirk—the one she was beginning to flash with annoying frequency—told me so. GNUS. The same four letters spelled GUNS.

We stayed in bed all morning and well into the afternoon. But not because I enjoyed the vocabulary lessons during eight consecutive Scrabble defeats. Throughout each heated contest, Tanya made cruel jokes about the intellectual inferiority of Americans. "Do people in your country read books? I heard Yanks watch telly eight hours a day. Isn't Jerry Springer the minister of education?" (Broadcast throughout Australia, *The Jerry Springer Show* is a slice of Americana that would have been best kept to ourselves. Thanks to satellite technology, however, 19 million Aussies believe that most Americans live in a trailer park and engage in sexual intercourse with trisexual siblings.)

I redoubled my spelling efforts. Not only for myself, but for nearly 300 million countrymen whose reputations rested on my shaky shoulders. THRUST. PATRON. SIGNAL. ABYSS. I thought hard and long, concocting words that used up as many letter squares as possible. Still, I was no match for the brainy Australian. In effortless deliberations that required mere seconds, she used all seven letter squares and placed them next to a letter already on the board—thus creating eight-letter blockbusters that gave her fifty bonus points. INCUBATE. CYSTEINE. TURGIDLY. QAWWALIS. "Qawwalis?" Not only was I miffed by the definition, but she had come up with one of those rare *Q* words that require no *U*. In the process she managed to use two *W*s. At first I thought she had made lucky letter draws. But no matter how many vowels or consonants she plucked from the mattress, Tanya came up with one victorious word after another.

Through the open window came a refreshing sound. Laughter. Something that was sorely missing from our deteriorating relationship. I looked out and saw a trio of teenagers, sunglasses wrapped around their faces, surfboards grafted to their hips. "Let's go to the beach," I said.

"Okay. As soon as we finish this game. You're just going to die when you see my next word."

She showed the word. I died.

"Let's bring the Scrabble board with us," she said.

"Let's not."

My opinion was apparently as worthless as my spelling game. Tanya gathered up the letter squares, dropped them in the pouch, and placed the Deluxe Edition Scrabble board in a beach bag.

We lay on a beach towel for the remainder of the day, wearing sunglasses and sweating in the sun, while Tanya kicked my vocabulary-challenged butt. When I looked up from the board and made a statement like, "Wow, it's a beautiful day," she'd say: "B.E.A.U.T.I.F.U.L. Beautiful. Maybe you could use that during the next game."

"Ha, ha, very funny."

"F.U.N.N.Y. Funny."

"Look, Tanya," I said, grasping at the last shreds of composure. "Don't you think you're taking this whole spelling thing a bit too far? Can we drop the Scrabble metaphors? Let's forget about the game and have some fun."

"F.U.N. Fun. That's an easy one, even for you."

Turning to look at her smirking face, I suddenly understood why Tanya had no job, no friends, no life. Why she spent her days alone on the sand at Bondi. She was a Scrabble addict. A Deluxe Edition word junkie. Vocabulary was her life. She didn't smoke, drink, eat meat, or use drugs. Didn't own a television, radio, or computer. In the three days we spent together, her telephone rang once. The conversation lasted four seconds. Tanya didn't read Hemingway or Allende. Wasn't keen on Martin Amis or even Stephen King. She read one book over and over and over again. She read it in the morning before our mandatory Scrabble matches. She read it at the kitchen table while eating lunch. And each night, after smacking away my wayward hand, she let her favorite book lull her to sleep. The *Oxford Unabridged English Dictionary*. This was her muse, her lover, her confidant. The obsession that drove me away.

Before retreating to my old room at the Bernly Hotel, I finally accepted the truth. Tanya seduced me with the apple three nights earlier, not because she was interested in sex or even friendship. She needed Scrabble fodder and she got it.

LIFE IN COOBER PEDY

◀┈┈┈┈┈┈┈┈┈┈┈┈┈▶

The McCaffery/Greyhound bus pulled into the terminal and flicked off its headlights. Stepping down from the coach in the darkness, I looked up at a blanket of stars, yawning, stretching my arms, and yet thrilled to have finally made it to Coober Pedy after the dusty twelve-hour ride from Adelaide. The only vehicle in the parking lot was a courtesy van with the name RADEKA's emblazoned on the side. As promised in the brochure, the van delivered me to Radeka's Downunder Backpackers Inn & Underground Motel. The drive took thirty seconds.

An underground motel may seem like a unique idea, but not in this tiny opal-mining town. More than half the dwellings in Coober Pedy are built underground to provide shelter from the intense summer heat and the chilly winter nights. According to what I'd read, the idea of "dugout" accommodation was first introduced by soldiers returning from the trenches after World War I. Dugouts maintain an average temperature of about sixty-eight degrees. Air shafts poke through the ceilings to provide ventilation. The units have plumbing and are wired with electricity. Coober Pedy's subterranean dwellings boast all the comforts of a conventional home.

The bus driver, Tony Karestsan, turned out to be co-owner of Radeka's. The only other passenger—a shy German girl who sat across the aisle from me on the ride from Adelaide—barely responded when Tony assumed his position behind the check-in desk and asked what country she was from. Turned out she came from a tiny town in Bavaria. Population less than one thousand. But I never knew the name of the town because when Tony asked her to repeat it, her voice dropped a notch. I didn't catch her name, either. Hannah or Heidi or something like that. (I found out later that Hannah or Heidi had just turned eighteen and had only ventured away from home during infrequent trips to Munich. She was here in Australia for a one-month adventure. And she was traveling alone.) Wearing round silver glasses and a crisp backpack that seemed bigger than herself, she accepted the security key from Tony. He pointed to the communal bathrooms. Hannah or Heidi simply nodded. Then she descended, like a nearsighted mole, into the underground sleeping dormitories. I checked in and slept like a bat in a cave.

Later that same morning, I woke up hungry and eager to check out the town. The moment I stepped into the scorching midday sun, a sheet of dust flapped in from the desert. One hand shielding my face from the blowing sand, the other shielding my eyes from the sun, I walked down Hutchison Street, the town's nearly deserted main drag. A lone crow clung to a telephone wire, quacking like a duck. A cluster of Aborigines sat quietly beneath the shade of a tree, waving limply as I walked by. Fading signs on tiny dust-blown shops sang the one-note song of Coober Pedy. Let's see: there was KOSTA'S OPALS, ARETA'S OPALS, THE OPAL FACTORY, OPAL CAVE, OPAL SHOP, OPAL FIELDS, STAR OPAL, BLACK OPAL, BEST PRICED OPALS, DISCOUNT OPALS, SUNSHINE OPALS, THE OPAL INN, OPAL COUNTRY SHOP, OPAL MUSEUM, and JEWELERS OF OPALS. Through a dusty doorway draped in clear plastic strips, you could walk into CRYSTAL'S OPAL SHOP, stomp the dust from your boots, and purchase—drum roll please—"opals, opals, opals!"

More signs along the street offered FREE NOODLING. Because this was an isolated mining town in the middle of the outback, it didn't seem strange that prostitution had been legalized. But the fact that it was advertised and *free* left me dumbfounded. Around the corner from Hutchison there was even a PUBLIC NOODLING AREA where, one supposes, people are allowed to noodle in public. Noodling, I soon learned, is outback slang for "fossicking"— sifting for opals through the excavated dirt from any of the more than 250,000 mine shafts in and around town. Warning signs depicting a stick figure plummeting headfirst into oblivion are posted everywhere.

Hutchison Street continued for maybe two or three blocks until the pavement merged into a flat brown nowhere. I turned around, retraced my steps. Among the many signs on Radeka's arenalike facade, one had a familiar ring to it. OPAL: SALES, JEWELRY, SOUVENIRS. Next door at St. Peter & Paul's Underground Catholic Church, a house of worship much closer to Hell than the Vatican might care to admit, a white cross jutting from a mound of earth lets you know this ain't the Devil's playground.

But as any good Christian will tell you, the Devil is never far away. When I reached the dust-blown roundabout between Tom & Mary's Greek Taverna and Traces Greek Restaurant, the quacking crow was silenced by screeching tires. A pickup truck came roaring through the roundabout, running over a pile of garbage in the process. Grinning like a loon, the driver threw me a look through a cracked and dusty window. The truck sped away toward the Stuart Highway.

When I realized the "garbage" was actually a dog, I trotted over and watched the albino mutt convulse on the pavement. Blood trickled from its raised and grimaced snout; its tail beat limply against the pavement. With a final whimper, the dog's head flopped to the ground. Another sheet of dust blew in with a whistling wind. The crow started up again. I waited to hear theme music from a Sergio Leone spaghetti western. Expected a young Clint Eastwood to materialize from the dust wearing a poncho and nibbling on a thin cigar. Instead, an old Greek showed up. I figured he was Greek because when he staggered out of the cloud of dust, a stained and ragged T-shirt unable to contain his protruding belly, he introduced himself as Nicholas Sarantopoulos and muttered in a language that could only have been Greek.

"You speak English?" I said. He responded in Greek. I'm not one of those American travelers who rolls his eyes in France or Spain when the locals don't speak my language. But this was Australia, for crissakes. English is the official language.

"No English?" I said.

He shook his head.

I pointed to the dead dog.

He shrugged his shoulders.

I shrugged my shoulders.

He pointed to the dead dog.

We stood on the desolate road, staring at each other, a flattened cartoon canine at our feet. The old Greek grinned a toothless grin and scratched a patch of woolly beard stubble. Without another word—Greek or otherwise—he limped away and disappeared behind a billowing curtain of dust.

Welcome to Coober Pedy.

After pizza in a deserted Italian restaurant on Hutchison, I walked across the street to the deserted Umoona Opal Mine & Museum. Hailed as "Coober Pedy's Premier Tourist Attraction," the state-of-the-art museum was once a working mine. I took a tour of the mine shafts and got a look at two contrasting "dugout" homes: a hand-dug version and one created with modern tunneling machinery. Both were spacious and attractive and would be the envy of anyone living in Manhattan.

In the underground theater I watched *The Story of Opal*, a riveting documentary played out on a three-screen panorama. One hundred fifty million years ago, the below-sea-level area around Coober Pedy was covered by ocean. When the water tables lowered, silica solutions dripped into cavities and fractures in the ground. Millions of years later, *voilà!* Opals, opals, opals. The precious gems were first discovered here in 1915 by Willie Hutchison, a fourteen-year-old boy who traveled from Marree by camel with his father to prospect for gold. While his father went out searching for water, Willie went snooping around the campsite and *voilà!* Opals, opals, opals.

After a day of walking up and down Hutchison Street, peeking at expensive opals I could not afford, I sat at the bar at Radeka's Underground Motel, watching a thrill-a-minute cricket match on television. Tony tried to educate me about "overs" and "unders" while serving another can of Victoria Bitter. His French girlfriend, Oui Oui, the co-owner of the property, fed watermelon to two pet lizards that lay motionless on the bar. "Zey love ze watermelon," she said, in what had to be the thickest French accent this side of Dijon. "Zey are ze most beautiful babies, no?" Oui Oui (her real name is Yveline Page) pinched another piece of watermelon flesh and fed it to one of the reptiles. Then she kissed ze lizard on ze scaly snout. *Merde!*

Lizard fetish notwithstanding, Oui Oui's story is the same as those of many of Coober Pedy's three thousand residents. She blew through town thirteen years earlier while on holiday from France. Marveled at the opal shops. Embarked on a prospecting expedition. Soon she was infected with opal fever. After a brief trip home to Brittany, she returned to Coober Pedy and has been mining for opals ever since.

Coober Pedy is the world's largest producer of opals. Yet there are no commercial mining companies at work here. All excavation is done by individual claim holders, wannabe millionaires who dig in and around town, often losing more money than they make. Among the cast of prospectors you'll find Australian Aborigines, white Australians, Greeks, Italians, Lebanese, Chinese, Indians, Irish, Serbians, Croatians, Czechs—in all, some fifty ethnicities are represented here. Although the Aboriginal translation of Coober Pedy is "white man's hole in the ground," the town may have become the world's most ethnically diverse hole in the ground.

Ashley Wood, the soft-spoken Westpac Bank manager (the only bank in town), sat beside me at Radeka's bar. Intelligent, urbane, resembling a young Truman Capote without the lisp or the flowing garments, Ashley seemed somewhat out of place in this rough-and-tumble mining town. But like everybody else, he pegged an opal claim and digs for riches in his free time. "On one shelf in my kitchen pantry," he said, "there's a box of cereal, a bag of rice, and a few sticks of gelignite." Similar to dynamite, gelignite is made of gelled nitroglycerine, potassium nitrate, and either nitrocellulose or wood pulp. According to Ashley, the powerful explosive is available at stores around town. "Everybody has a few sticks lying around."

And so explosives replaced cricket as the topic of conversation. Thank the Lord. Tony, Oui Oui, and Ashley told mind-boggling stories about feuding prospectors who blew up each other's machinery, about locals who solved disputes by hurling sticks of gelignite. I shook my head, laughing. This is the kind of folklore a traveler expects to hear after too many beers in an outback bar. Tall tales told by locals whose lives had driven them past the brink of exaggeration.

Having dealt with countless disbelievers like me over the years, however, Oui Oui whipped out a stack of Xeroxed articles from the *Coober Pedy Times*. "Read zese," she said, holding a lizard in one hand. "I zink you will not laugh."

I drained the can of Victoria Bitter, bent toward the stack of articles, and learned about a ten-year stretch in the long, explosive history of Coober Pedy, Australia:

25 September, 1991: An explosive tore through the side of a vacant house in the township of Coober Pedy at 10:00 P.M. on

Sunday. . . . This is the third recorded unexplained charge in Coober Pedy in the past six weeks. Some residents say there have been more. . . .

16 June, 1993: It was a scene reminiscent of a deserted battle-field, twisted fingers of steel pointing skywards. . . . The destroyed equipment was owned in partnership by Sammy Wong and Danny Stefanovic and one can only wonder what might have gone through their minds when coming upon this scene of absolute devastation. . . .

6 February, 1995: At around 4:30 A.M. on Saturday 28th of January, the Coober Pedy Times [building] was bombed. This resulted in extensive damage to the front of the building and damage throughout the office. . . .

14 February, 1996: At about 3:10 A.M. Tuesday, two police Commodores were blown up in the Desert Cave Hotel precinct. . . . An explosive device was detonated causing approximately $20,000 damage to the vehicles and superficial damage to . . . the Desert Cave Hotel. . . .

20 June, 2000: Mining equipment worth more than $100,000 has been destroyed in two bombings. . . . Coober Pedy has a long history of such bombings. Explosives, mainly gelignite, are considered a tool of the trade in the opal mining town and are easily accessible. . . .

5 July, 2001: On Friday 22 June 2001 at about 9:45 P.M. a miner's tunneling machine was destroyed in an explosion on 17 Mile Road. . . . Detective Francis Pagh of the Coober Pedy C.I.B. stated, "I find it particularly irresponsible for someone to set explosives on a main road and at a relatively early time on a Friday night. . . ."

The Coober Pedy Courthouse survived an explosion. The clubhouse at the grassless Coober Pedy Golf Course is believed to have been destroyed by a bomb. The Acropolis, Coober Pedy's most popular restaurant and a late-night gathering place for nearly a quarter of a century, was blown to bits by four gelignite explosions (bomb squad specialists later found thirteen undetonated gelignite sticks in the rubble). The home of Theodoros Christopoulos, as well as his car, blew sky-high in 1993. All these incidents occurred *after* police allegedly took control from gunslinging, "take matters into our own hands" townsfolk who had finally learned to respect a badge. For all intents and purposes Coober Pedy is the Aussie Wild West—a time warp at the bottom of the world where gelignite-loving opal freaks are alive and tossing. (Recently, a couple of teenage boys tossed a stick of gel into a phone booth and blew it to smithereens. When police asked why they had done it, the boys shrugged their shoulders and said they were bored.)

Quite unexpectedly, someone slapped me on the back, adding to jitters caused by too many explosive stories and not enough beers. George Aslamitzis, a Greek miner who is prone to sudden bouts of good-natured screaming, had dealt the blow. Worked into a frenzy by all this talk of bombing and destruction, he pontificated about the advantages of Nitropril over gelignite. Speaking in accented English and using melodramatic gesticulations, George explained how he and other miners make bombs with the explosive fertilizer compound.

"You take newspaper and roll into cylinder, like dis," he said, clutching the air with two curled hands. "Then you pour Nitropril, stick in fuse, you light, and *boom*." He clapped his hands for effect.

My wide-eyed reaction must have intrigued him.

"You want we blow something up?" he said.

"Ahhh . . . well, I—"

"You want?" he said, nodding.

"No, I'm not really into—"

He cut me off again, this time by slamming his hand definitively against the bar. "Tomorrow, we go mining!" he said. "I show you."

The next morning, I woke to a loud knock on my door. "Come, we go mining!" Tony and George took me to the claim they share. But I did not drive there with them. I rode in a souped-up camper-van owned by one of their friends, an eccentric German called Michael "Mick" Eisenmann. Aside from cash flow and country of origin, Mick's life seemed to parallel my own. Like me, he had given up his job to travel the world. "Money . . . Is . . . Not . . . Life." He told me this, pausing dramatically after each word, before stepping into the van. "This," he said, turning toward the outback and making a sweeping gesture with one hand, "this is life." He left a lucrative position at a German architectural firm and had been driving across the Australian continent with his girlfriend for nearly a year. This was his second trip to Coober Pedy. Dressed in extremely short shorts, a leather vest, and one of those feathered hats worn by men in Bavarian tourism brochures, he exuded warmth and friendliness.

We drove for maybe fifteen minutes along a bumpy dirt road. I rode in the sleeper compartment with Mick's girlfriend and a petite German friend who had just arrived. She would be traveling with them for a month. Beneath a deep blue sky uniformly dotted with cumulus clouds, giant mounds of excavated earth rose as far as the eye could see. There were thousands of these "mullock mounds" on either side of the road. And beside each one lay a cavernous hole up to ninety feet deep, just waiting for a stick figure to plummet into.

The truck stopped alongside a hill of rugged limestone. At the base of the acclivity, a rectangular doorway had been perfectly cut by a tunneling machine. This was George and Tony's mining claim. We unloaded extension cords, lamps, flashlights, and a giant hand-held drill from which a two-foot bit protruded. Someone carried a power cord into the dark recesses of the tunnel. I followed far behind.

"Watch for roos," George said.

I stopped in front of the gaping black doorway and turned around for clarification.

"Sometimes the kangaroos, they go inside to escape heat," George continued. Should a kangaroo come bounding out of the narrow tunnel with me in its way, George told me to flatten myself against the wall. "If not, the kangaroo, he run over you."

The thought of a charging kangaroo made me nervous. But someone—Mick, I think—had gone in before me. If something were to happen, it would happen to him first. I stood by the doorway, sweating in the hot sun, straining to hear a muffled scream, expecting a crazed kangaroo to come bounding from the tunnel with Bavarian blood on its paws. But the others began watching me suspiciously. Without making a conscious decision to do so, I bent into the tunnel and held my breath.

At the far end of darkness a dim light flickered. But at the entrance, sunlight allowed me to appreciate the perfect rectangular shape of the tunnel. The limestone had been eaten away by tunneling machines similar to those used to create dugout homes. I crouched over, waddling deeper into darkness. *The kangaroo, he run over you*. I couldn't get George's warning out of my head. So certain was I that a massive marsupial would come crashing into my chest, I flattened myself against the wall as a precaution. Instead of retreating as my instincts suggested, I slid against the wall until reaching the light.

In a space the size and shape of a small living room, I found Mick. He was fiddling with the power cord and still wearing that ridiculous Bavarian hat. Moments later, Tony, George, Mick's girlfriend, and the German girl appeared.

With the crowd gathered around, Tony began boring into a jagged wall. Rather than drilling perpendicularly into the limestone, he angled the bit sideways, tearing away sheets of rock in the process. Every few seconds he stopped drilling. George shone a light on the newly exposed rock. "Look to see glittering rock," he said, "or shiny pieces of color." This is how opal mining works: You drill away a sheet of rock, shine a lamp, look for glinting particles imbedded in the wall. A chunk of opal the size of a baby's fist, a rare find indeed, might be worth a few hundred thousand dollars.

Tony continued to drill. George shone the lamp. I got down on my hands and knees in the dust after Tony said he would give a portion of the money to anyone who spotted an opal. Right then and there, I understood how Oui Oui and other Coober Pedy migrants had been smitten by opal mining. It's like casino gambling. You toil away with Lady Luck in a windowless place with artificial light and a dream. The next day you could be a millionaire. Or you could lose your shirt.

After a couple of hours of fruitless drilling, we gave up and loaded the equipment into the back of the pickup. Truth be told, I was disappointed. Especially since Tony had promised a cut to whoever discovered an opal. Yes, I was disappointed. But George was pissed off. "Shit!" he had said, over and over, each time the drilling stopped and the lamp detected only limestone. He used other choice words as well. "Fuck!" was one of his favorites. "Motherfuck!" had been particularly useful in expressing his emotions. He used the word again and again while tossing power cables and various objects into the pickup. Suddenly, something came over him. A sense of peace or resolution. He nodded his head as if answering a question that only he could hear.

"Now," he said, looking at me with danger glinting in his eyes. "Now we make bomb."

I watched George roll sheets of newspaper into a tight cylindrical shape the way he'd talked about the night before. He closed the bottom of the cylinder, poured in Nitropril powder from a bag, and stuck a fuse inside. He disappeared around the near side of the hill and a few minutes later we spotted his wiry figure on top. Looking through my camera's viewfinder, I watched him plant the charge. He lit the fuse. Ran. A few seconds later the bomb exploded, shaking the earth beneath our feet and sending a limestone cloud into the crisp, outback sky.

I celebrated New Year's Eve in Coober Pedy. The night began at Radeka's with a couple of cans of Victoria Bitter. Ashley was there. As were Tony and Oui Oui. Tony would have to hold down the fort that night, but Oui Oui agreed to meet Ashley and me before midnight at the town pub.

Into the unseasonably cool summer evening we went on the sixty-second trek across Hutchison to the Desert Cave Hotel. It's the most expensive hotel in town, the same location where two police cars had been bombed a few years earlier. We walked past glass doors, through a pleasant lobby, and down into the underground bar where a few people, mostly locals, had gathered. Among them was a woman who smiled at me from across the room as if we were old friends. She was absolutely stunning. Dark hair. Full lips. A shapely figure carved beneath a simple frock. I smiled at her. She smiled again. But there was something strange about her eyes, something . . .

"You might want to stay away from that one, mate," Ashley whispered. I leaned toward him, my eyes locked on the dark-haired beauty, waiting to hear the bad news. She's married. Has a boyfriend. Is only into girls. "The other day at the bank," he continued, "I looked out the window and saw her walking down Hutchison."

Of course he saw her walking down Hutchison. Who wouldn't? Especially in a town like this. She was a butterfly in a land of one-legged frogs.

"Mate," he said, placing a brotherly hand on my shoulder. "She was walking down the street naked. One of the employees had to run out and throw a towel over her."

I looked at her, trying to imagine the frock as a bath towel.

"She's crazy," Ashley said, tapping an index finger against his temple. "She's lost the plot."

I watched her more closely. Saw the wide, scary eyes. The involuntary twitching. Who else but a crazy person would stand in the middle of a hotel bar on New Year's Eve scratching her armpit as if it were infested with fleas?

Ashley told me what little he knew about her. She had been in Coober Pedy way too long, choking on limestone dust, pummeled by the sun, haunted by an arduous relationship that had produced two or three offspring between mining excavations. All this had pushed her through a revolving door to madness. Watching her digging absently at the flesh beneath her frock, everything began to add up. The toothless Greek guy stumbling through the dust had lost the plot. The truck driver who'd deliberately run over the albino dog had lost the plot. George's "Let's make a bomb." Aslamitzis was dangerously close to losing the plot. Anyone who ever hurled a stick of gelignite into a restaurant or a private residence or the editorial offices of the *Coober Pedy Times* had lost the plot. So, too, had the beautiful woman with the pleasant smile and the inexorable itch.

We bolted.

At about half past eleven, after Ashley and I walked down the street and downed our first beer at the Coober Pedy Pub, it seemed that plots had been lost by all. Nineteen eighties disco hits— "Blame It on the Boogie," "Boogie Shoes," "Boogie Nights"— blasted the tiny dance floor where locals, Aborigines and white Australians alike, crashed into each other with a forcefulness that must have rattled teeth. (Judging by the number of people who were actually missing teeth, impact must have reached shatter strength.) Images of drunkenness were so prevalent and clichéd, the perpetrators looked like B-movie actors trained in melodrama. A giggling woman fell backward onto the dance floor and remained there, giggling among the scuffling feet, her skirt high above a pair of jumbo panties. I saw a grown man sprawled face-down on a table, arms dangling, as if he'd just been shot. A young Aborigine staggered up to me, his eyes narrow and glistening. "Emmitt Smith!" he said, slapping me on the shoulder hard enough to sting. "Emmitt Smith!" he repeated, setting fire to my shoulder again. Through the miracle of satellite television he had probably watched a Dallas Cowboys football game and somehow associated me, a laughable athlete, with the Cowboys' former star running back. In a room crammed with stumbling, staggering, semiconscious revelers, I managed to slip away from the young Aborigine and make my way to the bar. New Year's Eve in the Australian Outback. I needed a goddam drink.

When Oui Oui showed up, the two of us made our way to the dance floor. But every few seconds some out-of-control Dance Fever acolyte would come barreling into us, amused and impenitent—even after spilling his or her drink. This set off a chain reaction of flailing bodies that seemed apropos, consider-ing the amount of grog consumed and the pounding disco music that abruptly ended a few seconds before midnight.

The DJ's shrieking voice competed for attention with the shrieking feedback from the speakers. The roaring crowd piped down. The countdown to the New Year began. "Ten, nine, eight . . ." Oui Oui, the French lizard lover, reached out and grabbed Ashley and me. "Six, five, four . . ." We huddled, raised our champagne glasses. "Three, two, one . . ." The Coober Pedy Pub exploded with cheer. And so did my champagne glass after someone whacked me on the shoulder.

I swung around. Cringed.

"Emmitt Smith!"

Before the police showed up to break up the inevitable pub brawl, Ashley, Oui Oui, and I walked over to the Greek Club. Coober Pedy is a small town, but large enough to support a Greek

Club, an Italian Club, a Croatian Club, and a Serbian one. According to Oui Oui, the previous New Year's Eve party at the Greek Club had been one to remember. This one, she promised, would be the bomb.

We entered a reception hall as large as an airplane hangar and found perhaps two dozen people scattered among the rows of empty banquet tables. Platters of souvlaki, moussaka, and Greek salad lay uneaten on a credenza. On the stage, a lanky DJ hunched over a turntable. The tune echoing through the cavernous hall did not sound familiar. It wasn't disco. It wasn't rock and roll. It wasn't hip-hop or rhythm & blues. Wasn't even the music of Keith Urban, the Australian country singer who recently broke Air Supply's 1980s record with five consecutive top-five singles in the United States. The music echoing through the Greek Club in the middle of the Australian Outback was undeniably Greek. A few middle-aged locals, their arms raised high, were engrossed in the shuffling, circular celebration that is traditional Greek dance.

We slouched at an empty table that New Year's Eve—Ashley, Oui Oui, and me—drinking shot after shot of ouzo and watching dance moves I hadn't seen since *Fiddler on the Roof.*

At no time is Coober Pedy more desolate than on New Year's Day. I staggered down Hutchison Street on that dust-blown afternoon, alone and hungover, feeling like the sole survivor on a failed mission to Mars. Beyond the road, a flat, monotonous field of reddish-brown earth stretched to the horizon. So level was the landscape, you could probably roll a baseball down Hutchison all the way to Alice Springs. It's no surprise that *Red Planet*, starring Val Kilmer, had been filmed here. As were *Mad Max III* and *Pitch Black*, the sci-fi thriller "set on a distant, inhospitable planet where the heat of the day is almost unbearable."

The heat was unbearable, all right. The sun glared down at me as if I'd done something wrong. As it turned out, I had. Having ignored Oui Oui's New Year's Eve warning to stock up on food, hunger forced me from my underground shelter and out onto the fiery grille that was Hutchison Street. The pizza shop was closed. So were the two Greek restaurants. Ditto for every opal shop. Not a single open door could be found along the street. Not a single human being. The quacking crow had disappeared from the telephone wire. The Aborigines no longer sat in the uncertain shade of the tree. No life. No food. No movement. Only an intermittent growling from a belly that would not be satisfied until the following morning when I took the McCaffery/Greyhound bus to Alice Springs.

HARD ROCK, MADONNA, AND THE FLIES

←·····················→

They came at me relentlessly, buzzing past my ears like tiny propeller planes that eventually landed on my forehead and taxied across the tarmac of my face. They crawled into my ears, eyes, attempted to gain access to both nostrils. Whenever I opened my mouth, I feared that one of them would dive in, Kamikaze-style, sacrificing itself and encouraging the meek to follow. Flies! No visitor to the Australian Outback can escape them. During a three-day excursion to Kata Tjuta National Park, I was attacked, in broiling 110-degree heat, by hordes of the airborne buggers. But it was Madonna who ultimately made me lose my cool.

We departed Alice Springs at daybreak. David, a mild-mannered guide from Way Out Back Desert Safaris, led a group that included a newlywed Spanish couple, a sixty-year-old Swiss businessman traveling with his adult son, two Germans (brother and sister), a Canadian who operates a Zamboni at a hockey rink in Alberta, and yours truly. One by one we piled into the modified Toyota Land Cruiser, introduced ourselves, took seats in the cramped air-conditioned cabin, and settled in for an outback adventure.

During the four-hour highway jaunt to our desert campsite, I would have been happy to stare at the arid landscape or converse

with fellow travelers. But David insisted on playing music constantly, and at high volume. Cruising along the desolate Stuart
Highway—the only paved inland road connecting Australia's
north coast to the south—we were bombarded with a cacophony
of forgotten tunes by the likes of Pat Benatar and Meat Loaf. We
bit our tongues. Suffered through seven tracks from *Bat out of
Hell*. But after an hour or so, the Canadian Zamboni operator
could no longer keep his cool. He had to scream over the music so
that David could hear his objection. This set off a chain reaction
of complaints that gave rise to *Madonna's Greatest Hits*, played
over and over at ear-splitting levels for the next three hours.

We arrived at the campsite, ears ringing from Material Girl
monotony, and were immediately set upon by flies. They hovered
around our heads as we off-loaded provisions to a makeshift
kitchen. More flies swarmed the picnic table as we laid out bread,
ham, cheese, lettuce, and sliced tomatoes. We swatted at our outback smorgasbord, trying in vain to remove the undulating black
blanket that covered it. Lunch was an insectivore's delight.

We endured these annoyances in order to see the world's
largest rock. Uluru is, after all, a thousand-foot-high sandstone
monolith with a circumference of more than six miles. Looking
like a colossal meat loaf (the meal, not the musician), Uluru sits
incongruously atop the flat desert plain of Kata Tjuta National
Park, which the Australian government leased for ninety-nine
years after returning the sacred land to the Aborigines in 1985.
Our plan was to tread around a section of the surrounding track
and then retreat to the viewing area. From there we would take
part in the Northern Territory's biggest attraction: watching
Uluru change colors in the fiery sunset.

For more than an hour, beneath a ferocious white-hot sun, we
walked around a section of the rock, swiping at flies all the way.
Uluru really is a magnificent sight. If you can see past the flies,
that is. I gawked at the Aboriginal wall paintings that grace
Uluru's basal caves. Stared up in awe at the giant mountain of a

rock that seemed to have been dropped by aliens. But soon I could think of nothing but the insufferable heat. It was like walking through the world's largest convection oven. With each labored breath, I felt as if my lungs might ignite. When we finally reached the parking lot and climbed into the Land Cruiser, tragedy struck. The air conditioner had breathed its last cool breath.

The heat inside the vehicle was more stifling than the heat outside. I tried to open a window so we could at least feel a breeze, but the Cruiser's windows had been permanently sealed to prevent dust from invading the interior. Locked in a four-wheeled hothouse, we drove in sweaty misery to the viewing area.

A sprawling concrete parking lot, not unlike the painted asphalt at your local shopping mall, had been laid across the desert. It seemed odd that so many parking spaces had been concocted. But moments later, when the tourism nightmare began, the tremendous car park justified itself. Huge tour buses roared into the lot, spilling maybe two thousand oglers who, like us, had come to watch the sunset play upon Uluru's northwestern face. More people came in minivans, pickup trucks, SUVs. Tuxedoed waiters appeared as if by magic, pouring champagne into glass flutes held by affluent tourists sitting on portable chairs. Others swarmed behind the ropes of the viewing area, pointing cameras and waiting for the colors to change.

As the sun began to set, perhaps one thousand camera shutters clicked in unison. Uluru bathed in a magnificent nexus of hues—amber, orange, reddish-brown, burgundy. The massive rock seemed to glow as if releasing heat, as if sending a signal to faraway beings who may or may not have left it there. And then, just like that, it was over. Uluru's light faded, the tourists marched back to their buses. Within a matter of minutes the parking lot had emptied.

At the campsite the next morning, I was awakened abruptly. Not by sunlight or hunger, but by more goddam flies. One of them had crawled into my open mouth as I snored in my "swag."

A first cousin to the sleeping bag, a swag has the advantage of a flap that folds over your head and tucks into the sleeping pouch. Perfect for the outback, swags prevent dust from covering the user's face while he sleeps. Swags also help keep flies away (as well as spiders, scorpions, ants, and a long list of creepy-crawlies). Apparently, my flap had flipped. Who knows how long the fly had been crawling around my mouth. Who knows where the buzzing insect had been beforehand. Feasting on a dingo turd, perhaps? I leapt from my sleeping bag and spat it out, swatting at squadrons of critters that flew sorties past my face.

My fellow campers suffered as well. The Spanish couple stood face to face amid the scrub, flailing wildly as if in a domestic dispute. The pot-bellied Swiss gentleman slapped his own face repeatedly. The others swung and swatted to no avail. But David, the Australian guide, never flinched. A thicket of flies clung to the back of his shirt. They crawled on his arms, his legs, his face, and yet not once did he seem perturbed. The rest of us snatched our gear and jumped into the Land Cruiser with flies in hot pursuit. We slammed the doors. When David casually climbed in, he brought a swarm of buzzing buggers with him. Dozens of flies became trapped inside. But because the windows had been sealed, and because the air conditioner was not working, we drove onward, slapping relentlessly at our sweaty skins.

The next two days were as exhilarating as they were difficult to endure. We hiked several miles in searing heat through Kata Tjuta (Aboriginal for "Place of many heads"), a grouping of monolithic rocks west of Uluru. We camped in the open spaces of Kings Creek Cattle Station, where a doorless "bush toilet" allowed one to answer nature's call and watch the sunset simultaneously. And on day three, after a sweltering uphill hike through Kings Canyon, we returned to the smoldering Land Cruiser and wilted like day-old dandelions.

As soon as David keyed the ignition, Madonna burst into yet another encore rendition of "Like a Virgin." I turned to the

Canadian Zamboni driver. The Zamboni driver looked at me. Amid the wilted carcasses of our allies—the Spaniards, Germans, and Swiss—Canada and the United States issued a unified demand to Australia: "Turn that shit off!"

Madonna finally fell silent. But inside the steamy sauna of our Toyota Land Cruiser, which had begun to stink of sweat and toe jam from eight pairs of sore, shoeless feet, a swarm of outback flies took over the airwaves—buzzing, buzzing, buzzing with a diabolical glee that silenced as they landed and began to feed.

TURTLE-MAN!

On a sandbar deep beneath the Coral Sea, some forty miles off the coast of Australia along the Great Barrier Reef, a dozen fledgling scuba divers, myself among them, knelt side by side, air bubbles spewing from our regulators, face masks shielding our bulging eyes. We were interlopers in an alien world. Aquatic prospectors on life support. Every gurgling, machine-assisted, Darth Vader breath released an effervescent burst reminding me that we did not belong.

The divemaster, Peter Lewis, knelt before us in the sand. His eyes as calm and sure as his directions, he pointed at the two Swedes, Helga and Helga, indicating, by tapping together his index fingers, that it was time to buddy up. He then pointed at the two Germans, the two Brits, the Canadian and his Swiss girl-friend, Inga, and the two garrulous Italians—with regulators jammed into their mouths, they were forced to stop talking for the first time since boarding the boat in Cairns. Ultimately, the divemaster pointed to Ian (the Irishman) and me. The time had come. Our PADI (Professional Association of Diving Instructors) scuba certification drills were about to commence.

Peter ripped off my face mask and tossed it as far as the sea allowed. Eyes stinging from the sudden rush of salt water, I watched the mask sink to the ocean floor. I retrieved it a moment later and put it on, remembering, as I tilted back my head, to press hard against the top of the mask while blowing air from my nostrils. Just as we had practiced in the swimming pool, the rush of air created a vacuum that sucked out the water from the mask. I could see clearly again. My eyes still stung, but they were able to focus.

Next came buddy breathing. Standing upright, my flippers buried in the sand, I pulled the regulator from my mouth and waited for Ian to pass me his. Back and forth we went, taking breaths from Ian's regulator, practicing the safety technique that could someday save our lives. At the moment, however, a watery death was less of a concern than swapping spit with Ian. I hadn't ingested another man's saliva since passing a bottle of T. J. Swan among college fraternity brothers. This could save my life, I thought to myself, biting down once again on the frayed rubber mouthpiece. Ian gave me a thumbs-up. Looking back at him through the swirling sand kicked up by our flippers, I wondered if Ian had cooties.

Our final task was to remove our BCDs and put them on again. Simply put, a buoyancy control device is worn like a vest. Depending on buoyancy requirements, the two air pouches on either side of the vest can be inflated at the press of a button. A diver's weight, diving depth, and skill level, as well as the particular diving conditions, determine how much or how little the vest should be inflated. The tricky part about removing the BCD is that the heavy air tank is attached to the back. But neither Ian nor I encountered a problem. We slipped in and out of our respective BCDs, knelt side by side on the sandbar, and waited for the others to finish. Once they did, Peter clapped in slow motion. We turned to one another, all twelve newly certified PADI divers, and smiled with our eyes.

Divemaster Peter Lewis then did something that will stay with me for the rest of my life. He reached beneath his own BCD and pulled out a plastic bag filled with a white, mucky substance.

Upon closer inspection, I figured the substance was white bread. Wonder Bread. The label on the package said so. Ian and I exchanged a look. Judging by the number of twisting heads, the other divers were equally perplexed. Peter reached into the bag, pulled out a handful of muck, and sprinkled it above our heads as if it were magic dust. As it turned out, the muck *was* magic. In a matter of seconds, the sea came to life.

Hundreds of fish appeared out of nowhere to feed on the floating specks of Wonder Bread. Spotted blue angelfish, their yellow mouths pouting like unfed children, swam inches away from my face mask. Bright orange clown fish brushed against my forehead. I saw tiny blue-green puller fish, black and yellow–beaked coral fish, surgeonfish that looked as if they'd been painted by artsy schizophrenics. There were butterfly fish, cardinals, wrasse, gobies, blennies, triggerfish, parrotfish, and damselfish—all of which swirled around us in a blinding wall of color.

Still on my knees, I looked up, turned around, and nearly spat out my regulator as hundreds and hundreds of colorful sea creatures descended upon us from the opposite direction. The Great Barrier Reef is populated by more than fifteen hundred species of fish. From my genuflecting position on the sandbar, it seemed as though every species had sent a delegate to greet us.

Air bubbles rising crazily like confetti in reverse, I grabbed hold of Ian. Ian grabbed hold of me. We danced together on our knees, without realizing we were doing so, until the last of the Wonder Bread had been consumed. The marine parade dispersed almost as quickly as it had appeared. Still holding onto one another, face mask to face mask, our eyes locked. We snatched our hands away almost simultaneously and rose to the surface with the others.

Later that evening, as the dive boat pitched on gentle swells and a billion stars winked in a black velvet sky, the cast and crew gathered at the stern to watch the Snorkel Races. "Snorkel

Races?" I said, as Peter slapped me on the back and let out a full-throated roar. "Wot?" he said. "Ya never heard about the famous Queensland Snorkel Races?"

I shook my head.

"Well then, mate . . ." Peter's voice, as gruff and salty as a pirate's, had an emcee's quality about it. He scratched his scruffy beard, took another sip of Victoria Bitter, and told me what I didn't want to hear. "Perhaps ya should go first and show everyone exactly how the races are run. Aye, mate?" My dive mates let out a resounding cheer, although they knew as much about the Snorkel Races as I did.

Peter guided me toward a stool at the very back of the stern. I sat down. The crowd gathered around. "The object of the race is to see who can drink the fastest." Peter produced a fresh can of Victoria Bitter, popped the top. Someone handed him a dive mask and snorkel. "But ya have to drink the beer," he continued, "through the bloody snorkel!"

The international group of neophyte divers—the two Brits, the Germans, the burly Swedish girls who shared the same name, the Canadian and his Swiss girlfriend, the Italians—looked down at me and burst into laughter. All except my Irish dive buddy, Ian. The tall, lanky kid from Dublin had a great personality but extremely bad teeth. He smiled without parting his lips.

"Let me get this straight," I said to Peter. "I'm supposed to put on this dive mask and drink beer through the snorkel?"

"That would be correct," Peter said.

"But the mask covers my nose. With the snorkel in my mouth I won't be able to breathe."

"That's why they call 'em the Snorkel Races, mate. Ya have to drink bloody fast." Peter slapped his thigh and let out a howl. "C'mon, mate," he said. "Give her a go."

Before I could refuse, someone slid the mask over my face. One end of the snorkel was shoved into my mouth, the other end awaited beer delivery. I sucked one last breath before it came gushing through. After five wimpy seconds, I leapt from the chair, coughing up beer as I did so. The other divers took turns at the Snorkel Races. Even the quiet Swiss girl drank more than me. But that was okay. I needed to focus on the big day ahead. Our first open-water certified dive.

The next morning, bad weather threatened to cancel the dive. Dressed in wet suits and scuba gear and ready to make a splash, the twelve of us stood in the rain, waiting for Peter's decision. The sea, which had been so calm and blue just one day earlier, had turned rough and gray. No one wanted to cancel the dive, least of all the divers. We had spent considerable money on the week-long PADI certification course, which included three days in the classroom followed by three days at sea. If this—our very first open-water dive—were to be canceled due to weather, we would simply be out of luck.

The rain slowed to a fine drizzle. The boat continued to lurch. The sky seemed to lighten up a tad. That's when Peter gave us the go-ahead. A cheer went up among the divers, yet Peter's face turned grim. "Remember," he said, without a trace of last night's humor in his voice, "*stay with yer buddy!* If ya get separated from yer buddy for any reason, what do ya do?"

We answered as a group, one voice, one song. "We swim to the surface, locate our buddy, and go down again together."

"And if ya don't see yer buddy on the surface?"

"We immediately head back to the ship."

"Good on ya." Peter slapped his hands together and rubbed as if he were cold. "Remember, ya got an hour of air in yer tanks. Be sure to surface with at least fifteen minutes left on the gauge." With those final instructions ringing in my ears, I leapt overboard with a splash.

Sinking beneath the choppy surface, down to a depth of thirty feet, the sea showed no ill effects from the weather. There was no direct sunlight, of course. But as Ian and I set off on our first unsupervised dive—making sure not to wander too far from the boat—the ambient light proved to be sufficient.

We swam among the batfish, the groupers, cod the size of miniature submarines, propelling ourselves with effortless flicks of our flippers. We explored a giant coral reef—only a tiny, minuscule section of the Great Barrier Reef system, which extends for more than twelve hundred miles from a point near Daru, New Guinea, all the way south beyond Mackay, Australia. We played peek-a-boo with a moray eel. Swam upside down, just to see what it felt like. Peed in our wet suits because that's what real scuba divers do. At some point during our underwater antics, Ian pointed at his air gauge. Time was nearly up.

After pausing to take a last look at the yellow polyps sprouting from the coral-like baby sunflowers, I looked up and saw a dark shape in the distance. The shape was big. Big and round and seemed to be heading straight toward me. Hovering a few feet above the reef, my arms flapping, flippers flipping, regulator spewing bubbles at an alarming rate, I wasn't sure what to do. I turned to Ian. From twenty feet away, I could see his eyes bulging behind his mask. When the thing fully emerged from behind a murky blue curtain, my heart nearly leapt from my throat. A sea turtle. It was a sea turtle. A huge, placid, impossibly old sea turtle. It banked left before getting too close. I followed by no will of my own.

If yer lucky enough to spot a sea turtle and feel like takin' a little ride, slip yer fingers under the rear of the shell and pinch down with yer thumbs. If she looks back at ya once and keeps goin', good on ya. If she looks back twice, maybe ya should worry a bit. If she turns around a third time, ya better let go quick, 'cause she's 'bout to bite your arse.

I wasn't sure if Peter's classroom tale was fact or fiction. But I had been mesmerized by this giant sea turtle. The grandfatherly folds around its neck. The high hump of its mossy shell. The effortless way in which it paddled through the sea, slowly, method-

ically, one decade after another. Without thinking about the possible consequences, I powered forward, kicking savagely with my
fins, until I caught up with the turtle and latched onto the rear of
its shell.

Just as divemaster Peter had said, the turtle turned back to
look once. Twice. But instead of craning its neck for a third and
final glance, the turtle took off like an underwater Jet Ski.
Through the deep blue yonder we went, gliding along the magical
coral reef, banking upward toward a twisting, silvery sheet of
fish, and then down again, soaring above a giant clam and skim-
ming the sandy bottom at a speed I could never have reached on
my own. I was James Bond in *Thunderball*, cruising beneath the
surface on a stealth submersible. Jacques Cousteau on holiday. I
had become . . . Turtle-Man! Half human, half reptile, probing
the depths of the Coral Sea in search of four-flippered romance
and adventure. *Turtle-Man!* If not for the regulator jammed in my
mouth, I would have blurted out the theme song to *Flipper*. Instead, I blew rhythmic bubbles while the turtle—

Oh, shit! I let go of the gliding beast and watched it disappear
behind another murky curtain. Like an astronaut drifting
through outer space, I was weightless, alone, floating through a
big, blank nowhere. Dark shapes swam in the distance. But these
shapes had dorsal fins. I looked left, right, below, and above. Ian
was nowhere in sight. Neither was the coral reef we had been ex-
ploring before I took it upon myself to hijack a friggin' sea turtle.
I looked at my air gauge. Tapped it with my finger, the way they
always do in marine documentaries aired on the Discovery Channel. Fifteen minutes left. We were supposed to have been out of
the water by now. Ian. Where was Ian? Where the hell was *I*?

Trying not to panic, I swam to the surface as we'd been trained
to do. The rain had picked up again, pelting the swells with a
steady splatter that made a bad situation even worse. The waves
tossed me about, so much so that a clear line of vision proved
impossible. Even if Ian had surfaced and was looking for me at

this very moment, even if there was no rain, the undulating waves would make it difficult to spot each other. That's when panic set in.

On January 25, 1998, in these very same waters, American scuba divers Tom and Eileen Lonergan were accidentally left behind by their dive boat. A head-counting mix-up was blamed. The mistake wasn't discovered until the following morning. The bodies were never found.

Staring across the waves at the faraway dive boat, I wasn't worried that it would leave me behind. After all, the vessel wasn't scheduled to hoist anchor and set sail for Cairns until the following day. What worried me was the amount of air remaining in my tank—about eight minutes, give or take a couple.

From my position in the choppy water, the dive boat appeared to be about two hundred yards away. A couple of football fields. Okay. No problem. Eyes locked on the boat's position, I sank just below the surface and began kicking toward what appeared to be the correct direction. But at such a shallow depth on a stormy day, the current, undetectable though it was, proved to be my undoing. When I surfaced a few minutes later, the boat was no closer, and yet my air supply had dropped to a precarious level.

Down I went again, kicking my flippers as fast as they would allow. Thirty seconds later, I popped up to the surface to check the position of the boat and then went down again. And so it went. Down, kick, surface, look for the boat. Down, kick, surface, look for the boat. As if punishing me for separating from my buddy, the swells slapped my face each time I came up. The rain fell. The boat grew closer. My air supply evaporated.

With a final furious kick of my flippers, I shot through the water and grabbed hold of the diver's platform at the rear of the boat. Peter was there, standing on the platform. As was Ian, still in his wet suit, a look of relief etched on his pallid face. Judging by the worried faces peering from the deck, Ian had told the other divers about my sea turtle adventure.

With a suddenness inspired by anger or relief, Peter reached down and yanked me up and onto the platform. "Ya had us worried, mate," he said. "Why'd ya peel off from yer buddy?"

Cold, weary, and thankful to finally be aboard, I could not find the words to express my own foolhardiness. I apologized to both Peter and Ian, and snuck away to my berth after storing my dive equipment. While changing into dry clothes, however, my hands began to shake uncontrollably. A posttraumatic surge of anxiety. Reaction to the tragedy that might have been.

But later that night at the Snorkel Races, the mood changed considerably. Face mask properly in place, snorkel protruding from his upturned mouth, Turtle-Man downed twelve ounces of Victoria Bitter without taking a single breath.

Southeast Asia

WELCOME TO BANDAR SERI BEGAWAN

◄·····················►

You can study a map of Southeast Asia up close and with a magnifying glass and still manage to overlook the tiny, fractured country called Brunei. Two minuscule parcels of land, carved from the jungles of northwestern Borneo and separated by the Malaysian state of Sarawak, are all that remain of a powerful ancient sultanate that spread across the world's third largest island until 1840, when James Brooke dropped anchor here. Recognizing a great opportunity when he saw one, the bodacious British Army officer helped Omar Ali Saifuddien II, the Sultan of Brunei, suppress a nasty civil uprising. The Sultan rewarded Brooke by making him the first white rajah of Sarawak. Let's just say this was a *big* mistake. Brooke soon became Britain's consul general to Borneo. Although he helped put an end to piracy—a serious issue of the times—he imposed strict new laws and was knighted by Queen Victoria for his accomplishments.

As Brooke's influence grew, the Sultan's grip on the kingdom began to loosen exponentially. By 1848, a series of land concessions had reduced Brunei to a fraction of its previous self. But in 1929, when the dwindling Islamic empire seemed likely to vanish altogether into the jungle from which it sprouted, the country found salvation. It came not from the heavens, mind you, but rather from a hole dug deep into the ground. Oil. Black gold.

Bubbling crude. It was discovered near the coastal town of Seria. Just like that, one of the world's tiniest nations had become one of the richest.

I came here in an attempt to save money. While trying to book a flight from Darwin to Bangkok, I happened upon a Royal Brunei Airways flight that offered a dirt-cheap one-way airfare. There was a catch, of course. Instead of flying nonstop to Bangkok, I would have to fly first to Brunei—arriving at around 4:00 A.M.—and wait eight hours before boarding a connecting flight. To spare myself the agony of waiting, I decided to stay a few days. Although at times I found myself rummaging around for something to do, I managed to see one of Southeast Asia's most remarkable religious buildings and enjoyed the best hotel experience of my life. Who cared if the Kampung Ayer toilet facilities were a little strange.

The country's complete name is Negara Brunei Darussalam, which loosely translated means "Brunei: Abode of Peace." And what a peaceful abode it is. Serious crime is rare. Acts of physical aggression are relatively unheard of. Nightlife is practically non-existent, and the sale and consumption of liquor is strictly forbidden by Islamic law. Early each evening in Bandar Seri Begawan (pop. 60,000), the capital, the streets roll up with the speed and efficiency of a prayer mat. The tiny central business district becomes as quiet as a mosque. Not once did I hear a horn honk. Not even during the height of rush hour when the streets were jammed with late-model cars, more than a few of which flaunted the Mercedes emblem.

After checking into the Brunei Hotel, relatively inexpensive digs in the center of Bandar Seri Begawan (BSB), I walked the quiet streets for a while. Women, their heads draped in traditional scarves, moved silently along the narrow sidewalks, peeking into shop windows where hundreds of cheap and shiny wristwatches were on display. Orient, Bonia, Morgan, Alba,

Sezen—names I had never seen or heard of were exhibited as prominently as a Rolex in a Fifth Avenue boutique. The glass counters were stocked with imitation gold bracelets, necklaces, lockets, and rings of every imaginable form—many encrusted with fake diamonds and emeralds. Judging by the number of costume jewelry shops in downtown BSB, opulence, or at least the perception thereof, seemed to be all the rage.

Perhaps the gold rush had been inspired by the Sultan and his two wives. His Majesty Sultan Haji Hassanal Bolkiah Mu'izzaddin Waddaulah, the twenty-ninth in a long line of sultans, is a walking monument to wealth. Worth tens of billions thanks to the country's oil reserves and his position as absolute monarch, the Sultan of Brunei was once believed to be the world's second richest man, behind Bill Gates. Unlike Gates, who looks as if he buys his clothes at Wal-Mart, the Sultan radiates affluence and prosperity. His official framed photograph, along with the photos of his two loving wives, graces the walls of every business and institution in BSB. Dressed in scintillating regalia—a golden tunic accented by a golden sash upon which several golden medals are pinned, and a golden headdress glittering with real diamonds—the Sultan and his two lavishly dressed beloveds greet every passenger upon arrival at the airport, every guest upon entering one of the city's few hotels, every customer at the downtown Royal Brunei Airways office, and every patron at every shop no matter how small or large the operation.

After ordering curried chicken at the Al Hilal restaurant, I sat back in my seat at the scuffed aluminum table and took a look around. The tiny eatery was packed with men, perhaps thirty or so. The only female, a waitress, floated silently from table to table, delivering plates of steaming yellow rice. Three dusty chandeliers hung incongruently from the ceiling. A ceiling fan wobbled silently between them. On one wall hung the three royal photographs: the Sultan on top, his two wives positioned dutifully below.

Protruding from the other wall, the wall to which all heads had turned, was a small color television. Eyes wide, jaws flexing as they shoveled food into their mouths, the men stared at the flickering screen as if hypnotized. This particular program did not spout religious teachings. It was not a live broadcast of the Sultan's latest proclamation. Strange though it may seem, the gripping TV drama turned out to be a WWF wrestling match broadcast from the United States. Two men wearing tights—one pink, the other purple—took turns growling and slamming each other onto the wrestling ring floor. The Bruneians stared in wide-eyed wonder.

Aside from the Yayasan Sultan Haji Hassanal Bolkiah Complex, a posh shopping mall commonly referred to as the Yayasan, the city has three notable features: Kampung Ayer; the Omar Ali Saifuddien Mosque; and the Sultan's private palace—which is off-limits to visitors. The Omar Ali Saifuddien Mosque just happens to be one of the world's most stunning religious buildings. Named after the present Sultan's father and visible from nearly every point in the city, the fortresslike structure supports a mammoth golden dome and more than two dozen smaller domes perched high atop rectangular white pillars. Inside the main dome lies a Venetian mosaic comprising more than 3 million pieces. The walls are made of exquisite Italian marble, as are the floors upon which intricately woven prayer mats are laid.

Standing at a distance, I took one photograph after another. There were no visitors with whom to jostle for position. No tour groups to eclipse the view. (Having few attractions and a wealthy oil-based economy, Brunei isn't exactly a hotbed of tourism.) I gazed at the mosque and its shimmering image in the reflecting pool, awed by the spectacular vision, which would not be outdone until I beheld the Taj Mahal months later. On cue, the Muslim call to prayer, the *adhan*, began drifting from speakers suspended beneath the golden domes. The Arabic chant, sung by a *muezzin* five times each day, had a haunting rhythmic quality that settled over the city like a veil.

Beyond the Omar Ali Saifuddien complex lay the entrance to Kampung Ayer, one of BSB's famous stilt villages. Poised on rotting wooden stilts above the Brunei River, the crumbling shacks are connected by a network of crumbling wooden walkways. Half the city's residents, some thirty thousand Malays and Chinese, live in these above-water communities. The villages have their own schools and mosques. Still, most jobs are in mainland BSB. Many residents descend the stairs each morning and climb into one of the ubiquitous water taxis crisscrossing the Brunei River.

With all the Sultan's wealth—the *country's* wealth (after all, the oil fields belong to Brunei)—it's difficult to fathom why so many of his people seem to live in poverty. All 350,000 citizens enjoy free education, free medical care, notably high minimum wages, and no taxes. Everyone is entitled to a pension, as well as low-interest loans and subsidies for automobile purchases (which might explain the abundance of Mercedes-Benzes and BMWs). Nevertheless, as I walked across one of the rickety wooden walkways suspended above the river, many of the stilt shacks appeared rotten and uninhabitable. Even some of the better homes bore fading paint. A few had broken windows.

It was midafternoon on a weekday. Kampung Ayer was deserted, save for a few women hanging laundry outside their homes. The few locals I passed along the way greeted me with suspicious nods. I nodded and smiled back.

After maybe an hour of walking, I stepped into a ramshackle sundry shop manned by an Indian gentleman. Before asking to use the bathroom, I purchased a pack of Doublemint chewing gum. The tactic worked quite nicely. The merchant smiled and pointed to a back door, which I opened in great haste. Inside were several stacks of boxes, stock, I assumed, ready to replenish the shelves as needed. When I took another step, the floor planks

bent beneath my weight. I looked down. Through the spaces between the slats, I could see the Brunei River. Murky water
sloshed maybe fifteen feet below. Mindful of the sagging slats, I
peered behind the stacks of boxes and into an alcove filled with
bulging garbage bags. No toilet. No urinal. No nothing. I left the
storage room. The merchant had obviously misunderstood me.

"I'm sorry, sir," I said. "There's no toilet."

The man abandoned his post and motioned for me to follow.
Back into the storage room I went. The merchant turned to me
and pointed to a place on the floor where the planks appeared to
have been ripped up. As he left the room, I walked over. The hole
in the floor was large enough for an adult male to fall through.
Either the fissure had been purposely created, or some unassuming stockboy had fallen through the planks, never to lift a heavy
box again.

Through the jagged opening, the muddy Brunei River was
clearly visible. I heard the motorized roar of an outboard. Waves
slapping against the wooden stilts. Standing before the hole on
the stockroom floor, only a couple hundred yards upstream from
the holiest of holy mosques, I paused to consider an act performed daily by the shopkeeper and his more urgent customers.
After a moment, I straddled the potty hole, unzipped my pants.
The planks groaned beneath my weight. The entire floor could go
at any second. Which is one reason I could not. Proximity to the
mosque was another. I dashed from the stockroom and out of the
store, down the wobbling wooden walkway, past the Omar Ali
Saifuddien Mosque, the Yayasan, past dark eyes gazing suspiciously beneath traditional scarves, and back to my room at the
Brunei Hotel, where business could be conducted without guilt
or peril.

By day two, I'd seen just about everything Bandar Seri Begawan had to offer. Kampung Ayer. The mosque. The Yayasan
Sultan Haji Hassanal Bolkiah Complex, which, as it turned out,

was just another shopping mall. I even peered through the gates of the Sultan's Palace, hoping to catch a glimpse of greatness. The Sultan did not oblige. With my options dwindling, I took a bus to the Brunei Museum.

If ever you are stuck in Bandar Seri Begawan, be sure to visit the Brunei Museum. The gallery of Islamic art displays a fascinating collection of artifacts dating back to the twelfth century. In a dark room tastefully illuminated with spot-lighting, perhaps sixty copies of the Qur'an have been encased in glass. The smallest, from Iran, is only one and a half inches wide and two inches high. The largest, a nineteenth-century masterpiece from Turkey, is larger than an oversized atlas and written in brilliant golden script. Here you will find Qur'ans of every conceivable size and disposition. Colorful volumes written in gold ink and bursting with blue and red flower motifs.

In the weaponry section of the same room, there's plenty more to look at: a seventeenth-century Iranian ax head upon which animal combat scenes have been chiseled; two daggers sheathed in ornate golden scabbards with blind filigree motifs, from eighteenth-century Oman; a mail and plate shirt (basically a coat of linked metal chains with four metal chest plates, two on each side to protect vital organs) with an accompanying helmet; and an Ottoman flintlock rifle inscribed by Governor Makka Ahmad Basha, 1827. The plate on the butt of the rifle is decorated with a gold flower design. Such artistic detail makes the flintlock rifle far too beautiful for a weapon.

In a different room, visitors can chart the growth of modern Brunei through a series of chronological photographs in which the Sultan is prominently featured. There's a photograph of His Majesty the Sultan officially opening the Brunei International Airport in 1974. Next to this is a photo of His Majesty the Sultan officially opening Radio Television Brunei in 1975; opening Hassanal Bolkiah National Stadium in 1983; proclaiming the

Declaration of Independence from England at 12:01 A.M. on January 1, 1984; opening the Islamic Propagation Center on September 16, 1985; opening the Trade Center Building in 1991; and opening the Islamic Bank of Brunei in 1993. The *pièce de résistance* is a photo of His Majesty the Sultan officiating at the ceremony of the "Billionth Barrel Monument of Crude Oil Production" at Seria Oil Field in 1991. Perhaps no other photograph better captures the spirit of Brunei's economic progress.

Inspired by the Sultan's wealth, I placed a call to the Empire Hotel & Country Club, the best hotel in Brunei and a member of the Leading Hotels of the World. I was surprised to learn that the Empire offered an affordable weekend rate—a mere pittance compared to rates at luxury hotels in other countries. I made a reservation for the following day and prepared for twenty-four hours of five-star opulence.

Three things struck me as I entered the Empire Hotel: the expansive lobby, with a huge crystal chandelier in the shape of an inverted pyramid; the sprawling marble floor design; and the seven-story atrium, where white marble columns stood as wide and tall as redwoods. After checking in at the front desk, a "rooms representative" escorted me to my quarters. "Welcome to the Empire," she said, guiding me to the sleek, soundless elevator that whisked me to my floor. "But many of our visitors prefer to call this the 'Jesus Christ Hotel.'"

The Jesus Christ Hotel. This seemed odd, given the fact that we were in a Muslim country. "Why do they call it that?" I said.

"Perhaps when you reach your room, you will see."

Originally, the Empire was meant to serve as private accommodation for the Sultan's guests. Sometime during construction, however, the decision was made to transform the multimillion-dollar property (the final cost soared close to one billion) into a lavish five-star hotel. Be that as it may, the luxurious surroundings made me feel like the Sultan's invited guest.

The rooms representative escorted me down an elegant corridor, passing high oak doors spaced so far apart I wondered if we had mistakenly reached the banquet floor. She stopped in front of one of the oversized doors and swiped it with the card key, motioning for me to go in first. I stepped inside. "Jesus Christ!" The words came unexpectedly. The rooms rep chuckled. "See what I mean?"

Perhaps wealthy folks are accustomed to this type of elegance, but I most certainly am not. For some mysterious reason—a reason I was not about to challenge—I had been upgraded to a junior suite. The sprawling living room itself was larger and more elegantly furnished than any apartment I'd ever lived in. It had a proper oak dining table, comfy sofa; and, like each of the four hundred rooms and suites, mine had a private balcony facing the South China Sea. The custom-made king-size bed, fitted with Egyptian cotton sheets, would turn sleep into a coveted event. The bathroom was a marble en suite palace, with separate glass doors leading to a toilet, bidet, and shower. A giant sunken bathtub, seemingly big enough to dive into, capped off the room quite well.

The rooms rep left me to bask in opulence. I immediately picked up the telephone, called Royal Brunei Airways, and changed my departure to a later date.

Because I don't play golf and didn't feel like bowling, I ignored the flood-lit eighteen-hole golf course and the high-tech eight-lane alley. Instead, I watched *Lord of the Rings: The Two Towers* at the Empire's lavish three-screen cinema. An arched, thirty-foot ceiling tops the elegant lobby where designer sofas and plump leather chairs sit stylishly on a polished marble floor. Movie posters, encased in stately wooden frames, are positioned on easels throughout the lobby. It's as if the posters themselves are priceless works of art. The theater is furnished with deep comfortable lounge chairs instead of conventional seats, providing a level of relaxation I never thought possible at an action flick.

I worked out in a health club fit for a muscle-bound king.

Swam in a swimming pool as big as a small lake. Sitting next to the baby grand piano in the lobby lounge, I sipped tea from an Asprey china cup and pretended to be somebody. When I ordered breakfast, room service delivered four slices of bread wrapped in cellophane, and a polished silver toaster on a polished silver tray.

My three-night stay, with taxes and all meals (including the best cheeseburger in all of Southeast Asia), came to exactly $500. That was more than $100 above and beyond my daily budget for the one-year around-the-world trip, but the experience was worth every penny.

My most vivid memory is the arrival of His Highness Shaikh Khalifa bin Salman Al-Khalifa, the prime minister of Bahrain. The hotel literally laid out the red carpet for him. I stood along the edge of the runner, amid the multitude of oglers assembled near the lobby door. While the crowd waited, a uniformed hotel employee crawled on his hands and knees, removing flecks of lint from the carpet. After an hour of waiting, His Highness pulled up to the entrance in a Rolls-Royce. Dressed in flowing robes, he and his entourage stepped from the chariot and were whisked away by a team of hotel managers amid flashing cameras and murmurs from the crowd. The prime minister and his staff occupied forty-nine rooms, including the Emperor's Suite, which cost nearly $13,000 U.S. per night.

I wonder if he got the weekend rate.

THE PRINCE OF JEREDONG PARK

◄┄┄┄┄┄┄┄►

Walking through Southeast Asia's largest amusement park, the bright lights blinking cheerlessly against the black Bruneian night, the thrill rides hushed and motionless, it seemed as though the world had come to an apocalyptic end. Like the protagonist in Stephen King's *The Stand*, I might have been the sole survivor of a superflu virus that wiped out 99 percent of the world's population and left me scouring the planet for survivors. (In a chilling example of life imitating art, Severe Acute Respiratory Syndrome, SARS, was at this very moment affecting thousands and spreading panic around the globe.)

Here at the sprawling amusement park on the outskirts of Bandar Seri Begawan, no people moved along the meandering pathways. No one stood in line at the concession stands. Not a single person rode the bumper cars or the Pony Express or puked out his guts while plunging from the Giant Drop. Jeredong Park Playground, purported to be as large as Disneyland, was as vacant as a ghost town. I soon learned that SARS was not responsible for keeping the crowds away.

Behind the oversized windows of the Sky Tower, Jeredong's tallest and most prominent attraction, there were signs of life. A man. The operator, no doubt. He sat behind the window in front of the controls, feet propped up on the console, turning a page of the newspaper that now shielded his face. The news must have been riveting that day because I stood behind the maze of zigzag fencing, waving my arms in vain. When I launched into a dozen desperation jumping jacks, the operator still failed to notice me. So I made my way through the zigzag fencing, weaving back and forth in a solo effort that would normally be accompanied by hundreds. I stood at the front of the line that wasn't, my progress halted by a chain that had been looped between two posts. Still, the operator sat behind the window with the newspaper covering his face. Finally, I cupped my hands around my mouth and let my voice be heard.

"Yo!"

Nothing.

"Yooooooooooooo!"

The newspaper lowered just a tad, revealing two eyes that suddenly grew wide. The operator tossed down the paper, leapt to his feet, and opened the door to the enclosure. "Sorry, sorry," he said, smiling apologetically. "Welcome."

The Sky Tower is a large, round, rotating enclosure similar to a revolving restaurant, or alien spaceship, depending on what you've been smoking. Perhaps forty or fifty bodies could fit inside, but on this night there would be only two.

Pulsating rings of light shot up the tower as the spaceship began to ascend. The ship spun in slow motion, seeming to gather power for liftoff. The diminutive Bruneian looked up at me and grinned.

"Where are all the people?" I said.

"Today the park empty."

"Yeah, but why?"

"No many people come anymore?" He shrugged his shoulders and drove the Sky Tower to a dizzying height.

At the behest of His Majesty the Sultan of Brunei, Jeredong Park Playground opened to the public in 1995. During the first years of operation, locals flocked to Jeredong. Partly because it's the single most exciting activity in all of Brunei, and partly because the Sultan declared that admission to the park would be free. At least for a while. But even billionaire monarchs bow down to the realities of amusement park maintenance. Soon the public faced an admission charge. Attendance plummeted as fast as a fat man on the Giant Drop.

Through the windows of the revolving Sky Tower, I got a bird's-eye view of Jeredong. The property stretched across several acres of deforested land. A labyrinth of walkways lined with street lamps, and populated, from what I could see, by perhaps a dozen human beings, led to brilliant pools of light in the middle of which stood the thrill rides. Beyond the park, the lights faded into dense dark jungle and disappeared into the vast blackness of the South China Sea.

When my spaceship returned to Earth, I thanked the operator. He immediately picked up his newspaper and assumed the position. I walked along the empty asphalt walkway, past the dormant bumper cars and the Tilt-a-Whirl that did not tilt, until feasting my eyes upon a towering mechanical monolith. The Giant Drop. From the looks of it, brave souls were supposed to strap into the seat harnesses, which would rise slowly to the top. There would be a dramatic pause, a moment for patrons to be overcome by fear and apprehension before plummeting to what would surely be a grisly death. But there seemed to be no operator on duty. For as far as I could see, there wasn't another soul around. Until a man motored by in a golf cart.

"Hey, fella," he said. The voice was warm, British. "You want to ride the Drop?"

"Yes, please." I felt like a kid answering his daddy.

"I'll be right back." The Briton sped away in the cart and returned a moment later with a little man. The operator. He had vacated his post to play cards with other operators who were equally bored.

Into the harness I went. The operator threw a lever. I was cranked up to the dropping point high above the park. The great thing about being in a vacant amusement park is that there's no one around to hear a grown man scream like an eight-year-old girl. The harness, with me frozen in it, suddenly plunged as if it were an elevator with its cables cut. I screamed like an eight-year-old girl. Just before hitting the main floor, before disaster occurred at an amusement park that could easily cover up my death, the plunging harness and its shrieking cargo came to a precipitous halt.

When I staggered out of the harness, dazed and exhilarated, the friendly Briton looked at me and smiled. "Can I buy you a Coke?" he said. I've visited a few amusement parks in my time—Six Flags, Disneyland, even the beer-sloshing carnival that is Oktoberfest—but never has a park employee offered to buy me a Coke. Or anything else, for that matter. Flabbergasted, I hopped in the golf cart with the cheerful Briton and let him drive me to the beverage concession.

Milton worked as a park maintenance engineer. His job was to repair the rides, which, according to him, broke down with some regularity. Born and bred in Manchester, he had been working at a local amusement park when the Sultan of Brunei placed an ad in the local paper. The Sultan was looking for a maintenance engineer to work at Jeredong Park in Brunei. Milton applied. Got the job. A few months later he moved to Bandar Seri Begawan and received, as part of a generous compensation package, a free car, free apartment, and an outrageous salary that is the envy of maintenance engineers the world over.

"It's not a bad job," he said, between sips of his Coke. "The bonuses used to be better." Milton told me about the day he was summoned to the office by his supervisor and handed an envelope. Inside he found a bonus check for nearly $5,000 U.S. "All the employees got a similar bonus," he said. The Sultan was a generous employer.

"Are there any openings?" I said.

"Nah." He drained the Coke and tossed it in a rubbish bin.

"Things aren't as cushy as they used to be." He went on to say that Jeredong had fallen on hard times. Many of the rides were broken and waiting for spare parts that never arrived.

Milton drove me around the park, pointing first to a tunnel-of-love attraction where log boats floated along a man-made river and disappeared into a faux mountain. "We have offices inside there," he said, nodding toward the fiberglass peaks. "We watch videos, you know, stuff like that."

There was a sadness in Milton's voice. In spite of the salary and the car and the spacious apartment, he seemed bored and a little lonely. Most nights at the park were like this one, calm and painfully eventless. (Which is why Milton had time to buy me a Coke and drive aimlessly in a golf cart.) But on rare evenings his walkie-talkie would crackle to life with news of a dreaded "Code Blue."

"A Code Blue means someone is stuck on a ride," he said.

"Anybody ever get hurt?"

"Once, a guy died. But he had a heart attack on the Pusing Lagi."

"The Pusing Lagi?" I said.

"Yeah, it's a killer."

For the most part, Jeredong lacks the heart-pumping terror rides you might find at Great Adventure, Disneyland, or Six Flags. But the Pusing Lagi is quite another story. "It's an SLC," Milton said, wowing me with amusement park lingo. "A suspending looping coaster." The golf cart squealed to a stop. I looked up at the Pusing Lagi. Swallowed hard.

"Have a go, fella. You'll like it."

Unlike the other operators that night, this one was there at his station, ready and willing to send me on my merry way. I stepped onto the empty platform and climbed into the very first coaster car, which was unoccupied, as were the other cars linked behind it. I pulled the harness over my head, gave the operator a thumbs-up. As the coaster lurched forward, I looked down and saw Milton, the maintenance engineer. The smiling Briton waved from a reclining position in the golf cart and sat back to watch the show.

The coaster climbed slowly to the first rise and paused, only a second or two, before plunging into a two-G dive that pushed my stomach to the top of my throat. I screamed that eight-year-old girly scream and screamed even louder after hitting the first loop. My British friend had neglected to mention that a suspending looping coaster means the cars turn upside down, whip into a series of tight inverted curls, and then plunge to new depths of terror and lunacy. Hurtling along the looping track in the upturned position, blood rushing to my brain, I rode the Pusing Lagi like a man. At least for the first couple of minutes. As the coaster whipped around and around the twisting tracks, however, I couldn't stop thinking about a Code Blue. The wind rushed past my ears. The cars flew along the track. At one point, I almost pissed my pants. Before skid marks had a chance to appear in my shorts, the Pusing Lagi shuddered to a halt.

I took a deep breath. Opened my eyes. The operator was standing there on the platform, sizing me up for another ride. "You want go again?" he said.

"Hell yeah."

The Pusing Lagi lurched forward. Climbed the first rise. Paused, only a second or two, before plunging into a two-G dive that pushed my stomach to the top of my throat. Code Blue be damned, I was the Prince of Jeredong Park, the shrieking girly-man, riding a royal roller coaster above the deserted playground, again and again and again. . . .

VIRTUAL THIEVES

<······>

"Fire in the hole!"

The first explosion, soon to be followed by a second and a third, ripped through the crowded room filled with Bruneian teenagers. Next came the staccato bursts of machine-gun fire. A mortar blast. Cries from the dazed and wounded. The room shook from another powerful detonation and yet none of the survivors, including me, had the courage to dash toward the exit. Time froze. Tension mounted. A rocket-propelled grenade rocked our world. Drifting through the chaos came a voice—loud, automated, distinctly American. "Terrorists win! Terrorists win!" All I could do was shake my head and sigh.

The terrorists in this case were virtual. Computer-generated bad guys battling American troops in *Counter-Strike*, arguably the most popular online action game at Internet outposts from Buenos Aires to Bangkok. Here at the Netcom Internet Café in Bandar Seri Begawan, each of the forty or so computers held the attention of a teenage boy, his eyes locked on the animated soldier crawling through a computerized terror maze. The boys wore baggy pants and T-shirts. In spite of the sweltering outdoor temperatures, the kid at the station next to mine—and the two friends leaning over his hunched shoulders—wore wool skullcaps that had been pulled down artfully, just above the eyes. "Damn to fuck!" he said out of frustration. From the corner of my eye I watched him stab the joystick in a futile attempt at making a kill. "Shit. Shit. Shit!"

Game over.

Because *Counter-Strike* is an online video game, "gamers can battle real players throughout the world . . . strategizing and communicating with up to fifteen other players in a gritty realistic counterterrorist world." So claims Microsoft, the manufacturer. At a time when U.S. troops were poised to invade Iraq, it seemed ironic that a U.S. company encouraged boys all over the world to "choose from more than twenty-five real-life weapons, including shotguns, sniper rifles, pistols, and other military artillery for live multiplayer action."

I had been staring at my computer screen for as long as the kid had been staring at his. Instead of playing *Counter-Strike*, however, I was writing an epic e-mail to a friend. A warning window popped up in the middle of my computer screen. A payment of one Bruneian dollar was necessary for another hour of Internet time. I had exactly five minutes in which to pay the cashier or my half-finished e-mail would be snatched from the screen and zapped into a black hole in cyberspace.

I reached into my daypack, grabbed my wallet, removed a Bruneian buck, and headed toward the cashier. Walking between the rows of bobbing teenage heads, mortars and machine guns blazing in the background, I threw a look over one shoulder. Sure enough, my daypack remained exactly where I had left it. After paying the cashier, I returned to my seat and placed the daypack on the floor beneath my station. The three boys at the adjacent station turned to leave when I sat down.

A friend had expressed concern over my decision to visit a Muslim country when the American invasion of Iraq seemed imminent. (I came to Brunei in February 2003. War broke out in Baghdad the following month.) Anti-American sentiment had been on the rise all over the world. As was the case with a few fellow Americans I'd met on the road, there had been a shift in the manner in which I was received. The shift did not apply to local Muslims, mind you. The few Bruneians I encountered shook my hand eagerly after realizing I hailed from the United States. And yet the Western travelers—Britons, Australians, Argentineans, Spaniards, the French—sometimes bristled when they learned my nationality. "Oh . . . you're *American.*" No political attacks were launched. No anti-American statements made. Just an infinitesimal pause during a typical traveler's greeting. A pause that did not exist before the Bush administration decided to . . .

I was trying to find the words to express my feelings in the e-mail when, suddenly, there was a voice from behind.

"Excuse me, sir?"

I turned and saw the face of a teenage boy. The same boy who had been sitting at the cashier's desk when I paid for another hour of Internet time. He pointed to the floor beside my chair, where my wallet lay. My wallet! I picked it up and sighed. "Thank you, thank you," I said, shaking my head as he walked away. How could I have been so careless? I jammed the wallet into the bottom of my daypack and finished writing the longest of what proved to be a half-dozen long-winded e-mails.

An hour later, when another warning window popped up on the screen, I reached into my daypack and opened my wallet. The fold was empty. One hundred Bruneian dollars gone. Even worse, my ATM bank card had disappeared. All that remained was my MasterCard. I sat there, playing back the tapes, wondering how this could have happened. I searched the area around my station. Nothing. The boy who had spotted my wallet suddenly appeared. "What is the matter?" he said in textbook English.

"My money. My money is gone."

The boy stood there, his plump face warped by grief. Then a flash in his eye. "The boys, the three boys. I think I see them throw something on the floor when you come to pay."

"The boys at this station," I said, pointing at the computer next to mine.

"Yes. You must go to police. You must go to police!"

It was my fault. I had pulled the wallet from my bag for every *Counter-Striking* kid to see, and then left it in my daypack while paying the cashier. In the time it took me to get there, three opportunistic boys had opened the wallet, snatched what they could, and tossed the wallet to the floor.

"I know the boys," the boy said, his eyes wide and earnest. "You must go to police."

The bank card was replaceable. The money, a little more than fifty U.S. dollars, would be chalked up as a lesson learned. "What's your name?" I said.

"Mohammed."

"Thank you, Mohammed. Thank you very much. But I don't want to call the police."

"But you must."

"That's okay, really."

"No, no, no. You must go to police. I will take you." The look on Mohammed's face was so anguished, so sincere, I didn't have the heart to walk away. The fourteen-year-old took me by the hand and out onto the streets of Bandar Seri Begawan. We walked to a police substation on a street corner three blocks away. The tiny outpost had the look of a lemonade stand. With Mohammed as translator, I told my story to three policemen who leaned forward and listened intently. A report needed to be filed, they said. We must go to police headquarters a few blocks away.

Mohammed and I walked past an open-ended stadium where hundreds of Muslim girls ran out onto the grassy field. The humid air crackled with the voice of a man barking instructions into a megaphone. Mohammed offered the explanation before I had a chance to ask. "They practice for the Independence Day celebration." Some girls wore turquoise tunics and black pants; others wore white tunics with their school name (S.M. Sayyidina

Abu Bakar) emblazoned on the back. They all wore flowing head-scarves that flapped like wings as they ran.

There was no time to dawdle, apparently. Mohammed tugged my hand. "We must go to police," he insisted. "We must!"

From the stadium we made a right turn in front of the Omar Ali Saifuddien Mosque and stepped inside a nondescript office building. Again, with Mohammed translating, I recounted my story to a policeman at the reception desk. He pointed to an empty room and told us to wait there. The room was furnished with one metal file cabinet, two chairs, and an old metal desk upon which sat a circa 1960 Universal typewriter. On the bare wall were three large rectangles, each edged in dust—missing portraits of the Sultan and his two wives. Mohammed sat in the chair, his feet swinging playfully as we waited. Twenty minutes later, a cop came in and told us to go to another building.

We walked down a hallway, past unoccupied offices, out the door, and down an outdoor footpath that ran beneath an over-hang and led to a set of concrete stairs. On the second floor we walked through a doorway and peeked over the divider behind which a woman munched on a sandwich. Mohammed told her my story. She fixed him with a disbelieving stare and pointed to the back office. We walked past bleak offices with rundown furni-ture and sat in a room where a Malaysian soap opera played on a flickering TV screen. "Oh, Amir," the sobbing actress appeared to say. "I love you so much." Amir shook his head, dejected. He had probably been screwing a blonde. The drama was interrupted when a policeman peeked into the room and motioned for us to join him and another policeman in a different room.

Two cops interrogated Mohammed as if he were a witness to a murder. My noble friend recounted my story for the fourth or fifth time in less than an hour. I filled out the report. Answered questions that seemed to have no relevance to my case. "No, I have never been involved in an uprising."

We went downstairs to the room we'd sat in earlier. Another

cop—he appeared to have a higher rank because of age and stature—asked us to tell the story again. He filled out a log book. We shook his hand and left.

Once outside the building, Mohammed let loose a high-pitched giggle. "I never been to police station before," he said. "Thank you. It was very fun."

BAD NIGHT IN BANGKOK

I flew to Bangkok one warm and muggy night and landed, through no fault of my own, in the middle of a misunderstanding.

"You boxer?"

The question came at me from a Thai immigration official who stared at my passport photo and then appraised me. The same question came from customs officers, baggage handlers, even the guy who gobbled up my dollars from behind the counter and issued the taxi voucher. When I stepped outside the airport terminal and into a waiting cab, the driver looked in his rearview mirror and posed the question again.

"You boxer?"

"No, no, no . . . I'm not a boxer," I said, shaking my head for the twentieth time.

"American soldier?" He pronounced it *Ameddican soja.*

"No. I'm not a soldier."

"You strong body," he said. "Mike Tyson." Although I am taller and perhaps wider than the average Thai, comparisons to the beefy boxer were preposterous. From a Thai perspective, perhaps all black people do look alike. "Good, veddie good," he continued. He gave me a thumbs-up and dropped a heavy foot on the gas pedal. Thai boxing is the country's number-one sport. The hurt-him-any-way-you-can martial art permits the unrestricted use of feet, knees, elbows, and fists in a fast and furious clash of diminutive titans. I soon learned that boxers, Thai or otherwise, are held in the same esteem as gods. They garner respect in the ring and on the street.

The taxi sped down a highway on-ramp and into motorized mayhem. Battered automobiles weaved in and out of the flow of traffic like emergency vehicles en route to some horrible disaster. Motorbikes shot through the forbidden zone between lanes, and sliced across when space and courage permitted. Most bikers did not ride alone. I saw two, three, four, and in at least one instance, I saw five people positioned on a motorbike no larger than a 200-cc.

A man, probably the father, drove the bike. Stretched out on the gas tank in front of the driver was a five- or six-year-old boy. Behind the driver sat a woman—the mother, perhaps. A toddler was sandwiched between Mom and Dad. Bringing up the rear was a pre-teen girl whose skinny arms clung around her mother's waist. The girl's butt protruded from the seat like a bony bumper.

I watched through the passenger window as the biker family, suddenly and quite recklessly, sliced in front of a wobbling truck. The truck driver slowed accordingly, without altering the blank expression on his face. His eyes cut toward the taxi. The truck accelerated and then disappeared. This was driving, Thai-style. Traffic moved in a deadly game of Survival of the Quickest.

Above the speeding cars and the overloaded motorcycles and the wobbling trucks hung a noxious cloud of auto exhaust that turned the sun into a pale white blur.

"You want woman?" my driver whispered, as we raced toward the city.

"Huh?"

"You want woman?"

"No. No thanks."

"I get you young girl," he continued.

"No thanks."

"Young, veeeeeddie young."

"No. I don't want a girl."

"I bring to hotel for you."

"No."

"Cheap price."

"No!"

Silence. The driver stared at me in the rearview mirror. I could almost see his mind percolating with possibilities. Then, suddenly, his eyes widened. "Ahhh . . . ," he said. "You want boy. I get you boy!"

"Look," I said. "I don't want boy. I don't want girl. I don't want woman. I don't want man. I don't want sheep. You know what I want?"

His eyes gleamed in anticipation.

"I want hotel. Okay? Ho-tel."

We drove for the next half hour in silence.

When we arrived at the hotel, a young Thai ran to the car to greet me. I thought it strange that management found it necessary to employ a bellboy at a two-star dive. But I was beginning to learn that Bangkok is different from any place on earth.

The bellboy dragged my duffel to the room. I tipped him a dollar and tried to close the door, but he had leaned a forceful shoulder against it. He stuck his head inside and spoke in a conspirator's whisper.

"You want woman?"

"No."

"You boxer?"

I rolled my eyes and shook my head.

"You want—"

I slammed the door, lay on the spongy mattress, and watched the naked lightbulb sway above me.

After a long nap, I found my way to Patpong Road, Bangkok's infamous red-light district. No, I wasn't looking for women.

Even though the place was packed with strip joints. I wanted to see the liveliest area of the city. According to the guy at the front desk, Patpong was it.

Throngs of wide-eyed Western men squirmed past sidewalk vendors who hawked pirated Hollywood videos, CDs, DVDs, T-shirts, jewelry, and a hundred Thai concoctions that sizzled in greasy woks. Barefoot boys darted through the crowd. Groups of prune-faced men squatted on street corners. The shouts of Thai vendors sliced through the humid air. "My friend, my friend . . . I have veddie special price for you." The spectacle was bathed in blinking blue-red neon light from sex clubs that stretched along either side of the street. Naughty names sprang forward like per-verted apparitions from a teenage boy's wet dream: Thigh Bar, Supergirl, Pink Palace, Pussy Galore.

A short, wiry street vendor accosted me amid the chaos. "Oooh, you good body," he said. "You boxer?" I gave a tired smile, but before I could move on, the old Thai reached up and squeezed one of my biceps. "Veddie strong," he said. "Mike Tyson. Good, veddie good."

Within seconds, I was surrounded by a dozen Thais. "You boxer?" one of them cried. "Ahhh, strong body," said another. "Good, veddie good."

I tried walking away, but they clung to me like rock star groupies until a young boy appeared. He pushed a sheet of paper into my hand. It was an invitation to a nightclub, a means of es-cape. Upon closer inspection, I realized it was an invitation to a strip club. I'm hardly a prude, but my budget was tight. At a strip club—even a Southeast Asian one—I would surely go broke.

"No thanks," I told the kid. "I just want a beer."

"Singha, national beer of Thailand. Only sixty-five baht," he said.

"Is there a cover charge?"

"No cover charge," he said.

I nodded. The mistake was made.

The boy snatched me away from my admirers. We hurried

around the corner, down a back alley, and up a ramshackle wooden staircase that led to a door with a flickering neon sign above it. The sign read INDERELLA, but I realized a moment later that the "c" had burned out.

Once inside, I was overwhelmed by the stench of stale beer and cigarette smoke. Dim light shone on several female dancers who slithered against chrome poles rising from a horseshoe-shaped bar/stage. They wore only G-strings and the doleful expressions of weary Third World prostitutes. A few drunken European men watched drearily from their bar stools. Others sat in booths with girls young enough to be their granddaughters. From a battered jukebox came the familiar sound of KC & The Sunshine Band. "Do a little dance, make a little love, get down tonight!" The lyrical irony was too much to take.

I turned to leave, but the proprietor, an ancient Thai gentleman with a willowy gray beard, attached a firm hand to my shoulder and guided me backward to a seat at the bar/stage. My young guide stood behind him, nodding, encouraging me to stay.

"There's no cover charge?" I asked, not wanting to cause a scene.

"No cover charge," the old man said.

"Beer is sixty-five baht, right?"

"Beer sixty-five baht."

Reluctantly, I sat at the bar. When a stone-faced waitress delivered a bottle of Singha, one of the bar dancers stepped directly in front of me. She spread her legs wide in a shooter's stance, knees level to my eyeballs. Watching me through slits edged in hastily applied streaks of eyeliner, she bucked her hips in a pathetic parody of ecstasy. After only two sips of beer, I asked for the check. Much to my surprise, I owed 700 baht ($17.00 U.S. instead of $1.60). I told the waitress there must be a mistake. She walked away in a huff and returned a moment later with the old man.

"You pay seven hundred baht," he demanded.

"What for?" I said.

"Six hundred thirty-five for see girls. Sixty-five baht for beer."

"But you told me there was no cover charge."

The old man snarled. "You *Ameddican!*" he said. "You pay seven hundred baht!"

It was a setup. I'd been screwed.

The music stopped. The dancers stopped dancing. The lights brightened a notch. All the seedy patrons sat back in their seats as if a more interesting form of entertainment were about to begin. Suddenly, I was confronted by three security men—one wore a deep scar across his cheek. Dressed in black, the men stood in wing formation, arms hanging easily at their sides. They were hard, malevolent ex-boxers. Ass kickers of a daunting persuasion. Ever wonder what Thai boxers do after retiring from the ring? This is it.

I scanned the room, looking for the boy who had led me to this, the ultimate tourist trap. The boy had disappeared. If I had seven hundred baht, or a credit card, or traveler's checks—any of the legal tender conveniently left in my hotel safe—I would have gladly paid the inflated bill in exchange for an unmolested exit. But I left my room that night with only enough money for a few beers. I had maybe four hundred baht in my pocket.

The old man demanded seven hundred baht one final time. I tried to negotiate. Tried to explain that all I had was four hundred, but he wanted the whole shebang. He barked an order to the security men. They hesitated, trading glances as if uncertain as to how I was to be dispatched. Did they assume that I, too, was a boxer, even though I'd only thrown one lame street punch in my life? Were satellite images of Mike Tyson dancing like demons in their heads? Trembling, but trying not to show it, I rifled through my trouser pocket, found sixty-five baht, and slammed it on the bar/stage next to my bottle of Singha.

I drew up to my full height, brushed past the boxer closest to me, and wanted to say something streety, something to inspire paralyzing fear. But I don't speak Thai. All I could muster was

"Excuse me, please." I then swaggered toward the exit like a bad-ass, like Samuel L. Jackson in *Jackie Brown*. I braced for the impact of a roundhouse kick. Listened for the click of a switch blade. Waited for a beer bottle to shatter against my skull. Instead, I heard blood beating in my ears and the mean, low voices of the Thais who pursued me.

Like a scene from a recurring nightmare I used to have as a kid, the door seemed to float farther away with every step. I held my head high. Tried not to soil my Calvins. As I moved closer to the door, a fourth boxer appeared. He put a muscled arm against the doorjamb in an attempt to block my departure. If I stopped, the three shadows would call my bluff and give the patrons something to ogle at. If I continued, I'd have to somehow force the issue with the doorjamb guy. I took one step. Then another. The door retreated another hundred yards. In a matter of seconds four martial artists would start kicking the living shit out of me. And everyone in the joint—the fat European men and the young girls huddling beside them, the old man, the stone-faced waitress, the kid (wherever the hell he was hiding)—everyone was going to watch as if it were a scene from a Jackie Chan movie.

Clenching both fists, I approached the man blocking my exit. He stared at me with cold, black, lifeless eyes. Doll's eyes. Eyes that miraculously flinched after I looked him up and down and spoke in the daunting voice of Samuel L. "Yo, motherfuckah, you best be steppin' off." He dropped his arm. I pushed open the door. Then I ran. Lord knows how I ran. I ran with the knee-pumping passion of an Olympic sprinter. Down Cinderella's rickety steps. Through throngs of startled tourists. Onto a busy street corner where I flagged down a *tuk-tuk* and jumped in.

Thirty minutes later, sitting at a lonely bar in a deserted restaurant far away from Patpong Road, I clung to a bottle of Singha beer with hands that still trembled. I took the first shaky sip, realizing how close I'd come to getting killed. Then, suddenly, a noise from behind. They had followed me.

I spun around in a panic only to find a waiter standing there. He stood with both hands behind his back, head bowed, as if preparing to address someone of great stature. The waiter looked up. He smiled, cleared his throat again. In a small, reverent voice he said, "You boxer?"

SUBWAY TO CLEANLINESS AND PURITY

◄·····················►

On a hot Singaporean evening, exactly four days before Severe Acute Respiratory Syndrome (SARS) reared its ugly head, before schools closed, restaurants emptied, and more than fifteen thousand potentially infected locals had been placed under mandatory quarantine, I arrived in this high-tech city-state, unaware of the danger and looking for a place to lay my head. I could not have chosen a more appropriate establishment than the Hotel Phoenix on Orchard Road.

At first glance the Hotel Phoenix seemed like an ordinary state-of-the-art hotel. Spacious, contemporary lobby. Friendly staff. In-room computers with high-speed Internet access. Satellite television, one-touch temperature controls, room service prices that make you shake your head and wonder. But two features distinguished the Phoenix in unanticipated ways. First, the leather lounge chair. My room had been furnished with a Leisure 2 OS-730. Made in Japan by Osim Global Health Care, the handsome Leisure 2 boasts four different massage actions (rolling, kneading, pointing, tapping), which can be achieved at varying speeds while reclining at a 180-degree angle. I spent my first full day in Singapore not in the towering shopping malls of Orchard Road, not at the famous Singapore Zoo or in the Raffles bar where the Singapore Sling was invented. Trembling as if zapped by a low-wattage defibrillator, I spent that whole day ensconced in the Leisure 2.

When my travel-weary body had recuperated, I went to the front desk to inquire about the hotel's second distinctive feature: the card key. Aside from the normal function of granting room access, my card key or "Smart Card" doubled as a Metro Rapid Transit (MRT) pass. Guests simply present the Smart Card to the front desk clerk, who then slides the card into an electronic apparatus and . . . *voilà!* A cash credit of up to twenty Singaporean dollars is uploaded and the glittering Singapore subway system is at your service.

Following the clerk's directions, I walked next door to the Somerset subway station and waved the card above the laser reader on the turnstile. A digital readout displayed the twenty-dollar credit. The gate retracted and I entered what is arguably the world's cleanest and most user-friendly subway system.

Polished marble steps led to a polished marble platform where passengers sat quietly upon polished marble benches that gleamed—they actually gleamed—in the soft fluorescent light. (A sparkling aluminum elevator delivered elderly, disabled, and infant-toting passengers to the platform.) The station was immaculately clean. Not a shred of paper littered the area. No dust. No dirt. No cigarette butts. Because chewing gum had been banned on the island, the subway platform remained free of gum wrappers and the sticky wads that inspired the ban. Spacious. Opulent. Odor-free. Walking into the Singapore subway is like stepping into the lobby of the Ritz.

Unlike the crumbling subways of New York City, where passengers occasionally stumble from platforms to be flattened by trains, fried by the third rail, or devoured by rats the size of Volkswagen Beetles, no such atrocities occur at Singapore's major stations. Here at Somerset, the train tunnels are encased by walls of glass and brushed aluminum. The walls boast sliding doors that open in conjunction with the doors of each arriving train. On the subway platform, lined up at each aluminum door, you'll find yellow markings. Before boarding the train, passengers are instructed to stand behind the markings. This allows alighting passengers a disembarking courtesy you never seem to get in New York.

Like the half-dozen people standing silently nearby, I waited obediently behind the yellow markings. The platform was as quiet as a library, and no less reverent. No one spoke. No one munched on corn chips or sipped cans of soda because eating and drinking on MRT property is prohibited. Offenders are subject to a $500 fine. (Smokers face a whopping $1,000 penalty.) But human nature works in mysterious ways. Never do you crave something as much as when you're told it can't be had.

Slowly, furtively, I reached inside my pants pocket and found the half-empty bag of M&Ms. Using my index and middle fingers, I dipped into the opening and scooped a few candy-coated morsels into my hand. Standing among the silent Singaporeans, I waited for the perfect moment and then tossed the candies into my mouth. A single M&M, a red one, my favorite, unfortunately lost its way. It clattered to the pristine subway platform.

By the reaction of my fellow commuters, you would have thought I had assaulted an old lady. A barrage of disapproving glances came my way. The wayward M&M rolled against the marble and wobbled to a halt next to a woman who had been punching a text message into her mobile phone. Her finger paused in midair. She looked down at the red M&M and then at me. The look she gave reminded me of a scene from *Invasion of the Body Snatchers*. As the protagonist walked among the alien converts, she made the mistake of gasping at an alien dog with a human head. A dutiful alien pointed at her and screamed, alerting others who chased the frightened human toward a body-snatching pod that would ultimately change her into one of them.

Three chimes, like escalating notes on a xylophone, suddenly echoed through the Somerset subway station. A recorded voice,

British, female—a voice you might hear in the departure lounge at Heathrow—wafted from the P.A. system. "Ladies and gentlemen, the next train on platform A goes to Marina Bay." Passengers gathered behind the yellow markings. I bent over casually as if to tie my Nikes, and picked up the red M&M. So clean was the floor, I considered eating the candy. But before popping the morsel into my mouth, another set of scornful eyes fell upon me. I placed the candy in my pocket.

A moment later there was a whoosh of air that almost made my ears pop. The train had arrived. The doors opened. Those of us on the platform waited patiently for passengers to exit before stepping onto the train and whooshing away.

Raffles Station seemed even more impressive than Somerset. Original art hung on the walls near the turnstile interchange, where commuters passed their wallets, purses, and backpacks over electronic readers. Assuming these folks must have had MRT cards inside, and that the electronic readers were sensitive enough to scan through leather and plastic, I placed my Smart Card inside my wallet and my wallet inside my backpack. Following the lead of the woman in front of me, I dragged my backpack over the turnstile's electronic reader and looked at the readout. Cool. The price of my journey had been deducted, and my new balance appeared on the digital readout.

I rode the subway to the world-renowned Raffles Hotel and drank an overpriced Singapore Sling. On the wall behind the Writer's Bar hung a gold plaque dedicated to the hotel's more notable guests. It read: "The Writer's Bar commends Raffles Hotel's association with great writers including the novelists Joseph Conrad, Rudyard Kipling and Somerset Maugham. Today it provides a new generation of literary talent with an excellent and inspiring vantage point." With rooms starting at $350 U.S. per night, however, today's literary talent may have trouble affording Raffles's inspiring vantage point.

From Raffles, I rode the subway to the Singapore Zoo. (It required a transfer to a metro bus, which accepted my Smart Card.) Billed as the world's first "open zoo," it has no bars or cages. Animals and humans are separated by foliage-filled trenches that give the illusion of an open plain. The rare white Bengal tigers were a sight to behold. As were the Komodo dragons. And I could not understand why the elephants declined to step across the trench and squash the puny people pointing at them. But the most interesting attraction was the lizards. Not because of any obvious features, mind you. They looked . . . well, they looked like lizards. Their "illicit" behavior is what piqued my interest. With all the talk about same-sex marriage in the United States, a sign at the Singapore Zoo lizard compound seemed apropos. "Some lizard species exist as females only. To reproduce, the female needs stimulation from another female who plays the role of a courting male." This process is called parthenogenesis, and is common among insects and other invertebrates.

As we all know, same-sex parthenogenesis is becoming more and more common among humans as well. But the repressive Singaporean government does not tolerate this. In fact, homosexuality is outright illegal here. Do a Google search on the Internet as I did. You'll learn that male homosexuality is illegal in public and private places. Female homosexuality, on the other hand, is illegal publicly but not privately. You would think that in an autocratic society such as this, men would have more rights than women. Go figure.

Singapore embraces a litany of draconian rules that would make an ACLU lawyer drool on his brief. The first chilling statute greets visitors upon arrival at Changi Airport: DEATH TO DRUG TRAFFICKERS. The message, written in bold red letters and printed at the top of every immigration form, somehow manages to curb illegal drug use in a way that SAY NO TO DRUGS never will. In Singapore you can be fined for eating or drinking in public places, you can be prosecuted for munching on or distributing chewing gum, penalized for not flushing the toilet, flogged for committing minor acts of vandalism, imprisoned for same-sex titillation, vilified for reading a banned book, and you will be singed by the white-hot stares of passing Singaporeans if you speak too loudly on the street or wear clothing designed by anyone more provocative than Tommy Hilfiger. The price for order and cleanliness is an antiseptic society where character and individuality seem poised for extinction.

I contemplated ways to break the rules without getting myself arrested. Perhaps I could skip down Orchard Road, holding hands with Richard Simmons and Ellen DeGeneres. The three of us could chew great gooey wads of grape, strawberry, and cherry Bubblicious while belting out old Barry Manilow tunes to outraged pedestrians.

The lizards at the Singapore Zoo. What was I saying about them? Oh yeah, they're really interesting. . . .

After a long day of covert M&M eating on the subway, I returned to the Hotel Phoenix, sat in my Leisure 2 OS-730, and watched the local television news. Three people had been diagnosed with a mysterious flu virus. No connection was immediately made to similar outbreaks in the southern Chinese province of Guangdong and in Hong Kong. But the following day, six more flu cases were reported here in Singapore. Two of the afflicted were hospital staff. The government made an official announcement: Singapore had its first cases of SARS.

I decided to fly south to Bali.

After relinquishing my trusty Smart Card to the front desk clerk, I walked to the Somerset subway station and bought a one-way ticket to Changi Airport. As always, the train was spotlessly clean. The crowd quiet and well mannered. As the train whooshed away on a current of air, I noticed that one passenger was different from all the rest. She wore blue jeans and a crisp white shirt as did many of the Chinese and Malay passengers. Her bristly black hair did not seem out of place. Nor her eyeglasses. But the woman's mouth and nose were covered by a white surgical mask. In less than a week, everyone in Singapore would be wearing one.

BALI BY MOTORBIKE

◄┄┄┄┄┄┄┄┄►

Loneliness is the bane of solo travel. It sits in your belly like a hunger that may never be satisfied. When you're dining alone for the tenth night in a row, you long for companionship the way an alcoholic longs for a drink. When you can't speak the language, you become haunted by your own ineptitude. When you experience a memorable moment—one that comes and goes unshared— you soon find yourself wondering if the moment ever happened at all. Such was the case with me and the Balinese sunset.

Like a huge red molten coin, the sun slid toward the sea and set the world ablaze. Cherry-orange waves splashed onto the sand. The sky became a crimson cotton field. Slowly, teasingly, the sun dipped into the horizon. You could almost hear the sizzle as it sank. Watching from a wooden chair on Legian Beach, this was the fourth spectacular sunset in as many days. The fourth day of heart-wrenching splendor. Unlike the European couples standing in ankle-deep surf and the Balinese teenagers clustered on the sand, I had no one with whom to share the moment. So rather than spend a fifth evening simply watching the glorious sunset, I decided to ride into it.

I rented a motorcycle. With nothing but a backpack and a crude road map of Bali, I set off on a five-day circumnavigation of the island. Along the way I fell in love. She was not pretty. My

250-CC Honda flaunted a busted speedometer, a missing left mirror, and dents that conjured up a dozen accident scenarios. But she purred like a panther when I kick-started her engine and pulled back on the clutch. And she took me places I'd never been.

With a smile on my face and a twinge in my gut, I motored toward Denpasar, Bali's traffic-congested capital. At the first stoplight, and at every frenzied intersection thereafter, motorbikes and motor scooters squeezed through the gaps between idling automobiles as if jostling for pole position at the Indy 500. When the light turned green, hundreds of vehicles lurched forward, belching clouds of exhaust that made me wish I'd rented an air-conditioned Jeep. What amazed me more than the sheer volume of motorbikes were the loads with which they had been burdened. Fat burlap sacks were stacked high on the seat behind many drivers. Some carried bulging bundles of wood.

As I turned the corner, a cavalcade of motorbikes flew by. But one motorbike stood out above the madness. It had somehow been outfitted with a towering network of birdcages. The bike flew by too fast for me to see the type of birds it carried, but there were dozens packed in wooden cages that rose five feet above the driver's head.

Somehow, in the midst of the chaos, I was pulled over by a motorcycle cop. He swaggered over to me as I sat on the idling bike and began jabbing a finger at his own head. "Use your head," he was trying to tell me. But what had I done wrong? I wasn't the one driving with a five-foot stack of birdcages on my seat. He jabbed the finger at his head again. "Where your helmet is?" he said. Damn. I'd forgotten to put it on.

I reached down to the side of the motorbike and unhooked the helmet from its clasp. When I donned the helmet, the cop grinned and shook his head. "Too late for you," he said. "No bagus."

"No bagus?"

"No good. You have problem." The cop told me I would have to attend a court hearing. A spectacular fine would be levied against me. From the tone of his voice you'd have thought a vicious caning would follow the fine. Perhaps jail time. Castration. No punishment seemed too severe for he who rides motorbike without helmet. Then it came. The proposition. The cop removed his aviator sunglasses. His eyeballs slithered in their sockets. "Maybe you pay me now," he whispered. "U.S. dollar."

I paid the twenty-dollar bribe and made damn sure to buckle my chin strap before pulling away.

Once outside the city, the traffic cleared. I shifted gears, pulled back on the throttle, and fell into the rhythm of the narrow winding road. The road to Ubud is lined with Balinese arts and crafts. I zoomed past several villages, each specializing in a particular art form. First there was Batubulan, a hamlet of stone carvers. Hundreds of ornately carved Hindu sculptures formed a gauntlet through which I cruised. Next was Celuk (silver- and goldsmithing), Sukawati (handicrafts), and Batuan, which is known for paintings of everyday Balinese life.

After reaching Ubud, the epicenter of Bali's art scene, I stumbled upon the residence of Ketut Liyer. A local artist and Balian (medicine man), Ketut was busy counseling Made, an unemployed hotel worker. Like thousands of locals, Made lost her job as a direct result of the terrorist bombings in Kuta Beach. The bombings—which left more than two hundred dead and hundreds injured—sent shock waves throughout the Balinese tourism industry. Here it was, five months after the attacks, and the job market was as bleak as the Day After. To this end, the Balian prepared to put "magic" in Made's résumé.

She pulled the typed pages from inside her jacket. The Balian chanted softly. He held the pages in his weathered hands while Made watched the spectacle. She walked away smiling, the résumé imbued with the power to land a job.

For two days I lounged at Ubud's coffeehouses, rambled through its many arts and crafts shops, ate *nasi goreng* and *gado gado* at Satri's Restaurant—a fifteen-year-old mainstay on Monkey Forest Road. For two nights I slept at the home of a reclusive U.S. expatriate (a retired friend of a friend). My hostess lives in a rustic two-bedroom bungalow perched on the edge of a deep ravine. Her open-air living room faces a jungle of coconut palms through which orange light blazed as we drank tea at sunset.

She invited a fellow expatriate for sunset tea—an ex-tennis pro from Tennessee who now led expeditions into the wilds of New Guinea. He told fascinating stories about trekking through the Guinean jungle. About how he had suffered a mysterious infection that caused one hand to swell to nearly twice its normal size. About how he'd met tribal people who "had never seen a white man," or "a black man either," he added, looking up at my face. "At least not one from outside the island."

Intrigued by the possibility of real adventure, I listened as he spoke of creature encounters as if they were badges of accomplishment. I heard of wild boar and killer ants. Primordial shrieks in the night. "You haven't lived," he said, "until you've peeled a bloodsucking leech from your testicles."

Early the next morning I jumped on the motorbike and drove far, far away from the crazed Tennessean. I headed for Tirta Gangga, some seventy kilometers to the northeast. At one point I turned from the main road, bounced along a dirt track, and chanced upon the tiny fishing village of Kusamba. Locals emerged from their huts to stare at me, wide-eyed and smiling.

A middle-aged man in a T-shirt and baseball cap pointed at my arm and then rubbed his own. "Same, same," he said. "Same, same." Our skin was the same shade. This fact put a big smile on his face. "Same, same," I repeated. Like the tribal people in the Tennessean's story, perhaps these people had never seen a black man. An old man, skin withered on his naked chest, reached out to shake my hand. The man in the T-shirt pointed to his daughter, who nodded shyly and hid behind his leg. He explained, through a series of hand gestures, how they make a living turning seawater into salt for export to Japan.

With the wind in my face and the cheap plastic helmet strapped to my head, I zoomed past the station from which ferries sail to Lombok. Downshifting from fourth gear to third and then second, I slowed beneath a canopy of trees and gazed at Candi Dasa Beach. The recently erected seawall saved the seashore, but eroded its beauty in the process.

I stopped at weather-beaten roadside shops where whole families tried to converse in Indonesian while I drank bottles of mineral water in an attempt to beat the ninety-five-degree heat. When I finally reached Tirta Gangga at sunset, I screeched to a halt in front of the Tirtu Ayu Homestay.

Tirtu Ayu is a water palace built by a Balinese rajah in 1948. It's graced with swimming pools and ornamental ponds from which sculpted fountains spout. I spent a quiet, luxurious night in a marble-floored villa that featured a four-poster bed with an embroidered muslin canopy. The next morning I motored along a winding mountain road that offered dizzying views of rice terraces so perfectly landscaped they looked like emerald stairways to heaven. From there I sped along the northeast coast, stopping once at a roadside shack where an attendant stuck a funnel in my gas tank and poured petrol from a glass jar. My final stop was in the north coast hamlet of Lovina Beach, where I secured a thatch-roof seaside bungalow and slept to the irrepressible song of barking beach dogs.

At 5:30 A.M. the following morning, I squeezed into a boat with a Balinese fisherman and two German tourists. Together, we motored out to sea. For twenty minutes we sat in the creaking wooden boat, watching the glassy waters, waiting for a rounded snout to break the surface. The sun rose from a peach-colored horizon. The salt air tickled my face. I sat there, thinking about how fortunate I was to sit in a fishing boat on the Java Sea. That's when it happened. With a sudden splash, a dolphin shot from the water not twenty feet away from the boat. A second dolphin somersaulted behind the first as if it were a rehearsed routine.

More dolphins followed. Jumping. Flipping. Splashing. Grinning. Greeting the new day with a playfulness humans only dream of. Then nothing. Silence. One moment passed. Then another. Behind our boat, in the distance, a sudden splash. The boat sped toward the commotion and stopped. The sun inched higher. We waited. Watched the sea. A grinning gray snout broke the surface. Another show had begun.

The next morning I hopped on the Honda and leaned into the high-banked turns that twisted through the mountains near Singarja. After five days and more than three hundred kilometers of island biking, I found myself watching another spectacular sunset at Legian Beach.

Lovers strolled along the shore, pointing to the flaming horizon. Balinese children sat in the sand, staring at the same orangy half-light they'd seen every day since birth. I sat alone in my wooden beach chair, the sea air kissing my face, watching, wanting, and ultimately realizing that life doesn't get any better.

India

SACRED OFFERINGS

◆••••••••••••••••••◆

With more than a billion inhabitants speaking eighteen major languages and a thousand minor languages and dialects, India, the birthplace of Hinduism, is as fascinating as it is complex. Consider the fact that 83 percent of the population is Hindu and that, even today, most Hindu marriages are arranged. Or that the social structure is built upon a complex caste system that in many ways predetermines a person's destiny. Or that the population increases every year by a staggering 18 million souls—1 million shy of the population of Australia. But during my first morning in Delhi, as Hindu prayer music blasted from the temple across the street from my two-star hotel, the thing that captured my imagination was not language or population statistics or even another ear-piercing sitar riff from the temple loudspeaker. I was mesmerized, instead, by urban cows.

Looking through the dusty third-floor window of my room at the Hotel Ajanta, I saw three weary cows ambling down the dusty street. The sluggish mini-herd blocked the flow of motorbikes and sputtering cars, creating a traffic jam that somehow failed to evoke a single case of road rage. Imagine what would happen if three cows blocked traffic on Second Avenue in Manhattan. After being run over by a fleet of speeding taxis and bludgeoned by pedestrians who still had cow shit on their shoes, the dead or dying bovines would be dragged to the sidewalk where they'd be sliced, diced, and barbequed before the cops showed up. Not so in India. Cows are sacred here. Even the local McDonald's offers veggie burgers instead of McBeef.

According to Hindu Scripture, cows represent nurturing and fertility. Bulls, though more aggressive, command divine respect because the Hindu god Shiva is often depicted riding one. Due to these religious associations, the animals are virtually untouchable. They roam freely through tiny villages and large metropolitan areas alike, creating surreal images that would make Salvador Dali roll over in his grave and reach for a paintbrush.

I once saw a cow standing among a group of men on a busy street. Ruminating happily, tail flicking lazily against its own hide, the cow tilted its head as if contemplating human conversation. I watched a bull march straight down the middle of a crowded pedestrian lane and nudge people out of the way with repeated flicks of its horns. I saw cows reposing peacefully in the shade of trees, rummaging through garbage dumps, grazing in city parks, and eating from the hands of loving Hindus who care for the stray animals as if they are communal pets. And I watched in disbelief as these bovine beasts made Delhi's insufferable traffic jams even worse.

Consider, for example, my excursion to Jama Masjid, the country's largest mosque. Before leaving the hotel, I noticed a framed proverb hanging inside the elevator: IF YOU DON'T WALK WITHIN, YOU WALK WITHOUT. As I was headed to a house of worship, the pious message lifted my spirits, carrying me across the lobby and out into the heat of Arakashan Road.

The dusty, partially paved street is crammed with hostels that provide basic accommodation for as little as five dollars. Sandwiched between the hostels are an array of tumbledown enterprises: old wooden shops, mobile food vendors, shoeshine stands, rickety convenience stores. At regular intervals along the street, I saw crowded STD offices. Delhi must be flooded with patients suffering from sexually transmitted diseases. Or so I deduced after seeing so many STD offices. But I soon learned that STD stands for Subscribers Trunk Dialing. The "patients" were actually patrons making long-distance telephone calls.

Like many of Delhi's crowded two-way streets, Arakashan Road appears too narrow to accommodate even one-way traffic. Cars, buses, trucks, motorbikes, bicycle-rickshaws, bicycles, pushcarts, ox-driven carts, and the ubiquitous three-wheeled auto-rickshaws—all these vehicles collide in two-way vehicular pandemonium that miraculously manages to flow. At least until the cows show up.

I hopped into a passing auto-rickshaw and negotiated a five-dollar round-trip fare to Jama Masjid. For this low price, the driver agreed to wait two hours while I visited the mosque (of the many great things about India, affordability is right up there). After leaving Arakashan Road, my motorized rickshaw turned onto a major thoroughfare and was promptly overwhelmed by traffic. Vehicles came at us from a dozen different directions. Horns screeched, breaks squealed, engines revved and spewed big black exhaust clouds into the sky.

Like a rugby player slamming into the scrum, my driver wedged the auto-rickshaw into the swarm of vehicles. He manipulated the throttle with his right hand, inching into an open space, moving past a bicycle-rickshaw driver who possessed neither the quickness nor dexterity to commandeer a good angle. We pushed past wobbling ox-driven carts that could have rolled off the set of *Braveheart*. We moved past massive trucks that belched clouds of exhaust. Emblazoned across the side of several trucks were the words PLEASE HONK! Everyone did. We bobbed through a sea of rickshaws, past thrill-seeking pedestrians darting through the narrow gaps between vehicles. The honking horns laid a soundtrack to this vicious traffic game. Cows were off-limits, of course. But there was no limit to the number of people who might be killed.

The midafternoon temperature hovered around 105 degrees.

Heat and auto exhaust combined to brew an oily broth that splashed through the open carriage and onto my skin. Every few minutes or so, the driver would hawk up a big gob of spit and let it fly. Sound effects were as important to my driver as the size and trajectory of the globule being spat. As we inched through traffic, he made deep, resonating, gurgling sounds that were always followed by a thoroughly decisive hawk.

After one particularly impressive discharge, we found ourselves behind a big black cow that moved through the street in slow motion. Vehicles skirted around the revered animal as if an invisible force field protected it. But no matter how hard my driver tried, he could not navigate around the cow. Automobiles and rickshaws had us hemmed in on both sides and from the rear. We sputtered along, a few respectful inches behind the blessed bovine, waiting for an opportunity to pass. I sat there sweating in a pair of khaki shorts, my bare thighs sticking to the vinyl seat that had been split by a billion butts.

Suddenly, the auto-rickshaw angled left and stopped. From this precarious position, the cow's enormous posterior was mere inches from my face. That's when the unthinkable happened. The creature stopped in its tracks. Its tail rose high in the air. Nature took its course. It was like watching childbirth without the blood on the child.

Afterward, the cow took a few steps forward and plopped down right in the middle of the busy street, oblivious to the mess it had made—traffic, and otherwise. We finally navigated the congested streets leading to Jama Masjid, and I leapt from the auto-rickshaw, arranged a pick-up time with the driver, and then walked toward a smattering of tourists ascending the stone stairs. Before I reached the first step of the 350-year-old mosque, before entering one of three massive gateways and climbing the great minaret, before even taking three steps away from the auto-rickshaw, I stepped in something. Something soft and moist. A blessed offering from a sacred cow.

Following the lead of a faithful few, I removed my sandals (yes, I scraped the bottoms first) and left them with a pile of shoes at the top of the steps leading to one of Jama Masjid's grand gateways. Made entirely of red sandstone and white marble, the mosque, completed in 1658, is India's largest and most impressive. Its beauty lies not just in the arched porticos and the giant onion domes sitting atop the prayer structure at the back of the courtyard; the beauty lies also in the courtyard itself. Surrounded by high sandstone walls, the open space is large enough to accommodate as many as 25,000 worshippers.

Barefoot and humble, I began the trek across the courtyard. But the hot afternoon sun was unkind to naked feet. After those first few steps, my soles were set ablaze by the smoldering sandstone surface. I jumped backward instinctively, landing on the naked toes of a British tourist who was too polite, or perhaps too reverent, to scream. *She* apologized even before I could. Looking out at the courtyard, I noticed that a long, twisting, narrow tarp—a poor man's red carpet, if you will—had been haphazardly laid across the scorching surface. The tarp began a few feet inside the hot zone, angled toward the middle of the courtyard, turned left sharply toward the north face, and zigzagged to the far side. It ended abruptly in places, only to begin again a few feet later. At these gaps, sockless visitors were required to take a leap of faith, which, depending on individual luck or athleticism, might spare the leaper from the hellish sandstone floor.

I made it to the far side of the courtyard and up the steps to a terrace where an old man stood alone in a shaded corner. Dressed in a flowing white gown, he beckoned me with a trembling hand. He took my ticket and pointed a withered finger toward the entrance of the minaret.

From a touristy standpoint, the minaret is perhaps the most compelling aspect of the mosque. The old sandstone tower stands nearly a hundred feet high. Visitors are allowed to climb the ancient spiral steps leading to the viewing tower. From there the view of Old Delhi is said to be spectacular.

I walked through the doorway. After a few tentative steps up the twisting steps, I became shrouded in darkness. The spiral staircase was extremely steep, the turns amazingly tight. So much so that I used one hand for balance against the curving tower wall and the other to feel for higher steps not far from my face. The air, clogged by the musty scent of ages, helped make my ascent an uneasy one. I climbed higher. The dark claustrophobic interior occasionally gave way to light from a small opening cut from the thick stone wall. When I finally reached the top, I took a big gulp of air and stepped onto a small circular platform that was occupied by a young Indian family. A man. His wife. Two small children. They sat quietly on the platform, having already feasted on the view.

From atop the minaret the sprawling city of Old Delhi revealed itself. Hundreds, perhaps thousands, of ancient white buildings seemed to spread for as far as the eye could see. To the left, the huge onion domes of the mosque squatted proudly atop the lower structure. To the right lay the Red Fort, the seventeenth-century imperial palace of the Mughal emperor Shah Jahan. Sandstone walls surrounded the fort for one and a half miles, rising in places to thirty-three feet. A thirty-foot moat ran along the eastern edge of the fort. The moat was bone dry.

The sweeping cinematic images from *Gandhi* had not prepared me for such a view of Delhi. My Lonely Planet guidebook had not prepared me for the maddening, mood-killing, inescapable sound of a ringing cellular phone.

The phone rang again. Rather, the piercing, electronic chime sounded off again. The tune was a familiar one. "Jingle Bells." The incongruous melody ravaged my ears. *De de de, de de de, de de de de dee.*

"Allo?" The Indian gentleman sat akimbo on the platform, shouting into a battered Nokia. "Allo? Allo?" He pressed one button and then another, put the unit against one ear and cocked his head. "Allo? Allo? Allo? Allo?" He muttered something to his wife, who seemed dutifully appalled. They spoke in hushed Hindi. Or maybe it was Bengali, Assamese, Gujarati, Punjabi, or any of eighteen languages recognized by the Indian government. Perhaps they were trying to figure out why the call was dropped. Frustrated, the man jabbed the "end call" button. He put down the phone and waited—atop the 350-year-old minaret overlooking the ancient city—for another high-tech microwave transmission.

By the time the phone rang again, I was halfway down the spiral staircase. I stepped blindly down the cool stone steps, groping in darkness, listening to the haunting beep of "Jingle Bells."

Once outside the mosque, I found my tainted sandals and scanned the throngs, looking for my motor-rickshaw driver. Hundreds and hundreds of people milled about. Beggars. Street vendors. Tourists. Police. My driver must have seen me among the mass of humanity. The rickshaw pulled in front of the mosque as I descended the great stairs.

Off we went to Arakashan Road, through the traffic, the heat, the omnipresent cows, back to the Hotel Ajanta. Along the way I caught a whiff of something. I cocked my head. Sniffed. Sniffed again. Lifting one sandal and then the other, I could not locate the source of the odor. But my driver did. When we finally stopped in front of the hotel, he removed one sandal and beat it against the pavement until the shit flew off.

DELHI BELLY

Delhi Belly. Even iron-gut travelers have become intimately associated with the term. You can read about it in guidebooks or listen to graphic tales from tourists who have survived. Delhi Belly. Such gastric combustion can turn a normal bowel movement into a volcanic eruption on a par with the legendary Krakatoa blast. Delhi "oh-my-aching" Belly. Don't drink the water. Don't eat leafy green salads. Don't even *think* about eating fruit unless the skin can be peeled and discarded. Lord, if only I had followed that advice.

I happened to be sitting in the backseat of a chauffeur-driven car when Delhi Belly came into my life. Don't be impressed by the "chauffeur-driven" thing. My limo was, in fact, a sputtering Peugeot without air conditioning. For what you'd pay for a one-night stay in a three-star hotel in New York, however, my driver agreed to take me from Delhi to Agra and on to Jaipur before returning to Delhi on day three. A common route for tourists, the "Golden Triangle" covers more than four hundred dusty miles and reveals some of India's greatest treasures: the Pink City, Hawa Mahal, Agra Fort, and, of course, the magnificent Taj Mahal. The price included the car, driver, petrol, one night's accommodation in two different three-star hotels—even hotel accommodation for my driver.

As we drove past the outskirts of Delhi, the veil of rural India slowly lifted, revealing miles of parched earth for as far as I could see. Only a few scabrous trees dotted a landscape that a hazy white-hot sun had sucked the life out of. From the speeding car I saw crumbling brick structures around which peasants gathered. Sacred cows attempted to escape the heat by lounging in muddy holes. Flatbed trucks—stacked high with burlap sacks on top of which sat turban-wearing workmen—flew by. Looking at all this through the dusty car window, I felt the first painful stomach cramps. Next came a curious bubbling noise from deep within the bowels. I won't go into detail about what happened next. Trust me, you don't want to know. But when the car screeched to a desperate halt along the highway—miles from the nearest toilet—I staggered into the dusty field, bare-assed and poised for purpose. So powerful was the back-door blast, so fiery the discharge, I closed my eyes, clenched my teeth, and prepared to be launched into orbit.

Delhi Belly. I had it. I had it bad. My driver had to pull over two more times before we finally reached Agra that afternoon. I checked in at the hotel desk and made a mad dash for the in-room facilities. There I remained for some thirty wretched minutes. After crawling from the bathroom, haggard and dehydrated, I lay on the bed, attempting to gather my strength. It was about 3:00 P.M. The Taj Mahal closed at sunset. The following morning we would be leaving for Jaipur. The window of opportunity was closing. This would be my only chance to visit the world's most beautiful building. In spite of the cramping and dizziness, I threw myself out of the room and into the waiting car.

One look at the Taj Mahal was well worth the intestinal fortitude required to get me there. At the far end of the courtyard, past the towering red sandstone gate and the awestruck hordes rushing through it, beyond the sculpted geometric garden and the long, linear fountain slicing down its center, lay the most stunning building I've ever laid eyes upon. Sitting high atop a broad marble platform, the Taj Mahal is a dream in white marble. If Fabergé had designed palaces instead of opulent eggs, this is what he would have conceived. The grand structure has not one but four identical facades. Each one is graced with a 100-foot central arch and embedded with hundreds of tiny precious stones that make up an incomparable flower motif. A giant 240-foot translucent marble dome sits atop the building. The dome is said to shimmer in the moonlight.

Although the Taj appears to be a grand palace, it is, in fact, a grand mausoleum. When Mumtaz Mahal died during childbirth in 1631, her husband, the Mughal emperor Shah Jahan, became so distraught his hair is said to have turned gray overnight. Soon after, he made plans to build a final resting place for his beloved. It took twenty-two years and required the efforts of more than twenty thousand workmen, but in 1653 the Taj Mahal was completed. It stands on the southern bank of the Yamuna River, a 350-year-old tribute to lost love.

Armed guards patrolled the area in and around the building. I had the feeling I was being watched because I *was* being watched. So were the other visitors. Not only is India's preeminent symbol under constant threat of terrorist attack (this is the reason for the security checkpoint at the entrance), it's also a target for petty looters. If you look closely at the precious stones embedded in the marble facades, you'll see where some have been mysteriously pried out.

I sat on a bench in the courtyard, admiring the world's loveliest building, basking in its luminescent glow, when suddenly there was a rumbling from inside. Not in the interior chamber where Mumtaz Mahal's body lay, but in the deep, dark recesses of my warped digestive system. The runs. The trots. Mumtaz Mahal's Revenge. Whatever you want to call it, it was coming. I held my head in my hands, thinking solid thoughts, conjuring up images of concrete and steel. But in this battle of mind over matter, matter would not be denied. I rushed from the courtyard, through the towering red sandstone gates, and into the waiting car, which my trusty driver navigated through the crowded streets of Agra to deliver me posthaste to the hotel.

While dashing past the front desk on my way to the elevator, the desk clerk called my name. "We need to see your passport, sir," he said. I stopped, turned, leapt in front of the desk, swaying, clenching my cheeks.

"I don't have it with me," I said.

"We must see it."

"I don't have it."

"Is it in your room?"

"No."

"Where is it, sir?"

"It's in Delhi."

He picked up the phone. The hotel manager appeared instantly. "I really need to get to my room," I said. The manager shook my hand and guided me toward a sofa in the middle of the lobby. Sitting down required a colossal act of courage on my part.

He sighed as he leaned forward, as would a doctor before explaining that the tumor is malignant. "I'm sorry," he said. "All guests must provide a passport."

"I know," I said, nodding my head. "My passport is back in Delhi."

"Why did you leave your passport in Delhi?"

Sweat dripping from my temples, knees trembling, my belly thoroughly Delhied, I told the whole sordid story. . . .

Two days after my arrival in Delhi, I entered the Ethiopian Consulate hoping to procure a travel visa. I walked into the cluttered office of a grim-faced Ethiopian bureaucrat who sat behind his desk without bothering to look up. After allowing me to stand there for an appropriate time, he motioned to a chair. Everything was in order: my passport; inbound airline ticket to Addis Ababa, outbound to Cairo; passport photo; completed visa application; enough rupees to complete the transaction; and a credit card just in case. My passport would be held for two days, as is customary during such transactions. When I returned to pick up the passport, a brand-new Ethiopian visa would have been glued to its pages. Yeah. Right.

The bureaucrat surveyed my documents. "What about yellow fever?" he said.

"It's okay," I said, smiling. "I don't have it." My humor went unappreciated.

"You must have the yellow fever immunization before the visa can be processed."

"Okay. Where do I go for that?"

"The airport. There is a health clinic there."

I looked at my watch. It was 10:30 A.M. I told him I'd go immediately to the clinic and return with the immunization certificate after lunch. The bureaucrat issued a dismissive smile and returned to the bureaucratic tasks stacked on his bureaucratic desk.

Into the motorized rickshaw I went, sputtering across the city in the stifling heat through one chaotic traffic jam after another. Somehow we made it to the clinic in an hour. The doors were locked when I arrived. Business hours—according to a fading sign on the wall—were between 2:00 P.M. and 4:00 P.M. only. Why the Ethiopian bureaucrat failed to mention this I'll never know.

There were three hours to kill. I was hungry. The driver took me to the city center and dropped me in front of a rickety restaurant. This one was "safe," he said.

At the entrance, a trio of pots simmered on gas burners. Inside, beneath a low-hanging ceiling, sat a lone customer. I ordered curried chicken, which was delivered in less than thirty seconds. Way too fast. The piece of chicken was unlike any I'd ever seen. It seemed as though a wing and neck bone had been fused together to create a mystery part that no earthly chicken could produce.

The gnarly meat was served in a bowl with red spicy sauce, rice, and pita bread. No fork was provided. Given the shape of the bone and the measly amount of meat clinging to it, I contemplated my next move. Sneaking a look at the next table, I noticed the man had torn away a piece of pita bread and was using it to pinch meat from the bone. I followed his lead and asked for a Coke to wash it down.

When I returned to the immunization clinic, more than fifty people were already waiting in line. Men in long cotton gowns and prayer hats. Men in turbans. Men in jeans. By two-fifteen, the line had not moved and yet more people came seeking a yellow fever shot. Some stood in line behind me, but others crowded in near the front and butted into line. Had we been back in the States I would have said something. Hell, everybody who had been butted would have said something, too. "This is India," said the man directly behind me. He had no doubt seen my shaking head.

The line began moving slowly. But every time someone stepped through the door of the clinic, two more people rushed in from nowhere and slid in the front of the line. More than an hour had passed and I seemed no closer to getting inoculated than when I arrived. The clinic would shut its doors at four. I worried that those who failed to reach the interior by that time would be locked out and told to return the next day. Perhaps the same thought occurred to everyone else. Shouts rang out. An argument erupted after yet another man butted into the queue. Two men shoved each other. One walked away. In an act of solidarity that I have never seen before and will probably never see again, everyone in line threw his arms around the man in front of him, linking the line in an unbreakable human chain. Still, the chain swayed, bulged, threatened to break.

After another bout of shouting, a woman in a white lab coat burst through the door of the clinic to confront us. One need not speak Hindi to understand her outrage. Arms flailing, eyes bulging, ponytail wagging impatiently, the woman told everyone to go home. Apparently, the clinic would not allow such beastly behavior.

The queue dissolved. A few dozen disheartened men stumbled around in front of the clinic. I inched toward the door, head bowed, passport extended, hoping the inoculations would resume. To my surprise, they did. In the next moment I found myself in the reassembled queue, but this time I stood in front of it.

An assistant with a clubfoot ushered me inside. He, too, wore a lab coat, but unlike the female doctor his was unbuttoned and not so clean. He limped over to a table and picked up a disposable syringe. After tearing away the plastic packaging, he uncorked the needle and came at me. I returned triumphantly to the Ethiopian Consulate, only to find that it had closed for the day.

First thing the following morning, I presented my visa application to the very same Ethiopian bureaucrat. He examined the yellow fever certificate. Studied my airline tickets, passport, and photograph. "That will be seventy dollars," he said.

"Terrific." I pulled out a stack of local currency. "Let's see, that's about 32,000 rupees, yes?"

His eyes narrowed. This was not good.

"You must pay in U.S. dollars," he said.

"You're kidding me." An ice-cold glare told me he was not. "This is India," I continued. "Why am I forced to pay for an Ethiopian visa with U.S. currency?"

"Because you are American."

I opened my wallet and found exactly sixty-three dollars. Three twenties and three singles. Seven dollars short.

"You take credit cards?"

He shook his head.

I laid the sixty-three dollars on his desk. "Please," I pleaded. "Will you allow me to pay the remaining amount in rupees?"

He shook his head again. He enjoyed shaking his head. Almost as much as he seemed to enjoy pushing away the money and telling me to come back when I was prepared.

The motorized rickshaw driver drove me back to the Hotel Ajanta, where I cashed a few traveler's checks. Then it was out into the heat again, through the traffic, and to the Ethiopian Consulate where the world's most insufferable bureaucrat took my application and the seventy dollars and told me to come back in five days.

"Five days?" I said, perhaps too forcefully. "It's only supposed to take two. I need to have my passport back by Friday."

The bureaucrat spoke without even looking at me. "The consulate is closed tomorrow and Friday for holiday," he said. "You must return on Monday. Or perhaps Tuesday."

"But I'm traveling to Agra on Saturday. I need my passport right away."

The bureaucrat shrugged his shoulders and made a noise that might have been laughter. . . .

Having heard my woeful tale, the hotel manager stood up and cleared his throat. Night had fallen in Agra. A group of European tourists—returning, no doubt, from a visit to the Taj Mahal—crossed the lobby and waited for the elevator to deliver them to comfort. I longed to be among them, to drag my Delhi "oh-my-aching" Belly from the lobby before soiling my shorts.

"I am sorry," the manager said, shaking his head. "But you should not have left Delhi without your passport."

"Yes, yes. You are totally correct, sir. But can't you make an exception?" I crossed my legs.

"Every guest must present a passport. There are no exceptions."

"Well, why did you allow me to check in without a passport in the first place?"

The hotel manager looked at me curiously.

"Yes. I checked in before visiting the Taj Mahal. I showed my credit card, handed over my room voucher. The clerk gave me a key and that was that. It wasn't until now, four hours after check-in, that he demanded to see my passport."

"I understand that, but—"

"Had your clerk told me that a credit card wasn't good enough; had he told me that I must have a passport to check in, I could have left with my driver. At the very least I would have been able to sleep in the car. Now you're telling me I have to sleep on the street?"

"I am sorry."

"You're forcing me out into the streets of Agra and all you can say is sorry?"

"You should have brought your passport."

"You shouldn't have let me check in without the goddam passport." The manager gave me the evil eye. "Okay, okay, my bad. I shouldn't have come without a passport. But you have to admit, the hotel made a mistake as well."

Politely, but no less resolute, the manager went on to say that the "secret police" monitor the guest registry of every hotel in the state. "Passport numbers must be written beside each name."

"I know my passport number, it's—"

"We still need to see the passport."

"But where can I go? If you won't accept me as a guest even though my room is prepaid, neither will other hotels."

The hotel manager fixed me with a weary stare. "Sir," he said. "There is nothing I can do." But before walking away, he asked for my business card. Why, I'll never know. I rummaged through my wallet and found a crumpled card that had been hastily de-signed at Kinko's in Miami. Written in fluid Edwardian script, just below my name and address, were two words: *Travel Writer*. The manager focused on these words. Thirteen characters, in-cluding the space. Thirteen turned out to be my lucky number. His brow softened. His demeanor changed.

"Oh, so you are a travel writer."

"Yes, sir, I am."

"I am truly sorry for the inconvenience," he said. "Enjoy your stay in our hotel."

I sprinted to my room and leapt onto the toilet like a frog onto a lily pad.

GO SOUTH, YOUNG MAN

◀┅┅┅┅┅┅┅▶

It takes real trust—or gullibility—to travel more than fifteen hundred miles from Delhi to Mysore at the urging of an e-mail from a stranger. But that's exactly what I did. The unsolicited message appeared on the computer screen, between power outages, in the cramped and cozy Internet café on the first floor of the Hotel Ajanta. The e-mail had been sent by a man called Ram Prabhu who lived in a distant city on the far side of the world. A place called Cleveland, in Ohio. I had never met the mysterious Mr. Prabhu, but apparently he knew me. Well, sort of. He read about my trip in an article I'd written for the *Cleveland Plain Dealer*. Having learned of my plans to travel aimlessly around his native country, the altruistic Indian-American offered direction. "Go south," he said. "Most people who visit India never go to the south. I have a friend in Mysore who will take good care of you."

Perhaps by visiting Mysore and meeting Mr. Prabhu's friend I would come to know at least one person in this country of 1 billion. But *Mysore*? When contemplating the world's most dubiously named towns, Mysore, India, ranks right up there with Pukë, Albania; Anus, Philippines; Pus, Malaysia; Poop, Mexico; and Shīts, Iran. (Believe it or not, Iran is home to two Shīts: one in the province of Māzandarān, the other in Zanjān.) Even before my bus rattled to a stop at the steamy depot in Mysore, the destination managed to live up to its name.

The thirty-eight-hour odyssey began with a gob of spit. Not from me, but from the driver of my motorized rickshaw. The first phlegmy projectile hit the pavement seconds after we pulled away from the Hotel Ajanta en route to the Delhi train station. Through the maniacal early evening traffic we went, sputtering across frenetic intersections and smog-choked avenues, looping along roundabouts that spun out toward dark cluttered roads. Every two or three minutes the driver found it necessary to turn his head and spit into the wind. So constant was the spitting, so voluble the hawking from his uncorked throat, I began to regard it as part of a well-oiled driving routine: (1) Stop at crowded intersection; (2) Rev engine; (3) Wait for green light; (4) Pull back on throttle; (5) Hawk up a good gob and let it fly. *Stop. Rev. Wait. Pull. Hawk.* The Five Cornerstones of Rickshaw Driving must surely be written in the Rules of the Road because many of the drivers we encountered along the way seemed committed to the idea. *Stop. Rev. Wait. Pull. Hawk.* Motorized rickshaw spitting, Delhi-style. Passengers beware of the backwash.

As we sputtered to a stop in front of the train station, my driver hawked up a voluminous discharge that hit the curb and splattered like a water balloon. "The train station, sir." He announced this with a proper British intonation that made me feel as though I'd arrived in a Bentley.

A crowd had gathered in front of the open ticket window. The weary ticket agent processed one transaction after another without seeming to reduce the swarm. I stood at the rear while new arrivals nudged themselves up to the front, pushing me farther from the window. That's when worry set in. The train to Bangalore departed in about thirty minutes. It could take at least that much time to reach the ticket window. And what if I'd come to the wrong place? There were two major train stations in Delhi. I had relied on my rickshaw driver to bring me to the correct one. Following the lead of another line butter, I threw myself into the fray and made it to the window minutes later.

"Do not show your ticket to anyone." The ticket agent told me this while pointing toward the designated platform. "There are those who would steal it from you." With this warning in mind, I tucked my ticket into my pants pocket, dragged my duffel through the crowd and out onto the darkened platform. A few intermittent pools of light gave shape to the surroundings. Hordes of people, many in flowing gowns, drifted like ghosts along the platform. A hot, oily scent hung in the air. Sweat dripped down my temples. There were five, maybe six platforms that could be reached by climbing steep stairs and descending from the connecting bridge. I heaved my duffel onto one shoulder, staggered up the steps, and down to what proved to be the appropriate track. Track Four.

Moving toward the train, I was approached by men wearing chains. They wore five, six, seven chains at a time. These were not tacky fashion statements. Not the silver or gold decorative bands worn by guys who try too hard. These were heavy chains. The kind associated with warehouses and Master Locks. The thick, bulky, three- to four-foot links clanked together as they swung from the neck. "You want?" said one chain-wearing gentleman, moving like the Frankenstein monster. "You need?" said another, dressed in a robe of dangling irons. I had no idea why the chains were being offered until I stepped into my sleeping compartment and met Sandeep Mukherjee, one of three men with whom I would share close quarters for the next thirty-five hours. "The chains are used to secure your luggage," he said. "To make sure nothing is stolen."

Our tiny compartment was equipped with four beds. Sandeep sat on one bottom bunk. I sat across from him on the other bottom bunk. As departure time grew near, Sandeep told me he was traveling to Bangalore to take a position with a travel agency. But his most immediate hope was that no other passengers would claim our compartment. "It would be nice to have space," he said. "The trip to Bangalore is a long one."

As it turned out, the trip was made even longer by two men who snatched open the door and climbed to the top bunks without speaking. Wearing crumpled business suits and unknotted ties, the men perched themselves on the edge of the beds and remained there, withered and withdrawn.

Sometime later, after the train pulled away from the station and slid past the outskirts of Delhi, food was served by an attendant. Soup, a clump of bread, and a mushy yellowish substance wrapped inside something I could neither eat nor describe. The soup tasted like dishwater. Such a description is used flippantly when the French onion soup is topped with inferior cheese or the lobster bisque isn't up to par. But on the train to Bangalore, the dingy consommé tasted exactly like dishwater. Exactly. After my first and only putrid sip, I probed the lukewarm broth expecting to see soapsuds and flecks of dirty sponge.

Sometime after dinner, the train stopped. I pulled back the curtains and saw droves of people huddled around battered suitcases and sleeping on the dirty platform floor. Hundreds of people. Within the next thirty-five hours I would see thousands. Where were they going? Chennai, Mumbai, Hyderabad, Thiruvananthapuram? The Indian Railway System operates 6,856 train stations just like this one. Each day, 8,702 passenger trains carry more than 14 million people across 39,146 miles of track on the world's largest independent train network. With 1.6 million employees, Indian Railways is also the world's largest employer. As my train chugged away again, the platform giving way to glittering village lights, the sheer magnitude of the operation was too immense to contemplate.

Later that night, and several times during the following night, I woke to the familiar sound of a ringing cellular phone. Both men in the top bunks were carrying phones, but neither had the good manners to answer them once they had begun to snore. The man sleeping above Sandeep had his ringer set to a traditional chime. The cellular phone in the bunk above mine was programmed to play . . . you guessed it, "Jingle Bells." Hearing the tune over and over, I was driven to the brink of homicide. I kicked the top bunk hard enough to make the man cry out in the darkness. "Your cell phone is ringing," I said, derisively. He muttered into the phone and in less than a minute he was snoring again.

The getaway is gone. There is no place on earth where you can escape the ringing of a cellular phone. You will hear phones ringing in mosques, temples, churches, and synagogues. They beep on white sand beaches, grassy plains, mountain peaks, and crowded campsites. They cry out at book readings, conferences, during classroom lectures and visits to the doctor. They preclude face-to-face conversation in airplanes, cars, taxis, and buses (half the time it's the driver's phone), ferries, and in the cramped sleeping compartment on a train crossing the Indian countryside in the middle of the goddam night. When did the world become so talkative? Sit face to face with a friend or relative and you've got nothing to say to each other. Give the two of you a cell phone and suddenly you're calling fifteen times a day. Why? Why? Why? I don't know if Sandeep was affected by the constant ringing and the text message beeps, but during two long nights in that railway car I got maybe two or three hours of sleep.

Hours before arriving in Bangalore, I woke feeling sick. It wasn't only the lack of sleep and the cramped conditions and the ringing cell phones that made me feel bad. It was much more than that. My joints ached. My head throbbed. It seemed as though every ounce of energy had been drained from my body. Something bad was happening to me. I could feel it.

When the train finally stopped in Bangalore, I staggered to the crowded platform and nearly passed out. Not wanting to look like a tourist target, I leaned against a pole, casual-like, trying to regain my composure.

I tottered to the outer edge of the station, but had to sit on a bench to keep from falling over. The bus station was maybe a couple hundred yards away, but in my condition I didn't think I'd make it. Neither did the touts and hustlers. Like cheetahs loping toward the wounded antelope, they descended upon me. "You need transport . . . Where you go, sir . . . You stay in Bangalore long time . . . I am at your service, yes . . . What would you like, kind *sir, sir, sir* . . ." The words echoed in my ears as if I'd been drugged. Gentle hands set upon my shoulders, my arms. The sound of foreign whispers. The stench of sweat and curry. Thinking that the most gentle of muggings was about to take place, I stood up abruptly, grabbed the duffel handle, and rolled it in the direction of the bus station.

After buying a ticket to Mysore, I lumbered into a public bathroom that just might be among the filthiest I've encountered. On each side of the wet concrete floor there were three or four crumbling toilet stalls. The walls were made of stone, but the doors— in front of which waited two or three men—had been cut from sheets of corrugated metal. Out of nowhere came a loud banging noise. I covered my ears, but could not stiffle the throbbing inside my head. A bathroom attendant smashed his fist against one door, then another, and shouted something in Hindi that could probably be translated as "Hurry the hell up!" One of the corrugated doors swung open. A man rushed out. The attendant grabbed a bucket of water. He stepped halfway into the stall— making sure to turn his head away—and emptied the bucket without directing the splash. I turned around. Walked to the bus. My bladder would hold for a while.

After all the passengers had boarded the bus, the driver stepped off to open the rear luggage hatch. It seemed strange that

I was the only one with a bag to stow, but my mind was too weary to focus on details. I lifted the heavy duffel into the boot, thanked the driver, and took my seat on the bus.

The three-hour drive to Mysore seemed to last a lifetime. I remember nodding off, waking with my face dripping in sweat, and then nodding off again. I remember how passengers looked at me from the corners of their eyes. I remember the bus pulling over to a rest stop where I bought a Cadbury chocolate bar that melted before I could finish eating it.

When we finally pulled into the busy Mysore depot, I lumbered off the bus and stood near the back, waiting for the passengers to disembark so the driver could open the luggage hatch. The sun beat down mercilessly. The smell of gasoline permeated the air. I stood there, wilting like a wet weed, when suddenly the bus roared to life and took off with my bag in the boot. Almost everything I owned was in that bag. All my clothes. My guidebooks. Notebooks. Everything. I ran after the hulking vehicle, banging on the side as I went. But the driver shifted gears, pulled away, turned past the terminal, and disappeared.

I ran inside the terminal, heart banging against my chest, sweat dripping from my face, my head on fire. Into the masses I dashed—dodging women in colorful saris, bearded men, groups of wide-eyed children—to emerge, stumbling, on the other side of the depot. By the time I got there, six identical buses were parked and not one driver could be found inside any of them. I leapt onto one bus, then another, hoping to find the Cadbury chocolate wrapper I'd left in the seat pocket. Nothing. I ran outside in the hundred-degree heat. Onto another bus and off again. Surrounded by empty buses and throngs of people, I spun around, staring, cursing, unable to direct my rage at anyone but me. Suddenly, I saw a familiar face. A man who looked like my driver. But he shook his head and walked away when I pointed to the buses.

Finally, I saw him. The bus driver. He was drinking a soda and talking with a uniformed depot employee. "My bag," I cried,

lurching toward him, gasping for breath. "My bag is on your bus."
He walked calmly to the back of one of the buses and opened the
luggage compartment. There it was. My duffel. My life.

A wave of relief washed over me. But the chase had sapped my
strength. Hoping to get help from the driver but receiving none, I
leaned down and struggled to lift the heavy bag from the boot.
When I finally pulled it from the compartment and dropped it
heavily upon the ground, the driver looked at me and smiled. As
God is my witness he held out his hand and said: "Tip?"

SICKNESS IN THE HOUSE OF IRANI

I woke on the floor of a hotel room. How I got there was as much a mystery as the name and location of the hotel. After rolling over on my back and looking to the window, I realized, with a suddenness that made me jerk my throbbing head, that I'd been asleep all day. Darkness had fallen. From my position on the carpet I could see a faint luminescent glow from the street below. Did I pass out after arriving from the Mysore bus depot and stumbling into the hotel room? Had I fallen out of bed? Had I been drinking? Dressed in the same T-shirt and jeans I'd been wearing since boarding the train in Delhi some forty-eight hours earlier, I stood up and promptly fell down again.

What in the world was wrong with me? My legs had turned to jelly. The throbbing in my joints refused to cease. A limp hand to my forehead pushed away a coating of sweat that seemed to defy logic and air-conditioning. I struggled to my knees, crawled to the bed, and climbed in. There I remained in a state of delirium, until the early morning squeal of a car horn prodded me to action.

Although I hadn't eaten a proper meal in more than two days, hunger failed to raise its snarling head. My belly had other issues, which were best attended to in the toilet. Instead of searching for breakfast, I picked up the telephone and called Raian Irani. Mr.

Irani, a local businessman, had been introduced to me via an e-mail from Ram Prabhu, the altruistic Indian national living in Cleveland, Ohio. After dialing the number, I looked around the room again. Large television. Polished wooden desk. A modern bathroom. From the look of the furnishings and fixtures, I had checked into a place that exceeded my budget. Besides, the hotel was on a busy street. My condition would require lots of bed rest. Cheap digs and quiet were in order.

Mr. Irani's deep jolly voice greeted me on the telephone. I thanked him for e-mailing his phone number and said, regretfully, I'd have to cancel our dinner appointment. "I'm sick as a dog," I said. He understood, of course. "You didn't eat the food on the train, did you?" Silence. When I finally admitted the mistake, he chuckled. Despite the fact that I'd never seen his face, I could imagine Raian shaking his head. Changing the subject, I asked if he could recommend a quiet, affordable hotel. He told me about a place on the outskirts of town. "But won't you stop by for tea along the way?" Although my body disagreed, it was impossible to say no.

As is the case in many Indian towns, the beauty of Mysore lies in the people rather than the view. Through the window of a slow-moving car, I saw piles and piles of garbage through which bone-thin cows grazed. Open sewers ran along the street. Rickshaws and motorbikes and soot-belching trucks bounced along streets lined with litter. But the people were an entirely different story. There was a gentleness about them. A nobility (faith, perhaps) that seemed to transcend grief and poverty. Men moved gracefully along the sidewalk, heads wrapped neatly, mustaches waxed and curled at the ends. But there's nothing quite as elegant as a woman in a sari. Tall and short, young and old, thin and not so—Indian women traipsed down the sidewalks and along the busy streets, adding flashes of color and refinement.

When the car pulled through the gate in front of Mr. Irani's home, I realized he lived in a private paradise. The city had been kept at bay by four high walls surrounding a large, landscaped compound. Beneath shady trees, three homes and a swimming pool conjured images of a rustic resort. I would later learn that one home belonged to Mr. Irani, one to his brother, and the third was used as an office from which the brothers ran a small liquor distributorship.

Mr. Irani came out to greet me. He was a big man, with warm, intelligent eyes. In less than a minute after shaking my hand, Raian—he insisted I call him by his given name—insisted on something else. "You must stay as my guest," he said. Before I had the chance to refuse, before telling him how truly sick I was, a servant had already fetched my bag.

For two days I lay in bed. Twice each day, before lunch and dinner were served, a servant knocked on my door. "Master," he would say, with a tinge of Great Britain on his tongue. "Lunch has been prepared." An African-American descendant of slaves, I had a tough time dealing with the servant-master thing. After pleading with him to call me by my given name, the servant compromised. For the duration of my stay he called me "Sir."

Yazed, Raian's six-year-old son, made a habit of knocking on my door a couple of times a day. "Are you feeling better?" he would ask, his brow crinkled with concern. I lied and told him yes.

In spite of the two-day rest, the illness, whatever it was, had gotten worse. Twice each day I dragged myself into the dining room and sat at the table with Yazed, Raian, and his wife, Shahanaz. The table abounded with exquisitely prepared food: mutton, chapati, chutney, pickles, spicy relish, steaming bowls of white rice. A feast fit for kings and queens. And yet the fever, nausea, and subsequent lack of appetite made eating a nonevent for me.

On the third day I woke up knowing SARS had taken root inside my body. I displayed all the symptoms: headache, nausea, aching joints, dizziness, shortness of breath, chronic fatigue, loss of appetite. I'd lost four or five pounds—much of it during frequent trips to the toilet. Having recently spent time in

Singapore—which, along with Guangdong, Hong Kong, and Toronto, had become a hot zone for SARS outbreaks—I could establish an infection point. Now I was here in Mysore, having possibly contaminated Raian, his family, and half a dozen servants.

"God help us if SARS comes to India." The statement, made by a local health official, appeared in the *Times of India*. With India's teeming population and less-than-stellar health standards, a major SARS outbreak could have disastrous consequences across the subcontinent.

Convinced that I was Patient Zero, I shared the bad news with Raian. Surprisingly enough, he did not toss me out on the street. Instead, he drove me to a clinic. In front of the crumbling white building and along the dusty street, cows meandered freely. They seemed as much a part of the traffic flow as the motorbikes, cars, rickshaws, bicycles, and pushcarts. I remember stepping from the SUV and staggering past an ox-driven wagon. The massive bovine and its creaking load could have rolled straight out of the seventeenth century. I prayed the clinic was a bit more advanced.

I followed Raian up the stairs and into a room where a doctor appeared. Raian greeted him like an old friend. "Be careful," he said in that booming voice of his; "this old sod just arrived from Singapore." With a sleight of hand that would make Harry Houdini proud, the doctor pulled a surgical mask out of thin air. He began the exam, using an antiquated metal tongue depressor that was as heavy as a paperweight. I closed my eyes, but not before surveying the room. It looked fine. Comfortable, even. It reminded me of visits to the doctor when I was a kid. That's what suddenly caused me to worry. This exam room looked *too* much like the exam room from my childhood. The medical equipment appeared to be at least thirty years old. The tongue depressor was probably older. Although my jaw weighed heavily against my heaving chest, I managed to divulge my next of kin.

A few days and many antibiotics later, I recovered from what turned out to be a particularly nasty stomach virus. "It probably came from something you ate," the doctor said. The soup—the soup on the train! One sip of the dishwater broth had poisoned me.

Having risen from the dead, I went with Raian to see the Lalitha Mahal Palace—"A palace hotel that offers an experience of princely living in a real maharajah's palace!" Built by the Maharajah of Mysore in 1931 to accommodate his most important guests—none of whom was more important than the Viceroy of India—the converted hotel is without question Mysore's finest. Raian showed me the magnificent grand stairway, a sweeping marble acclivity that appears in every wedding photo of a gushing bride and groom. After strolling across Italian marble floors, beneath glittering chandeliers and sparkling glass domes, we drank brandies in the Billiard Room. There, at the polished oak bar, across from a swanky billiard table, Raian and I talked about urine therapy.

There's a whole movement in India dedicated to the practice of drinking urine. "It's called *shivambu*," Raian said. "It's supposed to extend the lives of those who consume it." One such consumer, former prime minister Morarji Desai, publicly boasted that he drank his own urine regularly. *Shivambu*'s most famous advocate and a poster boy for longevity, Desai, India's fourth P.M., lived to the ripe old age of ninety-nine. (As a whimsical parting gift, Raian gave me a copy of *The Water of Life*, a veritable how-to guide for *shivambu* wannabes. A glass of milk each day had been my regimen since childhood. According to the book, I should have been drinking pee all along.)

Along with Raian, Shahanaz, and young Yazed, I piled into the car and drove south to Udagamandalam for the weekend. Nestled high in the Nīlgiri Hills and surrounded by coffee and tea plantations, Udagamandalam (better known as Ooty, which rhymes with booty) was founded in 1821 by British colonists seeking respite from the scorching summer heat. It is still home to the

Lawrence School, Lovedale, which, not coincidentally, was in the midst of its 145th anniversary celebration when we arrived. Raian's teenage daughter, Vashti, is a student there.

A sturdy brick compound boasting a lofty clocktower and turrets, the Lawrence School sits atop a hill in Ooty looking very much like a building you might see in Cambridge. Originally built to educate the children of British Army soldiers, the school now tends to upscale Indian children. As part of the anniversary celebration, we attended art exhibits and equestrian events put on by the students. Vashti appeared on stage in a theater production, the name and thrust of which I cannot recall, and yet I sat in the audience with her family, beaming with pride each time she delivered a line.

That night we retreated to the Iranis' second home, just downhill from the school. After a scrumptious meal of lentil soup, spicy *Puri*, chicken *kholapuri*, and rice pudding, the five of us gathered around the blazing fireplace, immersed in tea and conversation: Raian, Shahanaz, Yazed, Vashti, and me—a drifter who finally felt at home.

Northeast Africa

STREET KIDS

◄·······················►

The children. It was the children who got to me first.

Walking down the dusty main road in the northern Ethiopian town of Bahar Dar, among weary-eyed peasants trekking in from outlying villages, among shepherds, shirtless teens, women balancing heavy baskets atop their heads, and even a naked man inexplicably holding a string and dragging a pair of tennis shoes through the dust, among the hordes of beleaguered Ethiopians walking down the road that day, it was the children who stood out the most. Wearing tattered clothing and hopeful smiles, they came at me in a rush—dozens of boys and girls, anywhere from five to maybe twelve years old.

All the children appeared to be homeless. Parentless. Left to fend for themselves in the world's fourth poorest country. AIDS had taken many of their parents. Others had been killed during the long, nasty war against neighboring Eritrea, which, ironically, happens to be the world's third poorest country (Mozambique and Somalia top the list). On a continent plagued by no less than sixty wars and armed conflicts since 1945, the children had lost once again.

"Mister, mister." The voices came.

"Please, give me . . ."

"Please, I need . . ."

"Please, no mother, no father . . . Mister, please . . ."

It wasn't a question of whether help was needed. The question was, how much? The sheer volume of children made any attempt seem futile. From a continental standpoint, the question boggles the mind. Of the nearly 900 million residents of Africa, almost half are children, a great many of whom are as homeless as the multitudes that now followed me. Most of the children asked once or twice before giving up and moving on to other people, other possibilities. But one boy continued to follow me as I headed back to my room at the Papyrus Hotel. Every time I turned around, his dust-coated face would brighten. "Please," he said, after I turned around again. "No mother, no father." Instead of asking for money, he pointed to his bare feet. "No shoes," he said. "Please, mister."

How could I refuse a homeless kid who looked into my eyes and asked for shoes? Especially when I saw beyond the dust on his face and realized, with a sudden jolt, that this homeless kid looked just like me. He had the same nose and lips from my grammar school photographs. Same high forehead. Same skinny, birdlike legs—albeit dustier than mine had ever been. I stood there on the busy road, staring at him, a million thoughts rushing through my brain. First and foremost came the realization that I could have been in his position, begging for shoes on a dusty African road. Slavery changed all that.

When the subject of slavery bubbles up during interracial conversations back home, occasionally I've been told, "Of course slavery was a horrible thing, but aren't you better off having grown up in America?" Being American, loving my country, warts and all, the answer is a resounding "Yes." But does my current position of privilege in the United States justify the capture and enslavement of my ancestors? Of course not. Still, slavery happened. I am who I am because and in spite of it. The resulting emotion is best captured when you consider the child of a rape victim. The child grows to be a man and is happy to be alive. But when he thinks of the violence his mother endured—the horror of his misbegotten conception—the guilt can be overwhelming.

I felt guilty. That's the best way to describe it. Looking at the dusty, shoeless, homeless Ethiopian kid, I felt guilty. When I smiled, the boy's eyes lit up. He smiled a smile the likes of which I had never seen before and will probably never see again. He called himself Bogale, which I later learned means "glowing, getting brighter." As Bogale led me to the market, that's exactly what happened to his face. At one point, he tugged my arm and pointed to a boy running toward us. The boy was obviously a friend of Bogale's. He had been tracking us. Lying low so as not to overwhelm a potential benefactor. (Had I been in his position, I would have done the same thing.) The friend wore a tattered sweater, dirty shorts, and nothing else. Bogale pointed to his friend's bare feet. "Shoes," he said. "Please, mister."

Off we went to the shoe stall, the three of us. Interestingly enough, shoes in Ethiopia—or at least in Bahar Dar—are priced according to size. This makes sense when you think about it. Why should a size nine leather shoe cost the same as a size fourteen when the fourteen requires so much more leather? The boys knew exactly which shoes they wanted. Shiny black jobs with leather uppers and rubber soles. They bounded over to the salesman, who gave me an approving nod before bending to speak to the kids in Amharic. Bogale needed a size thirty-four. His buddy, a size thirty-five. The price was calculated by multiplying the size by 1.75 birr. A pittance, even on my travel budget. And yet the barefoot boys refused to wear the shoes out of the store. I stared down at them, perplexed. After Bogale made a scrubbing gesture, I realized they wanted to wash their dirty feet before putting on the brand-new prizes.

The storekeeper placed the shoes in the appropriate boxes and the boxes in clear plastic bags. We left the open-air shoe stall, the boys swinging their bags and smiling. But something had been overlooked. Essential items that eluded me until Bogale dragged me to another stall and pointed to a bin of socks. Of course, of course. The boys needed new socks to go with their new shoes. Again, Bogale spoke to the merchant in Amharic.

After the appropriate socks had been selected, the merchant began pulling clothes off the racks. Studded denim jackets with matching pants, dress shirts, sport shirts, slacks, shorts, two baseball hats. Bogale looked up at me with one mischievous eye; the other eye squinted hopefully.

"I'm sorry," I said. "Only shoes."

"Okay, okay," he said. Instead of being disappointed, the boys smiled and shrugged their shoulders, having taken a shot at seeing how much they could get.

When I shook their hands and said good-bye, I assumed I had seen the last of them. But the following morning the boys were sitting on the curb outside my hotel. Bogale wore the same dirty shorts from the previous day, but at the bottom of his grimy legs he sported the new white socks and gleaming leather shoes we'd purchased the day before. Bogale's friend sat to his right, pointing at his own shoes and smiling. To Bogale's left, however, there were three new boys. All three were covered in dust. All three were apparently homeless. One of the boys, the youngest, pointed to his own bare feet, which were scabbed and encrusted with dirt. "Mister, mister," he said, his eyes wide and pleading. "No mother, no father."

My head down, a million thoughts racing through it, I walked alone on the dusty road, unable to assuage a lingering guilt.

LALĪBELA

By the grace of God and Ethiopia Airlines, I found myself crisscrossing the country, marveling at the two-thousand-year-old monoliths at Aksum, sailing to the mysterious sixteenth-century island monasteries of Lake Tana, strolling through Gonder's ancient castle, walking among the ruins of the Queen of Sheba's palace, and peering at the fossilized remains of Lucy—our 3.2-million-year-old human ancestor, the "missing link" that proves, once and for all, that humankind evolved from apes. But for all the archaeological treasures the country has to offer, for all the achievements that seem to go relatively unnoticed by the outside world, none is more mind-boggling than the rock-hewn churches of Lalībela. After hooking up with Mesfin Kebede, however, I would find myself gazing at the churches through the unholiest of eyes.

His full name is Mesfin Ali Kebede. I found him sitting behind an empty desk near the baggage claim at the Lalībela airport. When I picked up my duffel and rolled in his direction, the petite Mr. Kebede stood up and offered his services. "Do you need a hotel, sir?" he asked in perfect English. "Do you need a tour guide?"

As a matter of fact, I needed both.

In a dust-covered station wagon with a questionable starter and bad shocks, Mesfin and I drove fifteen miles, the lone automobile on a paved road winding through an auburn maze of tabletop mountains. Oxen plowed the dusty fields, prodded by men with raised whips. Schoolchildren, their books leashed and tossed over their shoulders, walked along the side of the road, waving as the station wagon passed.

Upon reaching the village, the car climbed a rutted dirt track lined with straw-and-mud homes in front of which more children stood and stared. There, high above a valley nearly two miles above sea level, we lurched into the driveway of the Hotel Paradise, which turned out to be anything but.

The "hotel" had no lobby or check-in desk. Just six box-sized units crammed together as if the contractors had packed up and drove away before building the rest of the property. There would be no electricity until 9:00 P.M. at Hotel Paradise that day. In fact, said Mesfin, as we climbed from the car, "there is no electricity in all of Lalībela today. Not until nine o'clock." The weekly outage occurs every Friday, he said. It was necessary in order to keep more power flowing for the following week. (Electricity came to this remote mountain village only four or five years before I did. I was lucky to have any juice at all.)

Mesfin disappeared into a nearby home and returned a moment later with the keys to room number six. I stepped inside, dropped my bag, and prepared to take a quick shower before going with Mesfin to see Lalībela's famous churches. When I opened the door to the bathroom, however, the dingy shower stall—and the cockroaches that scurried on its floor—gave me reason to appreciate my own body odor. I stepped outside, hurried and unwashed, ready for my guided tour.

"Do you like *tej*?" Mesfin asked, as we walked down the sloping road. Once the drink of Ethiopian kings, *tej* remains an Ethiopian favorite. The winelike intoxicant is made with honey and hops derived from the locally grown *gesho* shrub. "We can have a drink before we see the churches, if you like."

I liked.

We walked down the road to Jineakutoleab's, a slouching mud and straw *tej* house with shuttered windows. So low was the ceiling, I had to bend over to get inside. Three low wooden tables had been positioned on a straw-covered floor. Stone benches, covered in goatskin, lined the walls. Following Mesfin's lead, I sat on the goatskin bench and watched in the shuttered darkness as an old woman put a hibachi in the middle of the floor. On top of the grill she placed a piece of incense as large as a chunk of Kingsford charcoal. As soon as the incense had been lit, white smoke rose in a great billowing spiral. It spread across the low ceiling, filling the dark room—and my lungs—with the scent of burning lilacs. So thick was the smoke, I had trouble seeing Mesfin. I jumped when a server suddenly entered the room.

Moving ghostlike through the clouds, the old woman delivered a container of *tej* to our table. With a large bulbous bottom and long-stem neck, the glass container looked exactly like a laboratory flask. "It is a *birille*," Mesfin said, no doubt noticing my furrowed brow. A clear, viscous liquid sloshed around in the *birille* when Mesfin picked it up. Through swirling clouds of incense, I watched him put his lips to the stem and take a drink. He passed the *tej*, but before following his lead, I asked the all-important question. "Did they use bottled water to make this?" He shook his head, pointing to a clear plastic tube protruding from a barrel at the front door. The tube snaked along the floor, through the dirty straw, and disappeared to a back room that led to who knows what. Even in the smoky darkness I could see the air bubbles moving through the tube.

By drinking the *tej* I would almost certainly get sick. Just as I had gotten sick after drinking a frozen margarita in Mexico. Just as I had gotten sick after sipping soup on a train in India. Just as I had gotten sick after foolishly drinking a glass of tap water during a break between Polar beers in Caracas. But I had never tasted Ethiopian *tej*. I was hell-bent on having the experience and wasn't about to let potential illness get in the way.

I crossed my fingers. Mesfin nodded his head. I could almost feel the amoeba swimming down my throat as I took the first cautious sip. But the liquid in which the amoeba swam tasted pretty damn good. A bit like vodka and orange juice, only sweeter. I tilted the *birille* again. This time I took a man-sized swallow before passing it back to Mesfin.

There we sat, two men in a tiny smoke-clogged *tej* house, passing the *birille* back and forth at one o'clock in the afternoon. After two or three servings had been consumed at Jineakutoleab's, we paid the server and walked into the blinding afternoon sun. I felt as if I'd crawled from an opium den.

The quiet village of Lalïbela appeared different, somehow. The mud and straw homes seemed more substantial, the rutted road less rutted, the—

I tripped over a bump in the road and fell facedown in the dirt.

Mesfin could not stifle a giggle as he helped me up. "*Tej* is strong, no?" he said. "*Tej* is strong, yes," I replied, brushing the dirt from my T-shirt and looking to see if any of the villagers had seen me fall.

On we went to the churches of Lalïbela, one of us stumbling as we walked.

Sometime in the twelfth or thirteenth century, during the reign of King Lalïbela, leader of the Zagwe dynasty, eleven local churches were created from volcanic rock. Like pieces of cake cut from the center, huge square trenches had been carved by craftsmen out of nearby hillsides. From the resulting blocks of rock they fashioned steps, windows, doors, facades, and then scooped out the insides, leaving support columns and ample space in which to congregate. These elaborate churches, which were said to have been constructed instead by angels in the night, are connected by a series of secret tunnels and bridges.

Mesfin led me to a barren, hilly area that resembled an archaeological dig. There, sandwiched between four massive clots of earth—and looking like a Greek temple uncovered during an excavation—lay Bet Medhane Alem ("Saviour of the World"). Measuring 110 by 77 feet, Bet Medhane Alem is the world's largest rock-hewn church. Some seventy-two stone pillars, shaped from the earth, support the huge rock edifice inside and out. A vaulted rock roof lies above it. I walked down to the entrance behind Mesfin, amazed that something so massive, so ornate, had been cut out of an Ethiopian hillside more than eight hundred years ago.

The church interior was as dark as a tomb, and felt like one. The drum-shaped nave led to a chancel covered by heavy red velvet curtains. Religious paintings had been propped up on tables in front of the curtains: the infant Christ and the Madonna; Christ nailed to the bloody Cross. I still reeled from an overabundance of *tej;* the blood of Christ and the smirking Madonna and the ghostly air inside the claustrophobic rock-hewn interior began to make my head spin. When was the last time I attended church services? How long since my last confession? *Forgive me, Father, for I have sinned. It's been thirty-seven years since my last* . . . Wait, I'm not Catholic.

Just when I felt the Holy Ghost place his wispy hands around my neck and squeeze, an Ethiopian priest appeared. Dressed in a gown of indigo and crimson, his head wrapped in a bright white scarf, the priest stood in front of the velvet curtains holding a heavy metal ornament in one hand. "That is the famous gold cross of Lalībela," Mesfin whispered. "It is beautiful, no?"

At first glance, it looked nothing like a cross. The familiar shape had been lost in a twisting maze of ornamentation. Then again, my *tej*-tainted eyes could not be trusted. As we moved closer to the priest, Mesfin explained that the round protrusions on the top of the cross represented the twelve apostles. Four winged extensions near the bottom were meant to resemble doves.

"The priest will let you feel the cross if you like," Mesfin said. Honored, I stepped forward and reached for the famous nine-hundred-year-old cross of Lalībela. But when I tried to lift it from the priest's steely grip, he would not let go. In fact, he yanked it away from me and glared. "You are not allowed to take it," Mesfin said, criticizing my behavior in a soft but stern voice. "You are only allowed to *feel* it."

After bowing an apology to the priest, I proffered my hand. Still gripping the handle, the priest laid the cross upon my open palm. It was heavy. Extremely heavy. Mesfin told me it weighed more than fourteen pounds and was made of solid gold. No wonder the priest refused to let it go. (In 1997, the cross of Lalībela was stolen by an Ethiopian antiques dealer and sold to a European collector. Since the recovery, priests have become understandably protective.)

From Bet Medhane Alem we walked from one church to the next—Bet Maryam, Bet Meskel, Bet Danaghel, and others. Each time we were greeted by robed priests displaying a variety of priceless crosses. To get from Bet Gabriel-Rufael to Bet Merkorios, we had to inch along an eighty-foot tunnel. It was pitch black and blessed with the musty scent of the ages. Mesfin grabbed my hand, attempting to lead me down the dark path he'd walked many times before. Jolted by the feel of another man's hand, I instinctively jerked my hand away, choosing instead to negotiate the darkness on my own. Not three seconds later, I crashed into a solid rock wall. When Mesfin heard me cry out in the darkness, he managed to grab my hand again. This time I held on tight.

The best preserved and most visually stunning of the churches, Bet Giyorgis stands seventy-five feet high in the center of a seventy-five-foot pit. Looking down upon the perfectly carved three-tiered structure, I could see it had been created in the plus-sign shape of a Greek cross. The flat roof was engraved with three concentric crosses that began at the roof's edge and shrank toward the center. Flawlessly carved steps led to the platform upon which Bet Giyorgis stood. An elaborate door frame protruded from the front entrance. Onion-shaped windows, paneless and exquisitely carved, spoke of an Arab influence. It was a marvel of Ethiopian engineering. A testament to the staying power of a well-built building—holy or otherwise.

After a long but gratifying day of churchgoing, Mesfin walked with me up the road toward Hotel Paradise. Rather than return to my tiny room with no electricity, a room where scurrying cockroaches waited for me at the bottom of a grimy shower stall, I suggested we stop for a drink at Jineakutoleab's *tej* house. We sat together on the goatskin bench, inhaling four-alarm smoke from a billowing chunk of incense. We were attended by the same old woman. A couple of hours later, after polishing off three or four *birilles*, my little room at Hotel Paradise didn't seem so bad.

SECURITY RISK

‹·····································›

The most perpetrated scam in all of Cairo is the one in which a local convinces the newly arrived traveler that the hotel they are heading for is closed, horrible or very expensive and leads them off to another "better" place, for which your self-appointed 'guide' earns himself a commission." Having been duly warned by my *Lonely Planet Egypt* guide, and ready to fend off the touts, I stepped off the EgyptAir flight at Cairo International and headed to the immigration checkpoint. Turns out, it wasn't a tout who caused the problem.

Among the first passengers to funnel into the immigration interchange, I walked right up to an officer, who leaned forward in his booth and offered a weary smile. Wearing a crisp white uniform with epaulets, he seemed less like a tired immigration official than an officer on a cruise ship. The officer flipped through the pages of my passport. Failing to find what he was looking for, he began flipping through the pages again.

"Visa?" he said, looking up at me.

My first mistake, the one that opened the floodgates, was forgetting to stop and buy a visa after the mad dash off the airplane. (Unlike in other countries, passengers traveling to Egypt need not obtain a visa before departure. At Cairo International, visas can be purchased at one of several bank windows located just outside the immigration interchange.) Had the visa been properly affixed to my passport, the friendly officer would have no doubt stamped it and sent me on my merry way. Alas, my way was not to be so merry.

I apologized for the oversight. The officer smiled and pointed over my shoulder, having no doubt handled many passengers who had forgotten to buy a visa. Like the proverbial salmon swimming upstream, I moved against the rushing throngs and presented myself to a clerk at one of the bank windows. An Egyptian visa is essentially two postage-sized stamps—one orange, one blue—graced with flowing Arabic writing. After purchasing mine, I licked the back of both stamps, glued them onto an unused page in my passport, and returned to the very same immigration officer. He was busy processing a passenger, so I moved over to the next officer and immediately wished I hadn't.

Instead of waiting for me to approach the booth and hand over my passport, the new officer inexplicably stepped from the booth and confronted me. Of the hundreds of immigration checkpoints I've cleared since my first international trip some twenty years earlier, of the hundreds of furrowed brows and further questions, never has an official stepped from the booth to greet me.

Dressed in the same white uniform as his more amiable colleague, Officer No. 2 stood maybe six feet four and fixed me with the coldest of cold stares. Unsure of what was expected of me at that moment, I quickly offered my passport as if I were being mugged. The immigration officer did not snatch it from me, as expected. Instead, he grasped the passport and slid it from my hand slowly, menacingly, proving he was in charge. He stared at the passport cover and then looked at me. He turned to the identification page and then looked at me. He flipped through page after page, looking down at me from a lofty altitude and glancing at the entry and exit stamps: French Polynesia, Australia, Brunei,

Thailand, Singapore, Indonesia, India . . . After flipping through all the pages, he closed the passport, tapped it dubiously against his fist, and stared at me some more.

Had I broken some unwritten rule? Had he confused me with a terrorist? Was he offended by the fact that I wore a Kangol hat backward? Suddenly, the immigration officer spoke. His voice was exactly as you might imagine. Deep, harsh, intimidating.

"I'm sorry," I replied. "I don't speak Arabic."

He took one step closer. Close enough that our bodies almost touched. So tall was he, I had to lean way back in order to maintain eye contact. It was like sitting in the first row at a horror movie you didn't really want to see. "I do not speak English," he said, in perfect English. "Sit."

"Excuse me?" I said, as politely as possible.

"Sit," he repeated, pointing to the far corner of the room. There were a cluster of chairs in the distance.

"Sit there?" I said, snapping my head back around. "But why?"

"Security."

"Security? What did I—"

"Security!" he shouted, cutting me off. "Sit!"

Stunned and thoroughly unsettled, I stumbled over to the corner of the immigration interchange and sat down as instructed. Five minutes passed. Ten. Fifteen. If I had somehow aroused suspicion, why was it necessary for the officer to take my passport and leave his post? Could he not run the necessary computer checks from his booth? What was taking him so long?

Twenty minutes passed. In the meantime, my beloved duffel bag had been riding the luggage carousel all alone, just waiting for some enterprising character to take it. That's what this was all about. It was a setup. An airport conspiracy. My guidebook spoke about the touts lingering outside the airport. But what about the ones lingering within?

My life was in that duffel bag. Worried, I stood up and walked over to a group of three security officers. They wore the same white uniforms and pistols on their hips. "Excuse me," I said, ready to engage whichever one spoke English. But before dialogue could be established, one of the officers glared at me. "Security," he said, definitively, as if he had been briefed about my situation. He pointed to the chairs in the corner. I had no recourse other than to return there and sit.

Within minutes, another flood of passengers rushed into the immigration interchange. From my perch in Limbo Land, I watched long queues form in front of each immigration booth. Then I watched, dejected, as the queues slowly dwindled. No one was ordered to wait. Some five hundred people had been processed and still I sat alone in an immigration no-man's-land in the corner of the room.

Unable to wait any longer, I jumped up and marched back over to the same three officers who now seemed visibly angered because their conversation had been interrupted. Three snarling faces turned in unison. Undaunted, I let my feelings be known. "I've been sitting here for more than forty-five minutes. Nobody's told me why I've been forced to wait. Nobody seems to be addressing the situation. When am I going to be allowed to leave?" I stopped short of raising my voice, but my anger had nonetheless been uncorked.

The three men moved toward me as a unit, speaking in harsh Arabic, hands moving toward their weapons. I had stepped over the line. Me. A mild-mannered flight attendant. Until that moment my only brush with the law had been with a female cop. (Dressed in a bikini, a little tipsy from the strawberry daiquiris we'd been drinking, the off-duty New York police officer brushed up against me in the Jacuzzi at Club Med in the Turks and Caicos Islands.) The three Egyptian officers weren't going to be nearly as soft. I could already hear the pounding of a judge's gavel, the sound of my own pathetic sobbing, the clink of Egyptian prison bars. I would never see the treasures of King Tutankhamen. Never see the Great Pyramid of Giza, the ancient necropolis of Thebes, never walk into the fabled tombs of Luxor.

I would rot in an Egyptian prison and one day become a relic in my own right.

As the three officers badgered me in Arabic, the missing six-foot, four-inch immigration officer suddenly appeared. He walked slowly, nonchalantly, as if sauntering along the Nile on a lovely summer's day. He moved toward the four of us, tapping my passport against his fist.

Like a big kid no longer interested in a small toy, he gave me a dismissive look. "Security," he said, without giving any other explanation for my one-hour detention. The officer returned my passport. The four men stared as I turned and walked nervously from immigration. I found my duffel on the luggage carousel, cleared customs without a hitch, and then stepped outside into the stifling heat of Cairo.

Choosing from among the taxi drivers who pointed to their waiting cars and motioned excitedly for me to get in, I picked the one who seemed least eager. I climbed into the backseat. Gave him the name of my hotel. As we pulled away from the curb, he eyed me in the rearview mirror. "That is not a good hotel," he said, just as my guidebook had predicted. "I know one that is much better."

THE LONG CAMEL RIDE

◀┄┄┄┄┄┄┄┄┄▶

Slouching in the saddle like a weary Middle Eastern nomad, I rode the camel as it ambled along a narrow path between the Sinai Mountains and the Gulf of Aqaba. The sun glared mercilessly. Through polarized sunglasses I looked up and saw only white light. I reached into my backpack, took a sip of bottled water. It seemed almost as hot as the 105-degree surface temperature. With each inhalation of broiling air, my nose hair felt as though it might ignite. To make matters worse, a bothersome blister had formed on my buttocks. And with each wobbly stride of the camel, the blister rubbed against the saddle and grew.

From the moment of arrival in Egypt, I had been eager to ride a camel. While visiting the pyramids at Giza, however, I foolishly turned down an opportunity because the rides lasted only a half hour or so and were overrun with tourists. After traveling to Luxor and checking out the Karnak and Hatshepsut temples, I squandered another chance because the "Sunset Camel Rides" seemed a bit Disneyesque. I had hoped for a *unique* camel-riding experience. In Dahab, a tiny resort village on the east coast of the Sinai Peninsula, I found what I thought I was looking for.

Dahab is a haven for escapists who come primarily to snorkel and scuba dive in the Red Sea. The town boasts cozy beachfront restaurants, several scuba-diving centers, and a multitude of tour operators offering desert Jeep treks, sunrise climbs on Mount Sinai—and, of course, camel rides. I arranged for a full-day camel trek to the Bedouin village a few miles up the coast. Bedouins migrated from Arabia hundreds of years earlier and continue to inhabit the inhospitable areas of Egypt's Western and Eastern deserts as well as the Sinai Peninsula. They are a nomadic people who depend on camels for survival.

After a thirty-minute drive out of town, I was dropped off near the base of a rocky hill. There, alongside a camel, stood a young Bedouin boy. He couldn't have been more than twelve years old. Still, my driver introduced him as my guide. Then the driver disappeared. I do not speak Arabic. The boy did not speak English. Acute shyness prevented him from even looking me in the eye. It soon became apparent that any communication would be brief and nonverbal.

Never having ridden before on a camel, I was unsure how to proceed. My young guide yanked down on the camel's reins. The beast released a muffled roar similar to that made by Chewbacca the Wookie, Han Solo's very hairy sidekick from *Star Wars*. The camel then dropped to the ground, folding its legs before sitting. Next, the boy motioned for me to hop in the saddle. There would be no instruction. No explanation of how to mount, sit on, or control the animal. Lacking this knowledge, I threw one leg over the saddle and decided to treat the camel like a horse.

Camels and horses are not alike, I soon learned. With me in the saddle, the camel stood up on its hind legs first, as camels do, thrusting its rear end high in the air. Unprepared for the sudden shift of balance, I slid off the saddle and fell forward. As the camel's front legs rose, I found myself clinging to the animal's neck. I dropped to the ground, feet first, and gave my young guide a look that said, Yeah, I did that on purpose.

That was the first and only time I saw him smile.

The two-hour ride to the Bedouin village proved to be everything I'd hoped for. Atop my one-hump wonder, I bounced along the path, amazed by how easily the camel walked uphill, around boulders, and along harrowing cliffs near the water's edge. Aside from the soft rhythmic thud of camel feet upon rock, there was only the sound of waves lapping the shore. No birds. No animals. Just me, my camel, and the Bedouin boy, who trailed on foot.

When we reached a flat stretch, I turned in my saddle and shouted to my young guide. Holding the reins and bouncing emphatically in the saddle, I asked, tacitly, for permission to run the camel. The boy nodded his head. That was all the permission I needed.

With a few gentle kicks of my heels, the camel took off. It was a clumsy, wobbly two-hundred-yard sprint that had me bouncing in the saddle, an inexperienced jockey in the world's goofiest race. All that bouncing in the saddle caused the butt blister to burst. I pulled the reins. The camel stopped. While I tried adjusting myself in the saddle, the camel turned around on its own accord and took off running again. This time in the direction of the Bedouin boy, who stared indifferently as we scampered toward him.

The Bedouin "village" was merely a smattering of open-air shacks made of plywood and reeds. I rode into the area, passing clusters of veiled women sitting in the shade. They glanced and looked away. Several naked toddlers stumbled in the sand. They looked up at me, unsmiling.

After dismounting near one of the structures, I was approached by a robed woman who handed me a plate piled high with rice and salad. "Are you married?" she said, almost immediately. Startled by the unexpected question, it took me a few seconds to answer. In the meantime her daughter appeared. A young girl of maybe sixteen or seventeen, she smiled shyly, watching me eat in the open-faced shack.

"Are you married?" I asked the girl, after another mouthful.

She shook her head, embarrassed, and gazed into the dust. "I too young."

We sat there, the three of us, the implication hanging in the air when the mother smiled and nodded her veiled head.

In the shade of the Bedouin shack, stuffed with food and refreshed by cold bottled water, I stared across the wide blue Gulf of Aqaba at the rugged mountains of Saudi Arabia. The silence and the solitude lulled me to sleep.

When I woke a couple of hours later, the young girl and her mother were gone. Instead, the silent Bedouin boy crouched above the sand in front of me, watching and waiting.

If the two-hour camel ride into the Bedouin village had been fun and adventuresome, the return to Dahab was nothing less than laborious work. In part, due to the heat that cracked my drying lips; but mainly because of the burgeoning blister on my booty. One half of my glutei maximi had become a full-fledged open sore—a four-alarm fire that would rekindle each time I attempted to sit during the following three to four weeks. Although the return trip had begun midafternoon when the fire in the sky burned at full strength, the fire in my ass was even worse. With each wobbly step of the camel, I banged about the saddle, wincing all the way.

Like a horse sensing an inexperienced rider, somehow the camel understood my pain. It seemed intent on providing a more unpleasant ride than necessary. Instead of taking sure-footed gentle strides as it had done earlier that morning, the camel's clumsy steps became exaggerated. If a flat surface presented itself, the camel managed to step on an uneven rock. If a smooth rock lay in our path, the wily animal placed its lead hoof at the base of an incline, angling its body and forcing me to lean, like an Egyptian rodeo performer, from the hard and slippery saddle. The amiable creature I so enjoyed earlier that morning had morphed, inexplicably, into the camel from Hell. A lumbering, uncooperative, mean-spirited beast, trudging along a familiar desert path, following instinct instead of command.

We lurched along the rocky path between the mountains and

the sea, as Bedouins have done for more than two hundred years. When we finally reached Dahab, I eased out of the saddle, clutching my right glute in agony. Standing face to face with the ugly beast, I looked into the great bulb of its eye, searching for some sign of intelligence, for some understanding as to why I had been mistreated. I made the mistake of turning away, just for a second, to wave good-bye to the Bedouin boy. That's when it happened. A warm, gooey rope of camel drool oozed onto my shiny bald head and dripped down my sunburned face. With frantic swipes of both arms, I wiped away the disgusting discharge. When I glared into the face of the camel, it was smiling.

Eastern Europe

BEING SAMUEL L. JACKSON

Walking the cobblestone streets of Prague in summer is like strolling through a fifteenth-century fairy tale. Gothic church steeples protrude from clusters of trees and seem to prop up a blanket of blue sky. Stone bridges stretch across the sleepy Vltava River. A six-hundred-year-old astronomical clock chimes every hour on the hour from the Old Town Hall tower in Old Town Square. The Karolinum, former site of Central Europe's oldest university (where Kafka earned his law degree), is still here, as is the Estates Theatre, a neoclassical masterpiece where Wolfgang Amadeus Mozart premiered *Don Giovanni* in 1787. High on a hill, presiding over this medieval metropolis, lies Prague Castle—a sprawling complex of churches, convents, courtyards, and palaces—home to Bohemian kings for centuries.

It was here that the lie was hatched. Beyond the gilded splendor of Prague Castle, on the outskirts of the city, in a dark, cramped apartment on a quiet, wooded street. A lie so brazen, so clever in its conception, the lead perpetrator had to sit back in his chair and admire the beauty of it all. "Ahhh . . . yes, yes," Pino said, scrolling through celebrity images on the computer screen and glancing intermittently at me. "You look so much like Samuel Jackson." Pino's girlfriend, Monica, the ex-actress, nodded her handsome head. As did Alex, Jiri, and the two casting directors, Jessica Horváthová and Alena Kubálková from Cine-Jessy Studios.

At Pino and Monica's request, the casting directors were to supply a limousine, bodyguards, and a convincing story that would be leaked to the local press. Dressed in identical slacks, wearing fanny packs and mobile phones clipped to their belts, Ms. Horváthová and Ms. Kubálková looked at me and began deliberating in hushed Czech voices. Judging by the smiling faces and the indecipherable dialogue that followed, the deal had been done. The famous American actor, Samuel L. Jackson, star of such critically acclaimed films as *Pulp Fiction*, *Jackie Brown*, and *A Time to Kill*, would be making a surprise visit to the thirty-eighth annual International Film Festival in Karlovy Vary, Czech Republic. Whether he knew it or not.

Alex Staffa was the reason for my being here. In spite of the Italian surname, Alex is Czech, born and bred. He spends part of the year in Prague working on one entrepreneurial endeavor or another. The rest of the year he spends in the same Miami Beach apartment building in which I lived until recently. Whenever we bumped into each other in the hallway or in front of the mailboxes, Alex extended the same friendly invitation. "You must come to Prague," he said. "It is the most beautiful city in the world." Finally, I got the chance to see for myself.

Alex met me at the airport. He escorted me to the Hotel Sophia, and once I had showered and changed, he gave me a quick tour of the city. "There is Kafka's apartment," he said, pointing to an unassuming building on Celetná Street in which the literary legend once laid his head. "And right there," Alex said, after we had crossed the Charles Bridge and strolled through Old Town Square, "that's where Paul Robeson reached down with both hands and lifted me into the air."

At first I didn't believe him. Robeson, a Rutgers alumnus and Columbia University law school graduate, was a Renaissance man if ever there was one. He was the first black All-American football player, as well as a singer (one of the most popular con-cert artists of his era), actor (he appeared in eleven films, includ-ing the 1936 classic *Show Boat*), and civil rights activist who was ultimately vilified in America because of his outspoken demands for equal rights and a well-publicized affinity for the Soviet Union. It was true that Robeson lived in Europe for many years and spent time here in the former Czechoslovakia. But what were the chances that he had lifted a young Alex Staffa on this very street in Prague?

Alex's eyes glazed over. His silver head tilted toward the side-walk. When he spoke, the words seemed to come from far away. "I was just a boy," he said. "I had never seen a black man in per-son and could not stop staring at him." This phenomenon would soon be shared by hundreds of Czech movie fans when Samuel L. Jackson . . . er, when yours truly walked between a phalanx of bodyguards at the International Film Festival in Karlovy Vary.

One night Alex took me to FX Café on Bělehradská Street. The hip, bohemian eatery was packed with cigarette-wielding young people dressed in clothing that appeared to be stylishly wrinkled in an attempt to impress other cigarette-wielding young people. Waiting at our table was Jiri Kratochvil. Alex's longtime friend, Jiri appeared to be in his late fifties and wore the same stylishly wrinkled clothing as those who were half his age. Over dinner I learned that Jiri was a theater maven. He'd lived and worked in New York for many years and had the neurotic disposition to prove it. His eyes twitched constantly. His head jerked upward whenever anyone walked past our table. He might start a discus-sion about costume design or politics, and before Alex or I had the chance to speak he would suddenly begin pontificating about the evils of crack cocaine. Jiri's most striking quality, however, was an uncanny resemblance to John Malkovich.

So we readied ourselves for the film festival. Jiri Kratochvil would pose as John Malkovich. I would pose as Samuel L. Jack-son. To add spice to our entourage, the guy who lived upstairs from Pino and Monica—a mysterious American expatriate who called himself "Bob"—would accompany us, dressed as a shaman.

Regarded as "the most important international screening competition in Eastern Europe," the Czech International Film Festival features movies from former Soviet bloc countries, as well as independent productions from all over the world. But according to Pino and Monica, the event had become a haven for egocentric snobs. This was the motivation for the practical joke. When word got out that big-time movie stars Samuel L. Jackson and John Malkovich would be in attendance, the local glitterati would rush to be seen in their presence. Pino and Monica would get a huge laugh. The Cine-Jessy casting directors would gain valuable publicity for helping to pull off the prank. And for sixty of the most hectic minutes in our otherwise mundane lives, Jiri and I would be treated like royalty.

On the scheduled morning, Team Pino made the one-hour drive from Prague to Karlovy Vary. Pino pulled into the tiny Karlovy Vary airport, where a crack team of assistants had set up base. There were two makeup artists, four bodyguards, a photographer, and a whole slew of people whose functions could not be determined.

The two women rushed me into a bathroom and began applying makeup that would make me look more Samuel L. Jackson-ish. When they finished the job, I looked in the mirror. The face that stared back looked even less like the actor than before. Not that we looked anything alike in the first place. The only features we shared were skin tone and a predilection for Kangol hats. The scam wasn't going to work. It would be a fiasco. Hundreds of ogling Czechs would take one look and laugh me out of the republic. I tried to convince Pino and Monica to call the whole thing off. Tried to get them to reconsider. But money had been spent. A limo procured. Real live bodyguards, wearing black suits and sunglasses, were ready to spring into action.

Into the limo we went: Jiri, Bob, the two casting directors,

Pino, Monica, me, and four buff guys who looked like plain-clothes KGB agents. Bob wore a shiny silver gown and carried a wooden cane. He looked more like a gay wizard than a shaman. I wore my Kangol hat backward, as always, and a black polyester suit that a gentleman of Samuel L. Jackson's stature wouldn't be caught dead wearing. It didn't matter what Jiri wore. He actually looked like John Malkovich. Really he did.

Nestled in the Teplá Valley among lush wooded hills, Karlovy Vary is an old Bohemian spa town. Since 1522, when European royalty began flocking here to sample the healing mineral waters, Karlovy Vary has been the place to be. Frederick I of Prussia used to hang out here, as did Russian tsar Peter the Great. It's an aristocrat's retreat. The perfect place for film industry egos to be pampered.

My one-hour visit to the Karlovy Vary Film Festival was a blur. When our stretch limo pulled up in front of a crowd, the four bodyguards jumped out and held open the doors. The shaman was first to emerge. Next came John Malkovich. Finally, Samuel L. Jackson—the man who put the "pulp" in *Pulp Fiction*—stepped onto the sidewalk wearing dark sunglasses and dripping with attitude. The bodyguards played their parts perfectly. With Malkovich at my side and the entourage behind us, we moved toward the appointed restaurant, surrounded by four walls of no-nonsense muscle. Dozens and dozens of people—tourists, festival participants, locals—suddenly turned to look our way. Cameras flashed. Children pointed. The lead bodyguard thrust his hand forward, plowing through the crowd like a ship through rough water. A murmur rippled through the masses. Two American movie stars had landed. In the next instant we were gone.

A moment later we found ourselves in an opulent dining room with high frescoed ceilings and chairs that could have been antique. Uniformed waiters were allowed past the bodyguards and seemed to bow before taking our orders. We drank from crystal glasses and china cups. We laughed pretentiously at our own significance. But after Pino leaned over and whispered in my ear, the makeup almost slid from my face. "Ivetu Bartoŝovou wants to meet with you," he said.

"Who is Ivetu Bartoŝovou?"

"She is famous pop singer in Czech Republic."

"What does she want?"

"She wants to meet Samuel Jackson."

"What do I say to her?"

Pino shrugged and raised a bushy eyebrow. "Perhaps you tell her about your next movie."

The plan was for me to do the talking. Jiri might blabber us into conversational quicksand. Besides, he had a thick Czech accent that could easily be detected during his Malkovich impersonation.

Moments later, a Czech bombshell walked past the bodyguards and seemed to tremble while standing before our table. All lip gloss and bubbling breasts, she grinned so hard I thought the poor girl would burst. After introductions were made, she sat down beside me, hands fidgeting, grinning ear to ear. The speed at which bullshit began to flow from my mouth could not have been measured by conventional means. "*Pulp Fiction* was my favorite movie." I said this in response to Ivetu's first question. "But Travolta was a pain in the ass to work with."

The pop singer raised her eyebrows and yet managed to keep grinning.

"Oh yeah," I continued. "He's the biggest prick in Hollywood. Everybody knows I should have been nominated for Best Supporting Actor instead of him."

Her grin began to falter.

"Did you see the movie?"

"Umm . . . *Pulp Fiction*?" she said. It sounded like *Pyoolp Feekshun*. Her accent was so cute I almost stopped lying. Almost.

"Yeah, *Pulp Fiction*."

"Ahhh . . ."

"Who had the best scenes, me or Travolta?" I was really getting into character.

"What?"

"Which one of us had the best scenes? Samuel L. Jackson or John Travolta? As Hollywood movies go, typically the supporting actor who shines brightest in a particular film is considered for the nomination. Not the guy who played Vinnie Barbarino on *Welcome Back, Kotter.*"

"What?"

"You see, Hollywood ain't all glitz and glamour, sweetheart. I can tell you horror stories about being screwed out of a role just because—"

Pino interrupted me with a tap on the shoulder just when I prepared to launch into a tirade about incompetent film directors. The time had come for us to make the grand walk. I said good-bye to Ms. Bartoŝovou. But before doing so I extended an invitation to lunch should she ever find herself in Beverly Hills.

News of our arrival had spread through Karlovy Vary. Malkovich and Jackson were herded along a pedestrian walkway that ran through what appeared to be the center of town. Elegant old hotels jutted out from the hillside. According to one bodyguard who whispered to me as we walked, most of the hotels had been bought by wealthy Russians, who "stick a Czech guy at the front desk to make it look legitimate."

Hands clasped commandingly behind my back, I walked between Malkovich and Shaman Bob, soaking up attention from the many folks who pointed and stared. It was nice, the adulation. My ego grew in direct proportion to the number of Czechs who recognized me from my films.

Moments before climbing into the limo and returning to Prague, a young woman came bounding toward us. Two bodyguards stepped in her path, blocking her approach with 450 pounds of combined bulk. Always willing to appease an adoring fan, however, I, Samuel L. Jackson—the man who put the "pulp" in *Pulp Fiction*—motioned for the bodyguards to let her through. Green eyes jiggling excitedly in their sockets, a bright smile spreading from ear to ear, the woman held a baby in her hands. How sweet, I thought to myself. She wants me to kiss her child.

"It *is* John Malkovich!" she screamed, all of a sudden. *"John Malkovich!"* She almost threw her child into Jiri's unexpecting arms. Then she flung her arms around him, posing for photographs that did not include me.

"Malkovich?" I muttered, as I climbed into the limo and waited for the flashing bulbs to cease. "I'm bigger than John Malkovich."

THE LAST MUNICIPAL BICYCLE IN VILNIUS

On an overly optimistic summer day in June, two years before my arrival in Vilnius, Lithuania, Mayor Artūras Zuokas launched a bold municipal program. Hoping to ease traffic congestion in the city center and at the same time encourage citizens to adopt a healthier lifestyle, Mayor Zuokas arranged for the delivery of four hundred brand-new orange bicycles to the capital. Anyone wishing to use a bicycle could do so, free of charge, between 5:00 A.M. and 10:00 P.M., but only within restricted zones in Old Town, the downtown area, and nearby neighborhoods. All that was required of the borrowers was that they return the bicycles to one of ninety pre-positioned parking racks scattered throughout the restricted zones. The bikes would then be available for the next conscientious citizen to use.

Detractors of the program believed the bicycles would be stolen. Mayor Zuokas believed in the inherent integrity of his constituents. "This will be a test of morality for the people of Vilnius," he said in an article published in the *Baltic Times*. "They can control themselves." The municipal bicycle program even had its own enthusiastic, albeit awkwardly worded slogan: "The Bike's Invented—Ride Orange!"

The citizens of Vilnius rode orange, all right. Boy, did they ride orange. In a bicycling frenzy never before seen in Eastern Europe, anyone with two feet and a propensity to pedal took advantage of the mayor's hopelessly naive gesture. By the end of that first weekend, some twenty-five municipal bicycles had been wrecked, and more than three hundred vanished into thin Lithuanian air.

Contrary to the mayor's published comments, it appeared the citizens of Vilnius could not control themselves. Enterprising Vilniusians sold the orange bikes on the black market for as little as five U.S. dollars. A freshly painted bike with an altered "Vilnius City Municipality" inscription could reap three times as much. Needless to say, plans for an additional six hundred orange bikes were scrapped.

Artūras Zuokas did not give up completely, however. Determined to make use of the kilometers and kilometers of new bicycle paths in and around the city center, the good mayor proclaimed that the few remaining municipal bicycles would be made available to visitors at the main tourism center on Vilniaus Gatvé. The orange bikes were to be rented at the bargain-basement price of one litas per day, or about thirty-seven cents.

Never one to turn down a good deal, I showed up at the tourism center on a gray and drizzly summer day in Vilnius. Behind the counter were two smiling clerks, ready to direct me to one of the many tourism opportunities the city had to offer. As I remember it, there was a huge map of Lithuania on the wall behind the counter. Dozens of leaflets and brochures touted river cruises, Old Town tours, a visit to the Užupis Republic—a quirky bohemian artists' colony with its own unofficial president and constitution. Off to the side of the counter, leaning casually on a silver kickstand, was a bright orange municipal bicycle.

"I believe it is the last one in the city," said the clerk, as I walked over to admire the bike. When I asked if the "Ride Orange!" fiasco was true, she recounted the story of Mayor Zuokas's disastrous program, detail by pedal-pumping detail, shaking her head between chuckles.

After paying the one-litas fee, and completing a release that required my signature, hotel name, telephone number, e-mail address, passport number, religious affiliation, blood type, fingerprint, and next of kin, the last municipal bicycle in Vilnius was released into my possession.

It was a woman's bike. A small, bright orange, crossbar-less deal that was much too short for my long, skinny legs. Undaunted, I walked the bike through the doors and rode through the drizzle, knees akimbo, hoping to accomplish at least thirty-seven cents' worth of sightseeing before my clothes got soaked.

There are no black people in Lithuania. Trust me. A black man riding an orange bicycle—an infamous "Vilnius City Municipality" bicycle, no less—through the rain-slick streets was something the locals didn't see every day. I pedaled down the slippery sidewalk of Vilniaus Gatvé and came upon two female pedestrians walking arm-in-arm. I turned to smile while riding by. Their eyeballs rolled masterfully in their sockets, and yet their heads remained locked in the full frontal position, swiveling not a centimeter. Lithuanians are masters of the sidelong glance.

Following a bicycle sightseeing route hastily put together with the help of the tourism center clerk, I rode a few short blocks to the Frank Zappa monument. Yes. Strange though it may seem, Vilnius, Lithuania, is home to the world's only monument to zany American rock legend Frank Zappa. His stone bust sits atop a thirteen-foot stainless-steel column in a small courtyard next to Psichikos Sveikatos Centras, which, judging by the name and the strange bug-eyed people shuffling in and out, I assumed to be a psychiatric institute. What a fitting location for a zany musician who once said: "If we cannot be free, at least we can be cheap!"

I sat there, straddling the bike in the drizzle, wondering why on earth such a monument was erected here. Frank Zappa is not of Lithuanian descent. He never set foot in the country. There was absolutely no connection between him and Vilnius. Why, come to think of it, was I sitting on an orange bike in the goddam rain, staring at the bust of a man whose weird-ass "music" I never liked in the first place?

As it turns out, Saulius Paukstys likes Zappa's music. In fact, Paukstys is the president of Lithuania's Frank Zappa fan club. He *loves* Zappa's music. He relates to the message. During a time when Lithuania had been squashed beneath the Soviet jackboot, Zappa's antiestablishment attitude made him a cult figure here. After the country gained independence in 1991, Paukstys convinced Parliament to erect the memorial. The unveiling was accompanied by fireworks and music from a Lithuanian military band. Zappa, a purveyor of nontraditional existential tunes, probably rolled over in his grave and puked.

From the Frank Zappa monument, I rode through the wet streets, past the Doric columns of Vilnius Cathedral, and down Pilies Gatvé (Castle Street), the main entrance to Old Town. I parked the municipal bicycle next to a light pole and secured it there, using a flimsy cable lock supplied by the tourism center. Two men, no doubt experiencing a flashback from the bike scandal, pointed to my little orange bike and laughed.

Sitting beneath the canopy of an outdoor café, warmed by an electric lamp, I sipped hot chocolate, admiring the antique lanterns and flower-lined balconies jutting out handsomely across the winding cobblestone lane. The drizzle had stopped momentarily, but the flat gray sky remained. Short, stout ladies, their heads wrapped in scarves, closed their umbrellas and seemed to close their hearts. Old men stared grumpily at the cobblestones. Everyone, it seemed, wore a somber face: the mothers hurriedly pulling their children along the street; the shopkeepers, their faces as closed as window shutters; even the middle-aged men. Especially the middle-aged men.

According to the *Guinness World Records*, the Republic of Lithuania holds a dubious distinction: It has the world's highest suicide rate. Recent statistics show that for every 100,000 Lithuanians, 52 commit suicide. In 2001, for example, fewer Lithuanians died in car accidents than by their own hand. Men thirty-five to fifty are most likely to do the dirty deed.

A cloud of sadness seems to hang over the city, even when the weather is not gray and rainy. But when it does rain, when the sky is gray, the gloom is a tangible thing. I sat at the café, unable to feel the warmth of the electric lamp, looking into the faces passing along picturesque Pilies Gatvé. No smiles. Scarce signs of emotion. Only the occasional sidelong glance in my direction. I downed the remaining hot chocolate in one gulp, but could not manage to warm my bones. Determined to shake off the gloom, I unlocked my municipal bicycle and rode farther along Pilies Gatvé, pumping my knees as I pedaled.

I flew by the Church of St. Casimir, famous for its crown-shaped cupola, which can be seen from most points in the city. I rode past the Russian Orthodox Church of St. Paraskeva, where Peter the Great baptized Abrahm Hannibal, the Ethiopian slave-turned–Russian general. I rode past the Russian Byzantine Church of St. Michael and the Gothic Church of St. Anne, where Napoleon and his French cavalry holed up en route to an 1812 defeat in Moscow.

After turning around and zooming down Pilies Gatvé once more, I rode into the nineteenth-century New Town, up Gedimino Prospektas, past the newly planted trees sprouting along a newly laid pedestrian walkway teeming with young people. Young smiling people. People who had come of age during a time of freedom. Two teenage girls smiled, waved briskly, and then ran away, giggling at their own bodaciousness. A slouching, hooded teenage boy, skateboard tucked beneath one arm, raised his fist, as if we were passing on the streets of Detroit. "Waz up, bro?" he said, in perfect American street parlance. I laughed so hard I damn near fell off the bike.

Just when my spirits were beginning to soar, I made a mistake. I locked the bike and visited a museum. Not the kind of museum you should visit alone on a dark and rainy Eastern European day.

The Museum of Genocide Victims is housed in a monstrous stone building on Gedimino Prospektas. Built in 1899, and initially occupied by the Vilnius government of the Russian Empire, the building tells the sordid tale of Lithuania's oppression. From 1920 to 1939, it housed the courts of the Polish occupying power. From 1941 to 1944, it served as the headquarters for the German secret police (the Gestapo). After 1944, when the Russians booted out the occupying Germans and imposed their own brand of tyranny upon the Lithuanians, the building served as a KGB prison. The last political prisoners were released in 1987, but the Russians didn't vacate the premises until 1991, when Lithuania's independence had finally been declared.

The prison is exactly as the Russians left it. Twenty-three cells in a dark, depressing basement, which is now part of the Genocide Museum complex. I walked down the stairway, the museum's only visitor, and stepped into a long, narrow corridor. Bare lightbulbs, extending at intervals from a high-arched ceiling, gave off barely enough light to cut through the gloom. Twenty-three doors lined the corridor. Some of the doors were open; others were closed. As I moved to the first, my footsteps echoed against the cold stone floor. I peeked through a viewing slit, and felt shivers run up and down my spine.

It was a water-torture cell. A small room with concrete walls and a sloping concrete floor. From the middle of the floor rose a small round platform, perhaps a foot in diameter. According to the information plaque, a naked prisoner was given the choice to stand in ice-cold water, or balance on the platform. Most chose to shiver on the platform above the water. As the minutes turned to hours, as hunger and drowsiness created the desired effect, the prisoner would ultimately fall into the frigid pool and be forced to stand on the platform again.

Another door opened to a six-by-six-foot isolation cell. The recently arrested who refused to talk were tossed inside, forced to strip to their underwear, given three hundred grams of bread, a half liter of warm water, and allowed no more than five hours' sleep. Prisoners were kept in this tiny windowless room, a room with no heat, for up to seven days.

In the padded cell, a straitjacket hung from the back wall. During interrogations, the jacket arms were pulled so tight across the victim's torso, his shoulders would ultimately separate. He would then be left for hours to wither in agony, his screams absorbed by pads covering the walls and ceiling.

I didn't linger long enough to see the barn doors, beyond which dead bodies were once left to instill fear in passing locals. Didn't linger long enough to walk across the elevated glass floor to see the original blood-soaked concrete beneath it. After placing my palm on a locked steel door, behind which lay the remains of victims killed by the KGB, the proximity to horror became too much to bear. I ran down the dimly lit corridor, up the stairs, past the elderly museum attendant, who never bothered to look up.

With a heart no less anguished than the next Lithuanian who gives the *Guinness World Records* something to talk about, I stepped out onto the soggy streets of Vilnius. The drizzle had turned into a slashing rain. I unlocked the municipal bike and rode down Gedimino Prospektas. The street had all but emptied, save for a few desperate souls hunched beneath gray umbrellas. The buildings stood in shades of gray. The street had turned gray. The sidewalks. The clothes worn by previously mentioned souls. Above it all, a dark gray sky unleashed a torrent that soaked my clothes and chilled my bones. For the first time since my bicycle outing, there were no sidelong glances aimed in my direction. I moved along Gedimino Prospektas, somber and unsmiling, a black man riding an orange bike through a town devoid of color.

TROUT FISHING AND
OTHER ESTONIAN ESCAPADES

◄∙∙∙∙∙∙∙∙∙∙∙∙∙∙∙∙∙∙∙∙∙►

Triinu Onton—a six-foot, twenty-one-year-old Estonian beauty—took me fishing in her homeland. Instead of floating in an old wooden boat, our lines dangling in one of fourteen primordial lakes at Lahemaa National Park, instead of boarding a larger vessel and trawling the Baltic for herring, instead of choosing from a wide range of conventional angling options, we found ourselves standing on a grassy knoll near an isolated stretch of highway and staring into a murky man-made pond.

Looking less like a fishing hole and more like an oversized sinkhole filled with rainwater, Valkla Forell had been stocked with trout. Dozens of fattened fish swam just below the surface, waiting to be hooked by hungry patrons, cooked by the smiling proprietor, and consumed at one of several picnic tables clustered along the side of the pond. After paying a small activity fee, Triinu and I were given seven-foot fishing poles and a helping of tiny brown pellets—the kind commonly fed to hamsters and gerbils. Excited and sufficiently equipped, we took to the task of fraudulent fishing. The task ended not with a trout dangling from the end of my line, but in a flurry of violence and raw sex.

Had we been given worms for bait, it would have been easy to run the hook through its flesh and drop the squirmer into the artificial pond. But each time I tried pushing the hook through the food pellet, the rock-hard bait simply crumbled. A woman's touch, it seemed, was all that was required. Instead of jamming the pellet onto the hook as I had done, Triinu eased it onto the tip of the hook and sent me on my way.

I swung the line into the water, expecting an instantaneous bite. After all, the shallow pond was literally crammed with fish. How difficult could it be to catch one? And yet nothing happened. Not a single bite. Not even a nibble. From my position at the edge of the pond, I could actually see the pellet dangling in the water. A fat trout, maybe a three- or four-pounder, swam right up to the bait and investigated. Like a spoiled house cat presented with an undesirable snack, the trout seemed to sniff the pellet before making a U-turn and casually swimming away.

Perplexed, I lifted my line from the water, swung it a few feet to the left, and dropped the hook smack dab in the middle of a school of fish. Gills flexing, tails wiggling effortlessly as they hovered around the pellet, the trout stared dumbly for a moment and then disappeared. Perhaps they weren't so dumb after all.

Yours truly wasn't the only angler having trouble. Triinu stood a few feet away, feet wide apart, pole extended, her face a mask of Baltic concentration. On the opposite side of the artificial pond, two young ladies stood in a similar stance. Blonde, curvaceous, and strangely dressed—considering that they were fishing for trout at a murky man-made pond—their miniskirts were so incredibly tight, so impossibly short, even the subtle jerking of their fishing poles produced a view I will remember for life.

Looking as if they had just emerged from Club Hollywood (a den of techno music and iniquity in Tallinn's medieval Old Town), both ladies wore lipstick and frowns. Judging by the way they stared into the water, the frowning had been triggered by the persnickety trout, rather than the fact that their high-heel shoes were sinking into the soft earth at the edge of the pond.

Two blond men, the boyfriends no doubt, were angling unsuccessfully nearby. Out of frustration or hunger, one of the men suddenly threw his fishing pole to the ground. He picked up a different kind of pole, one with a large fishnet attached to the far end. Holding the lengthy pole, the blond Estonian carefully dipped the net into the pond. He waited a few seconds, eyes scanning the movement beneath the water's surface, and then yanked the net up and out. His unorthodox fishing technique landed a wriggling trout that neither fishhooks nor food pellets had been able to snare.

I watched in horror as the Estonian reached for a heavy wooden club—the use of which had been sanctioned by the proprietor and included in the activity fee. Holding the wriggling trout in the grass, the blond man raised the club high and brought it down with a powerful *thwack!* The trout stopped wriggling. The Estonian stood up. He carried the dead fish over to the proprietor and sat quietly at one of the picnic tables, waiting for his dinner to be served.

Triinu and I exchanged a glance. My self-appointed tour guide—a friend of a friend—Triinu had taken me to the artificial fishing pond as a spur-of-the-moment alternative to Tallinn's crowded restaurants. But dinnertime had come and gone. Our meal had yet to be procured. A sudden growling in my stomach, and the frustration in her eyes, impelled me to the most logical course of action.

Following the Estonian's lead, I tossed my fishing pole to the ground and picked up the fishing net. It was much heavier than I expected. Even with both hands grasping the thick wooden pole, I had trouble positioning the net in the water beneath an unsuspecting trout. When a victim finally wiggled within range, I yanked upward with all my might. The weight of the water stifled the snatch, however, allowing ample time for the fish to swim away.

Realizing the net had been too deep, I brought it closer to the surface, sliding it ever so stealthily beneath yet another fattened trout. With less water to clear, I snatched upward in one fluid motion and scooped up a hefty four-pounder.

Down on my knees, holding the poor wriggling creature in the grass, I raised the wooden club and closed my eyes before bringing it down. Unlike my Estonian predecessor, who had crushed his trout's skull with a single devastating blow, I only managed to tap mine on the noggin before letting go. Seizing the opportunity, the trout wriggled through the grass, heading toward water, toward life. I reached over and caught it just in time. Again, I brought down the wooden club. Again, the trout shook off the pathetic blow and tried wriggling away. A voice—deep, insistent, Estonian—suddenly came from behind. I turned to see the blond man raise an imaginary club. He nodded encouragingly and brought down his hand with a ferociousness that twice I had failed to muster. I looked to Triinu. She nodded her head. I looked across the pond to the long-legged ladies in miniskirts. They flashed beaver. Driven to the brink of madness by the pantiless duo and the vision they unwittingly provided, I swung the wooden club with the force of a sledgehammer. The trout stopped wriggling. I carried the dead fish to the proprietor and sat quietly at one of the picnic tables, waiting for dinner to be served.

Beneath a midsummer sky that refused to darken in spite of the late hour, Triinu Onton and I dined on grilled trout basted in a butter and garlic sauce. And what a tasty meal it was. As we rose from the table and walked to the car, I threw one last glance over my shoulder. The two Estonian men were long gone. But the two blondes in miniskirts remained. They stood as stiff as fenceposts at the edge of the Valkla Forell artificial pond, fishing poles dangling, faces pale and wilting, their skirts riding higher and higher.

Despite having grown up in a frigid Baltic country, weaned on *verivorst* (blood sausage), *suitsukala* (smoked fish), and hearty

Estonian folk songs, Triinu Onton burned with a passion that led her to become a spectacular salsa dancer. Such provocative dancing might have been unthinkable from 1944 to 1991, when the country endured a repressive occupation by the former Soviet Union. Had couples been caught dancing salsa during the four-year occupation by Nazi Germany (1941–44), they might have piqued the ire of Gestapo agents. But in 1991, when the yoke of Communism lifted and Estonia gained its long-awaited independence, the country began to change. The Estonian language reasserted itself after nearly five decades of subjugation. Bananas, a previously uncommon sight, appeared in abundance on the counters of new Western-style supermarkets. MTV began broadcasting, for better or worse. And on one fateful day in 1997, Miguel Verdecia arrived in Tallinn.

"I was working at the Eeslitall Hotel here in Old Town when I first saw him," Triinu said. "I walked into a ballroom and there were all these people dancing to this incredible music. A good-looking dark guy was in front, showing the dance steps to everyone."

So began Triinu's love affair. Not with Miguel (the Cuban dance instructor is married to a Finnish woman), but with salsa music, dance, and Latin culture. She took dance classes with Miguel and joined a local club for salsa devotees. She immersed herself in salsa music and practiced the dance steps relentlessly. She learned to speak Spanish fluently, thanks in part to hours spent deciphering lyrics from hundreds of salsa tunes. And while other Estonian girls her age tripped to the latest techno music, Triinu danced the night away to the music of Los Van Van, Cuba's most prolific salsa band.

The six-foot Estonian salsa queen received an e-mail from a mutual friend, "Doc" Graham—my flight attendant colleague and one of the most wordly people I know—and agreed to show me the pleasures of her country. First, there was the eye-opening evening of trout fishing. Next, as incongruent as it may seem for Estonia, came the salsa lessons. On an unseasonably warm summer day we headed not to Club Havana, a pulsating salsa hangout in the heart of Tallinn's fifteenth-century Old Town. Triinu took me instead to Pirita Beach.

Summer in Estonia is as short as the miniskirts worn by long-legged locals at man-made fishing holes. Accordingly, warm sunny days are not to be taken for granted. The beach was packed. Old women sat on blankets, their lips turned down at the corners in spite of the wonderful weather. Young girls stretched out on beach towels, their pale bodies pleading for more sun. Teenage boys stood in clusters, cigarettes dangling from crooked mouths. Elderly men paced the shoreline, hands folded behind their backs, their bare feet trudging through clumps of seaweed that littered the beach for as far as the eye could see. Children built castles in the sand. Armies of six-foot nymphs, their bodies sculpted from white marble, rose from their blankets and towels to wade in the icy Baltic waters.

Aside from the curious sidelong looks I received for being the darkest person on the beach, what stood out most as Triinu and I sat down in an unoccupied patch of sand was a deep and utterly profound silence. I heard no cries, joyous or otherwise, from the children. No shouts from the teenage boys. No sudden bursts of laughter from the girls. Private conversations failed to even register as whispers on my sonar. It was as if I were watching a Travel Channel segment about Baltic beaches and someone pressed the "mute" button on the remote.

All that changed when we met up, as planned, with Miguel Verdecia. Triinu pointed to her erstwhile salsa instructor as he walked the beach alongside Carlos Correa, a fellow Cuban salsa instructor. Miguel waved to us from more than a hundred yards away. A flash of color in a sea of whiteness, I had been easy to spot, even at a distance. So were they.

A small group of salsa acolytes accompanied Miguel and Carlos—four or five Estonian women and a couple of Estonian men. Triinu traded kisses with all of them and then introduced me. Interestingly enough, the Cuban government had sent Miguel from Havana to Moscow to train as an airline pilot. Somehow he ended up in Helsinki, where he married a lovely Finn and opened Baila Baila, Finland's premier Latin dance school. Carlos trained in Moscow as well. An engineer by trade, he, too, ended up in Helsinki and took a job as a dance instructor at Baila Baila. Then there was Katlin, a drop-dead gorgeous Estonian with jet-black hair down to her waist. Katlin worked at a local car wash. Jana, a platinum blonde, one of Triinu's closest friends, worked as a lawyer, I believe. I don't remember all the names, or the particular connections to Triinu, but I do remember the Russian girl. Antonina was her name.

Due to cultural differences and the legacy of Russian occupation, Estonians and Russians don't normally mix. Before World War II, Russians made up only 4 percent of the Estonian population. But after the war, and the large-scale industrialization that took hold in the Baltics, the Soviet government encouraged its citizens to migrate to Estonia. Some 30 percent of the population is now Russian. Generally speaking, Russians party with Russians. Estonians party with Estonians. Russians tend to keep Russian friends. Estonians are inclined to befriend one another. (I once asked an Estonian what she thought of Russians. "They are all thieves," she said. I posed the same question to a Russian. His response? "Estonians, they are so stupid.")

This is one reason I so vividly remember Antonina. She was the only Russian in the group. An ethnic minority. Someone whose position I could relate to. Besides, she had tremendous tits. A mutual love for salsa had brought her to our seaside gathering on Pirita Beach. When the music began, whatever differences existed began to melt away.

Carlos, the showman, popped a salsa CD into a boom box. The

unmistakable voice of Celia Cruz exploded above the previously quiet sands of Pirita Beach. Surrounded by hundreds of stone-faced beachgoers on that bright and sunny Saturday afternoon, Carlos grabbed Triinu by the hand. The smiling Cuban pulled the willing Estonian to his chest. So began our salsa beach party.

Carlos gently pushed Triinu away, and then spun her around as if she were a human gyroscope. They swung each other around the sand like exasperated lovers. The two expert dancers embraced, spun away, embraced again. In perfect tune to the electrifying music, Carlos wiggled his hips playfully against Triinu's. She moved effortlessly back and forth, following his lead, wiggling her hips with savage reciprocity, churning her feet in that constant, sensuous, rhythmic combustion that is salsa.

By this time, Miguel and Katlin had gotten into the act. Soviet-trained airline pilots aren't known for their gracefulness on the dance floor, whether it's composed of sand or polished wood, but Miguel proved to be an exception. He was smoothness personified. Barely kicking up the sand, he spun Katlin around so often and with such dizzying speed, her long black hair sliced through the air like helicopter blades.

The two Estonian men displayed none of the showmanship of the two Cubans, but they moved with a technical proficiency that their salsa instructors, Carlos and Miguel, could be proud of.

Of the three remaining females, two leapt from the sand. One joined Carlos and Triinu, the other merged with Miguel and Katlin. Two salsa threesomes. One salsa beat. Never before have two men handled four women so effortlessly and so well.

That left Antonina and me.

The big-breasted Russian girl reached for my hand. Moving with the passion of a Venezuelan stripper, Antonina managed to awaken a certain part of my anatomy, but could not rouse my slumbering feet. Holding my hips, she tried to guide me through the one-two-three, one-two-three, back-and-forth basic salsa movements. Given time to practice, perhaps I would not have stepped on her feet so often. Had I been able to understand either the Russian or Estonian she hurled at me so eagerly, perhaps I would have been able to follow instructions. If two thousand blank-faced Estonians had not been staring from their beach towels, perhaps I would have been able to handle the pressure.

Frustrated by my inability to perform, Antonina stopped moving and gave me one of those looks. The same pitying look a woman offers her lover when his johnson won't rise to the occasion. My johnson works just fine, thank you very much. It's my feet that occasionally fail me.

After an afternoon of sweat-dripping salsa dancing (I watched from a beach blanket along with throngs of astonished Estonians while Carlos, Triinu, Miguel, Antonina, and the rest of the group kicked up the sand), Triinu's father pulled up in an unassuming vehicle and picked up the two of us from the beach parking lot. Triinu and I were just friends, a platonic pair brought together by the high-speed ferry from Helsinki and an e-mail from a mutual friend. But her father did not know the boundaries of our relationship. His twenty-one-year-old daughter was in the company of a man twice her age—a stranger from the West, a "dark" one at that—and yet he smiled warmly and invited me into the car, chatting happily to his daughter in their native Estonian.

Imagine what might have transpired had I been in the United States, the state of Utah, for example. Instead of spending an afternoon on the shores of the Baltic with a twenty-one-year-old Estonian brunette called Triinu, imagine I had just spent an afternoon on the shores of the Great Salt Lake with a twenty-one-year-old American blonde named Trish. Instead of shaking my hand and smiling pleasantly as Mr. Onton had done here in Estonia, Trish's dad would have had a conniption. Even though Trish and I were just friends.

Further complicating matters was the fact that Triinu had taken it upon herself to invite me to an intimate gathering in the Estonian countryside. It was her grandfather's eightieth birthday. His family and friends were at this very moment descending upon the isolated farmhouse he shares with his wife, unaware that a stranger was about to crash the party. Had *Trish* and I been heading toward a gathering of country folk in the sticks of Utah, I would have thought twice about attending. On second thought, I might never have been invited in the first place.

As it turned out, Triinu, her father, and I were the first to arrive. We pulled up to a small wooden house, pale yellow paint flaking from the weathered slats. Several tables, upon which sat cellophaned platters of food, had been erected in the yard among vines and blooming flowers. As the car engine died and we slammed closed the doors, out of the house came Ferdinand Tammekivi.

A spry octogenarian if ever there was one, Triinu's grandfather wore a plain white T-shirt that could not contain his protruding belly. He was a tall man. A few inches above six feet, perhaps. Age and a slightly hunched back could not completely hide the strong, brawny man he no doubt was in his youth. Suspenders looped around his wide, sloping shoulders. A smile spread across his ruddy face. Having yet to finish dressing for his birthday party, he hugged his granddaughter, traded greetings with his son, and then stood before me, his eyes warm and expressive. "*Tere päevast*," he said, extending his massive hand. The newly anointed eighty-year-old nearly crushed my tiny mitt as he pumped it three times and ushered me into his house.

The house was littered with empty liquor bottles. Pints, fifths, half gallons, liters. I saw an empty bottle on the dining-room table. Bottles lining the kitchen sink. Triinu's grandmother, Elfriede Tammekivi, a friendly hostess in her own right, greeted me with kisses as if I were her own grandson, and then pointed to the bathroom at my request. I stood in front of the toilet, relieving myself, staring at a liquor bottle on top of the commode. The empty bottle bore the same label as all the others. It read: OLD FERDINAND. On the label, directly below the name, was a photograph of an elderly man, his warm eyes and ruddy cheeks unmistakable beneath a furry Russian hat. Ferdinand Tammekivi, it turned out, was the producer, purveyor, and marketing genius behind his own brand of moonshine whiskey.

I emerged from the bathroom only to be met by Ferdinand Tammekivi's long extended arm, at the end of which he held a shot glass filled to the brim with homemade Estonian whiskey. He nodded anxiously, the way people do when they want you to try something they know you'll enjoy. I took a tiny sip, barely tasting the robust whiskey. Ferdinand's eyes grew wide with disbelief. "*Ei, ei,*" he said, shaking his head and motioning for me to drink the whole thing. I held the glass between my thumb and forefinger, said a silent prayer, and tossed back an ounce of Old Ferdinand. The homemade firewater set my chest ablaze.

The coughing fit that followed did not dampen Ferdinand's enthusiasm for sharing moonshine alcohol. As I stood there gagging in the living room, he snatched my shot glass and filled it again. Apparently, the eighty-year-old whiskey aficionado knew how to party.

Eyes wet with tears, a second killer shot of Old Ferdinand in my hand, I was led into the bedroom by a gushing Elfriede Tammekivi. She pointed to the bed, a notion that sobered me instantly, considering the fact that a beautiful Estonian blonde was sitting there. "This is my sister, Kille," Triinu announced from behind. Kille nodded, smiled a little more, continued stroking the little gray pussycat she held in her lap. There were more little pussies in a box on the side of the bed. Kille gestured to them and smiled.

Elfriede's gushing had nothing to do with her granddaughter, as it turned out. According to Triinu's translation, the Tammekivis had just bought a brand-new bed. The Estonian grandmother was proud of the acquisition. Elfriede pointed again, smiling and nodding her head. She pressed one hand down on the mattress, as if to prove its worthiness and motioned for Triinu and me to sit.

Wedged between the stunningly beautiful Triinu Onton and her equally appealing eighteen-year-old sister, Kille, I sat on the Tammekivis' new mattress, feeling a bit out of sorts. Wiping her weathered hands with an embroidered towel, Elfriede Tammekivi retreated to the doorway, pride beaming in her eyes as the three of us sat together on the bed. "Yes, yes," she seemed to be saying to me, nodding enthusiastically and prattling away in Estonian. "Enjoy my bed. Enjoy my granddaughters. Enjoy the pussies." Without seeming to detect the slightest sense of impropriety, Elfriede Tammekivi, Estonian homemaker and the grandmother of at least two, sauntered out of the bedroom and closed the door behind her, leaving a depraved American on the bed with her beloved progeny.

Sandwiched between two nubile girls on a brand-new bed—the pride and joy of Ferdinand and Elfriede Tammekivi—I felt the sudden need for that shot of Old Ferdinand. I tossed it back, shut my eyes, endured that burning sensation as the liquor rolled like lava down my throat. As my belly and conscience were consumed by flames, I leapt from the bed as if *it* were on fire and stood gallantly by the bedroom door.

"What is wrong?" Triinu asked, her voice soft and innocent as she and Kille stroked the little gray kitten. Both girls looked up at me, their wide doelike eyes blinking steadily, foreheads pinched and furrowed.

"Don't you think this is a little strange?" I said, looking down at both of them.

"What?" Triinu said.

"You know, your grandmother leaving the three of us alone . . . in her bedroom . . . on the bed."

The sisters exchanged a curious look. They obviously had no idea what I was talking about.

"What are you talking about?" Triinu said.

Eastern European innocence and the jaded Westerner. Somebody should write a book on the subject. As the three of us left the bedroom and walked outside, all I could do was shake my head and wonder.

More than two dozen people had gathered in the yard. Friends, family members, acquaintances from the nearby Harju village. Triinu's mother was there, as was her mother's mother, a frail woman less than five feet tall. During the Russian occupation, Triinu's grandmother spent four years in a Siberian work camp. There was a man playing the accordion. Wearing white shoes and an even whiter smile, the lean, attractive Estonian Pat Boone roamed among the guests, squeezing his instrument and singing warmhearted Estonian folk songs.

When Triinu, Kille, and I emerged from the house, all eyes locked on yours truly. A flurry of conversation, none of which I could understand, buzzed between the wafting accordion rhythms. I was presented to a virtual receiving line of guests, each of whom shook my hand, smiled warmly, and greeted me in Estonian. We munched on *verivorst*—the blood sausage tasted gummy, but not bad at all—but were spared the horrors of other blood-related Estonian goodies such as *verileib* (blood bread) and *verikäkk*. Made with clots of blood and pieces of pig fat rolled together in flour and eggs, *verikäkk* remains a culinary adventure in which I will never participate.

And we drank rivers of Old Ferdinand.

When one of Triinu's relatives, a pilot for a local airline, found out that I, too, was an airline employee, he carried over a half-gallon bottle of Old Ferdinand and traded shots with me. One gulp. Two. Three. "Stop!" My head was spinning. The booze and the blood sausage were too much for me. But the Estonian pilot seemed unfazed by the liquor. He tossed back another shot, took my empty glass, and poured me another one.

I sat on a wooden bench holding the sloshing shot, dizzy as a dingbat, while the pilot held the bottle in front of my face. With one stubby finger, he pointed to four words printed in the corner of the label. I squinted through a drunken fog, unable to make out the words—perhaps because they were written in Estonian:

MAHT = VARIEERUV
KANGUS = PIISAV

CAPACITY: VARIES
STRENGTH: SUFFICIENT

When the pilot turned to place the bottle on the table, I dumped the rotgut whiskey in the grass.

The accordionist squeezed off a sour note, halting the music momentarily. The chatter died down. The blood sausage stopped bleeding. My world stopped spinning, if only for a moment. We lifted our glasses to Ferdinand Tammekivi (yes, the pilot poured me a refill), who now stood on the lawn, surrounded by the people who loved him. The accordionist played a lovely melody, at which the newly crowned eighty-year-old blushed. You didn't need to speak Estonian to understand the Happy Birthday lyrics. But when the accordionist broke out with a folk song to which everyone sang, and the Old Ferdinand whiskey continued to flow, you needed to be Estonian to drink another shot without falling flat on your butt.

BLACK RUSSIAN

A fter reading alarming news articles in the *Los Angeles Times*, I worried about traveling to Russia. Xenophobia appeared to be alive and well and running rampant through the streets of Moscow. Not a good situation for a person of color. "Whenever I come in contact with a guy, I either get hit on or spit on," said University of Nebraska student Leonna Griffin, an African American from Bellevue, Nebraska, who spent her junior year at the Moscow Linguistic University and Moscow International University. Jeannot-Michel Abessolo, a thirty-one-year-old doctoral candidate from West Africa, has been "spat on, beaten, scorned and otherwise insulted nearly every day, and often several times a day." Ugandan pharmacology student Hannington Ssenynonjo spent twelve days in the hospital after being attacked in a subway car by more than twenty Russian youths. When Jules Rakotondravoavy, an immigrant from Madagascar, went out one night to buy milk for his infant daughter, "he was jumped from behind and beaten." His Russian wife, Yelena, echoed the sentiments of liberal Russians. "I am ashamed of my own people," she said.

Racially motivated assaults have become so widespread in Moscow that the Kenyan Embassy provided the Russian government with the names of twenty-three countrymen attacked during a one-year span. Among the names were those of two Kenyan diplomats, as well as the ambassador's own son.

In spite of the *Los Angeles Times* article and the Kenyan Embassy's list and the uneasy feeling in my gut, I found myself in Russia, the only black face among the pallid crowds moving along the sidewalk on Nevsky Prospekt, the busiest boulevard in St. Petersburg. Within minutes I was accosted by a Russian thug. He came at me beneath the multicolored onion domes of the Church of the Resurrection of Christ, the same spot where Alexander II got whacked in 1881. I had been standing there, admiring the Byzantine architecture, the sacred frescoes, the outrageously vivid domes that seemed to have leapt from the pages of a Russian candy catalogue, when suddenly I found myself face to face with a tough-looking badass called Boris. That was his name. Really. When the muscles in his forehead relaxed, he tapped his own chest. "Boris," he said, in the thickest of Russian accents. Then he pointed to a girl standing on the sidewalk a few feet away. She stood there demurely, hands behind her back, eyes wide and hopeful. Boris smiled, revealing two shiny gold teeth among his pearly whites. In the next instant, he whipped out a camera.

Judging by their awkwardness (the two Russians stumbled about, looking lost among the bustling urban masses), the three gold teeth (the girl had one too), the handy camera, and the communicative gestures, Boris and his girlfriend were visiting from the Russian countryside. He wanted me to take their photograph. But when I reached for the camera, Boris snatched it away and motioned to his girlfriend.

Dozens of pedestrians threw passing sidelong glances as the girlfriend rushed over on the crowded sidewalk. She said something to me in Russian. Something sweet and deliciously indecipherable. Right then and there I realized that Russian, along with Italian and Brazilian Portuguese, ranks among the world's sexiest languages. As if to prove the point, Boris's girlfriend laid her head against my chest the way a lover would. Boris nodded approvingly, his gold teeth glinting in the summer sun. As he pointed the camera and pressed the shutter, his girlfriend kissed me on the cheek. So forceful were her lips, so warm and passionate her embrace, I worried that Boris's smile would turn into a grimace.

Instead, Boris threw a tree trunk of an arm around my pencil neck. We stood there on Nevsky Prospekt—the most storied avenue in St. Petersburg and perhaps in all of Russia—arms around one another, smiling, a picture of interracial solidarity in a woefully intolerant land. With the camera in the capable hands of his girlfriend, Boris gave a thumbs-up and flashed his gold-tooth smile. I noticed that his huge hands were swollen and scarred. They were the hands of a workman. Or a brawler.

"*Spasiba*," he said, pumping my hand when we finished posing. "*Nichevo*," I replied. (I knew exactly two words in Russian: *spasiba* [thank you], and *nichevo* [no problem], and was happy to have traded both in our two-word conversation.) Boris gently squeezed my shoulder and smiled again. His girlfriend waved good-bye and took Boris by the hand. A moment later they merged with a stream of Russians rushing inexorably down Nevsky Prospekt.

Peter Blandori shook his head. "Jeez," was all he could manage. Although my Italian-American travel buddy had been standing next to me when Boris and his girlfriend approached, they completely ignored him. Peter was obviously a foreigner, and yet the Russians never asked him to pose with them for a photograph. They never gestured to him or even seemed to acknowledge his existence. They had been fascinated, instead, by my skin color. A fascination that—depending upon who was doing the looking—could just as easily elicit a gob of spit or a flurry of nationalistic fists.

We continued down Nevsky Prospekt, two foreigners among thousands of silent pedestrians: thickset *babushkas* wearing drab scarves and carrying plastic bags; clusters of uniformed Russian sailors; shirtless teenage boys; jacketed businessmen; and dozens upon dozens of tall, shapely, posture-perfect women whose outfits left nothing to the imagination. A blonde in form-fitting powder-blue shorts sucking on a lollipop. A brunette in a tank top, the word CHICAGO stretched phonetically across her swollen chest. Women in translucent blouses and spotless white slacks and miniskirts through which thongs were clearly visible. Nevsky Prospekt is not only the city's shopping and entertainment hub, it is a 4.7-kilometer fashion catwalk.

Move over, *Babushka*. Thanks to *glasnost* and Gorbachev, Russian women have a whole new attitude.

In front of the Stroganov Palace, where Beef Stroganoff was invented by a French chef in the mid-1700s, two women separated from the throngs and pounced. Mere mortals in comparison to some of the supermodels strutting down the sidewalk, they rushed toward me, pleading in Russian. One of the ladies produced a camera while the other nodded excitedly. When I shrugged and smiled, they handed poor Peter the camera. Two adorable Russian girls held me in their arms. Two firm kisses were delivered, one on each cheek. The camera flashed. One of the women snatched the camera from Peter without acknowledging his efforts. Holding the camera between them, the two women skipped away like giddy twelve-year-olds. I'd never experienced anything like it. Neither had Peter, apparently. Having been snubbed again, he was beginning to develop a complex.

Time and time again, people came at me on Nevsky Prospekt, thrusting their smiles and cameras. Women. Men. Teenage boys and girls. It was the skinheads of Moscow that posed a racist threat. Not the curious folks along Nevsky Prospekt in sunny St. Petersburg.

I posed for photos in front of the Literary Café, where Alexander Pushkin—Russia's most beloved poet, the great-grandson of an Ethiopian slave—ate his last meal before being mortally wounded in a duel. Sandwiched between a grinning father and daughter, I smiled beneath the glimmering spire of the Admiralty, headquarters of the Russian navy between 1711 and 1917. Cameras flashed in front of a subway station, in front of eleven Cyrillic newspapers at a newsstand, on the stone bridge traversing the murky Griboedova Canal. And when Peter and I walked into a Nevsky nightclub later that same night, attention focused on me again. This time the action was more stimulating.

I had been leaning against the wall next to Peter, drinking a beer, listening to the music, and watching women on the dance floor. Dressed in miniskirts and high heels, an army of Russian nymphs moved with an erotic energy you rarely see at nightclubs in the United States. Unless, of course, you happen to be in a strip club. Tall and gorgeous, blonde or brunette, the Russian women danced with each other, or alone, gyrating suggestively, hands tracing the curve of their own hips, backs arched, lips parting, breasts angled upward like Tomahawk cruise missiles set to launch. It was the ultimate male fantasy. A lesbian's dream come true. When a supermodel-caliber brunette walked up to me and smiled, I thought I'd died and gone to Victoria's Secret.

"*Privet,*" she said. Beautiful, braless, and wearing a translucent blouse that made my pupils dilate each time the disco lights blinked, she held me in an icy green-eyed gaze. So shocked was I by her sudden appearance, so mesmerized by the fullness of her lips, the warmth of her smile, the perfect teeth, the hair, the perfectly symmetrical six-foot, two-inch impossibly curvaceous frame upon which a pair of skintight pants had been painted, I simply stood there and stared.

"*Privet,*" she repeated, her sultry voice minimized by the thumping dance music.

Something in her eyes set off a silent alarm. The steadiness of her gaze, maybe. Perhaps the manner in which she blinked. But in the very intense heat of the moment, the warning failed to register. What did register, however, was the sudden shift in attitude among the patrons. A couple of stone-faced Russian guys, dressed in black leather jackets (even though it was nearly eighty degrees outside), leaned from their bar stools and glared at us. Miscellaneous men, their faces hard and unsmiling, peered through the crowd. Two women turned around, smiling, their eyebrows raised. Everyone seemed interested in the white Russian girl and the black American guy together in the corner near the dance floor.

"*Privet,*" I replied, finally, having no clue as to what I had said.

The brunette spoke to me in urgent Russian. Nodding eagerly as if fluent in her language, I listened instead to a voice of my own. *The two guys in leather jackets look like the jealous type. Leave now. Forget about the girl. Grab hold of Peter, sprint toward the exit, and don't look back. Leave now, or you'll be sorry.* But I didn't leave. Captured by beauty, motivated by much more than wanderlust, I stood in the face of red lipstick and danger, trying my best to communicate.

Unable to compete with the blaring music, the brunette took my hand and led me through a curtained doorway and into a lounge area. Along the way, I threw a look over my shoulder at Peter. He shook his head. "Bastard," I could almost hear him say. The men in leather jackets were shaking their heads as well. I don't know the Russian word for "bastard." But whatever it is, I'm sure they used it in reference to me (and not in the same playful spirit as Peter).

Even without the music, I could barely communicate with the brunette, who called herself Elena. When she finally realized I spoke only English, Elena sighed and rolled her eyes. "Me no sex you," she said, almost apologetically. "Me friend." It was a line from page one of *The International Player's Manual*: "*No, really, I don't want to sleep with you* [insert name here], *I just want to be your friend.*" But men were usually the ones who used that hackneyed line on women. Not the other way around. Beautiful women need only put on an outfit like the one Elena wore so well. Nature usually takes its course from there.

So why did Elena want to be my "friend"? Was she looking for someone with whom to practice English? Or was she looking for something altogether different?

I pondered these questions as Elena's mobile phone rang. *"Da,"* she said, nodding sluggishly, her lips a marvel of genetic flawlessness. *"Da . . . da."* She spoke briskly, holding my hand until finishing her conversation. Looking straight into my eyes, her voice became insistent. "Me no sex you," she said, again. "Me friend." This was her English repertoire. The only way she knew to ease whatever concerns I might have. And yet somehow I understood that she wanted me to go with her.

"Where?" I said, willing to go anywhere.

Russian. Russian. More indecipherable Russian. Elena pointed to the exit. With one long, graceful, meticulously manicured hand, she made a motion to indicate that we could drive somewhere. Somewhere private. It was wrong. I knew it was wrong. I felt the wrongness deep down in my gut. But standing before the sumptuous Russian temptress, and the erotic possibilities she presented, being right was the last thing on my mind.

Arrangements needed to be made. Taxi, private car, bus, horseback, whatever. But no matter how desperately we tried to communicate, the language barrier kept getting in the way. Frustrated, Elena released a great sigh. She rolled her eyes, shook her stunning head, and then kissed me on the lips. She apologized, or so it seemed, and then walked away, leaving me amid a sea of peering eyes to contemplate the night that could have been.

Postscript: After relating the incident to a Russian tour guide the following morning, I was told that Elena was probably a prostitute, a thief, or both. It's not uncommon for an enterprising woman to lure a foreigner from a nightclub to an obscure apartment where the unsuspecting lover boy is drugged, robbed, in some cases beaten to a pulp by a male accomplice, stripped naked, and left in the street.

Western Europe

SAUNA PARTY

When I arrived in Helsinki, Doc Graham, my airline colleague and occasional travel comrade, was there to meet me. Smiling, carefree, his bleached-blond head incongruous with his African-American complexion, Doc possessed an invitation to a Finnish picnic that, according to him, promised to be "off the friggin' hook." (Doc neither drank nor used profanity, qualities I have so far been unable to forswear.) The day-long outing was an annual affair hosted by employees from a certain Scandinavian airline, the name of which will not be mentioned due to the dubious events of that day.

On the appointed morning, Doc and I showed up at Eteläsatama Harbor, where a plethora of sea craft, small and large, prepared to transport passengers on harbor cruises or excursions to Tallinn and Stockholm. Our prepaid admission to the picnic included the round-trip boat ride from the mainland to a small secluded island some forty-five minutes away in the Gulf of Finland. There we would be entitled to all the booze a human being could possibly consume in one day.

We boarded a bright red double-decker craft filled with maybe seventy smiling people, most of whom were employed as cabin crew and office staff at the unmentionable Scandinavian airline. There were representatives from other airlines as well. Two subdued couples (the only other black folks in the bunch) from Air Jamaica; delegates from Swissair and KLM. Doc and I were the only personnel representing a U.S. airline, which, for the same reasons as the Scandinavian carrier, will remain nameless.

It was a picture-perfect day. The kind of warm summer day that would make Finns jump for joy, if not for their lack of self-expression. The sun shone brightly, its rays glancing off the harbor in shimmering golden sheets. In spite of the early hour (scarcely after 10:00 A.M.), half the passengers were already drinking beer. Alcohol, I soon learned, is the elixir from which Finnish self-expression spouts.

I sat on the crowded top deck while Doc mingled with friends below. A tall, attractive Finnish woman sat down in the empty seat beside me. She wore bright pink lipstick. Her carefully sculpted fingernails were coated in glossy pink nail polish. She carried a tiny pink purse. To complete the ensemble, her Nokia mobile phone had been covered in a matching pink case. Finnish Barbie. The epitome of garish coordination. In spite of the outfit, or perhaps because of it, she was as polite and composed as a woman could be.

"You are American, yes?" she said.

"You are Finnish, no?" I replied.

And so the day began.

As it turned out, Finnish Barbie was employed as a flight attendant for the unmentionable Scandinavian airline. When our boat began chugging away from shore, she launched into a litany of complaints, beginning with Scandinavian winters ("They are depressing") and ending with pontifications about European airline food ("For the most part, it is good") versus food on American carriers ("It is shit"). By the time we docked on the island, Finnish Barbie had already downed two beers.

The wooded island seemed deserted, save for a small wooden shack and a concrete platform—a remnant of the house that burned to the ground the previous summer. The house was disposable. The wooden shack was not. It housed the all-important sauna, the entertainment base around which the picnic revolved. There would be no music. No sack races. Barely any food. The sauna would be the main event. The sauna, along with copious drinking.

After disembarking, it became apparent what the twenty-dollar price tag had afforded each guest. Liquor. Lots of it. Cases of it. Beer and alcoholic cider. Bottles of wine, gallon jugs of wine, even those waxy boxes of wine that you only see in European liquor stores. There were containers of vodka and whiskey and seemingly anything else that could be poured into a plastic cup and consumed.

Doc and I spent the first hour or so sitting on the edge of the concrete platform talking shop with our Finnish colleagues. He sipped orange juice while I worked on an alcoholic cider. Finnish Barbie, in all her pink magnificence, began hitting the vodka bottle as if it were Evian. The pink lips that once moved with such crispness had already come unglued. Within no time she had completely lost her composure. I watched her stagger over to the picnic table. She picked up a wine bottle and contemplated the label with one squinting eye. With a suddenness that made everyone in the vicinity jump, she dropped the bottle on the table with a *thunk!* In the end, she poured herself another vodka and was soon rip-roaring drunk.

Finnish Barbie wasn't the only person stumbling around the island that day. A blonde woman who may or may not have been an airline employee staggered backward and fell over a log. Thirty minutes earlier, she had been as prim and proper as an ambassador's wife. Now she was lying in the dirt, legs sprawling, crisp white panties in full view of seventy Finns, none of whom so much as batted an eye. One man tottered into the woods, never to be seen again. A woman sat in the dirt, staring at the Baltic as if hypnotized. Never before had I seen conservatism slip so quickly into outrageousness. I chuckled and headed for the sauna.

The Finnish sauna is a national institution. At last count, some 1,212,000 saunas were operating in private apartments. Another 800,000 had been installed in summer cottages and at public swimming pools. Before alcohol rendered nearly every picnicker mute, every one I talked to claimed to have access to a sauna at a summer cottage. With more than 2 million saunas gushing steam in a country of only slightly more than 5 million, Finland boasts the world's highest human-to-sauna ratio. Morning, noon, and night, locals can be seen tramping to and from a sauna. In summer and in the dead of winter. So dedicated are Finns to the art of getting naked in a steamy enclosure, Finnish soldiers have been known to build tent saunas during military maneuvers.

I walked into the changing room, stripped, and wrapped a towel around my waist. Somehow, I couldn't do the naked sauna thing with strangers. I walked into the steamy sauna just as a plump male flight attendant poured water over the coals. Inside the sauna sat six men and women. All were naked except me. The chubby male flight attendant took it upon himself to flog one of the women with a birch branch. Then he came over to me. "Don't worry," he said. "This is the Finnish way."

He smacked me on the back with the branch. The idea, according to my *Lonely Planet Finland* guide, is that a flailing birch branch opens the blood vessels. You were to sit in the boiling heat as long as humanly possible, while somebody spanked you with a birch branch. When you could stand no more, when you seemed ready to pass out from heat exhaustion, you were to exit the sauna, sprint naked down the wooden pier, and hurl yourself into the frigid Baltic Sea. The chubby guy did it. The girls did it, too. When my turn came, I toweled off and got dressed.

After most of the alcohol had been consumed, and many of my airline colleagues were stumbling around the island like extras in a zombie flick, I returned to the changing room to look for my towel. There I saw something that made me stop and stare. The blonde woman, who may or may not have been an airline employee, was lying on a bench, as naked as the day is long, her ankles pinned behind her ears by a middle-aged man who pumped his pelvis into hers as if operating on hydraulics. Instead of moaning and groaning, as you might expect spur-of-the-moment lovers to do, instead of panting and grunting, they were laughing. They were not caught in the throes of passion. They were laughing, for crissakes! They laughed as if they were playing Twister and the blonde woman slipped and fell on the blond guy's dick. *Ooops! Hee, hee, hee. I have fallen on your penis, Erik. I think I will fall again. Ohh . . . I like falling. Falling is much fun. Hee, hee, hee.*

I stood there, unable to believe what I was seeing. This wasn't a part of the Finnish sauna tradition. My guidebook specifically states that the sauna is "not, as many foreigners would believe, a place for sex." I plan on contacting the editors to suggest a rewrite for the next edition.

When my paralysis finally broke, I stumbled outside, stunned and the slightest bit jealous. Among the sloshed and swaying masses I saw Finnish Barbie. She stumbled around like a punch-drunk Rocky Balboa, refusing to go down for the count. Perhaps she was looking for her pink mobile phone or her pink purse inside of which she would undoubtedly produce a bottle of pink nail polish to redo the paint job that had been ruined by the makers of Absolut.

A few minutes before boarding the double-decker boat, a woman walked up and handed me a drink. We had barely spoken during the picnic. Unlike most of the others, she seemed lucid and relatively sober. When the time came to board the boat, we sat together on the lower level, talking about nothing in particular. Moments later, Finnish Barbie came stumbling in and plopped down on the seat across from us. Legs gaped open, hair like frozen fur, she threw a drunken glare that sent shivers up my spine. Gone was the composure she'd worn so well that morning. Gone was the crispness and the little pink purse. She muttered something in Finnish and promptly passed out.

As the boat chugged across the Gulf of Finland toward Eteläsatama Harbor, a commotion brought everyone on the lower level to their feet. Everyone except Finnish Barbie, that is. While everyone else craned their necks to see what was happening, the pink princess snored with the vigor of a Nordic beast.

The skipper's angry shouts had been directed at two people. The only two people crazy enough to brave the early evening chill on the exposed upper deck. A man and a woman. Both blond. Both naked. The blonde woman may or may not have been an airline employee. During pauses between the skipper's unheeded commands, we could hear the man and woman laughing.

INSIDE THE EROTIK MUSEUM

On April 30, 1945, the same day Adolf Hitler blew his own brains out in a Berlin bunker, Captain Beate Uhse, a female Luftwaffe pilot, leapt into an airplane with her two-year-old son, a nurse, and a wounded mechanic, and flew from Berlin to the northern region of Schleswig-Holstein. When British troops arrived a few days later, Captain Uhse's aircraft became one of the first to have its swastika painted over. As was the case with all German pilots after World War II, the not-so-noble sky-girl had her piloting privileges unceremoniously revoked.

Hungry, unemployed, and burdened with a young child, the enterprising single mom came up with an idea. Determined to provide German women with a choice, Fräulein Beate Uhse began distributing "Script X" birth control advice, which soon expanded into a mail-order business. From these humble beginnings she built the world's largest and most successful adult-entertainment empire. Today, the Beate Uhse Group boasts more than eleven hundred sex-industry employees in more than a dozen European cities.

Fräulein Uhse has since departed to that great porno distributorship in the sky, but her multimillion-dollar sex empire remains. It boasts publishing and video divisions, a thriving mail-order section, a sex museum, and a nationwide network of more than eighty Beate Uhse Erotik stores, into one of which I so innocently stumbled one fine summer day, while walking along Joachimstaler Strasse in downtown Berlin. The kinky mannequins in the window had caught my attention. Clad in black leather shorts and spiked dog collars, they jumped out and dragged me, kicking and screaming, into a twisted German sex world.

Up and down the darkened aisles I walked, gawking at porno magazines, kinky sex toys, and XXX adult videos with inspirational titles like *German Goo Girls, Willie Wanker & the Fudge Packing Factory, Dude Where's My Dildo?* and my personal favorite: *Hung Wankenstein.* Hung had been blessed—or cursed, depending on how you look at it—with a massive twelve-inch schlong.

Among the more interesting sex contraptions was a boxed kit with the words COPY DICK emblazoned on the front. "Cast a copy of your own dick," the ad copy announced. I picked up the box and read on. Through crude illustrations and simple text, I learned how to "pour the nontoxic liquid on your hardened member and end up with your own COPY DICK!" The three-step instructions seemed simple enough:

1. Cast a plaster mold of your erection
2. Mix the silicone compound
3. Remove the mold, and here's your COPY DICK!

I'm sure COPY DICK wows the crowds at Berlin house parties. Especially when Hung Wankenstein pours the silicone.

From the sublime to the inflatable, I soon found myself in the blow-up doll section. Amid the rubberized blondes and brunettes, their lipsticked mouths open in the traditional "O," Tyrone, the "dark Latin stud," stood out. The only guy in the crowd, Tyrone appeared to have been misplaced. I thought of flagging down a sales clerk to have the Latin stud moved to a more appropriate section. But instead of doing so, I picked up the box. According to the ad copy, Tyrone was

> A new and improved version of your favorite stud. A fantastic lover for her (or him, come to that). Dark eyes, black hair, trained body, and impressive penis—20 stiff centimeters long, open mouth and rear orifice. He is always ready to leap into sexual action for you.

I burst out laughing, wondering how any human being—male or female, straight or gay, German or otherwise—could become aroused by inflatable plastic. Realizing the impropriety of my sudden outburst, I scanned my surroundings, hoping that none of the smattering of customers had noticed me. Somebody did. He wasn't laughing.

Perusing the handcuffs and leg chains farther down the aisle was a tall, muscular man with spiked white hair. He wore a leather vest, crisp new jeans, and looked exactly like Billy Idol (if Billy had fallen asleep for maybe five hours in a sun-tanning machine). The man's skin glowed a sickly reddish-orange. His face erupted in a network of wrinkles that made him look even scarier when he smiled. And when his greedy eyes fell upon me, tearing at my T-shirt, burning into my crotch, I had to stifle an impulse to run. Why me? Why had I suddenly popped up on his gaydar? Then it hit me. I was standing in an aisle in Germany's most popular sex shop, holding a box containing Tyrone, the amazing lover who "is always ready to leap into sexual action." My interest in Ty had been purely platonic. Judging by the way Billy Idol looked at me, however, he thought me and old Ty were two peas in the same kinky plastic pod.

What better time to evacuate the Beate Uhse Erotik Store and meander to the Beate Uhse Erotik Museum on the third floor? I tossed Tyrone into the row of inflatable dolls and hurried to the elevator. When the doors opened on the third floor, I stepped out—too quickly, in retrospect—and was nearly impaled on a huge penis protruding from a naked statue. Beate Uhse apparently had a wicked sense of humor.

Softly lit, like any other meticulous museum display floor, the room was filled with Asian sex art: elaborately carved Balinese fertility demons, etchings of female genitalia, sexually explicit sculptures, kinky Indian miniatures, and giant tortoise-shell dildos capable of inflicting serious damage on anyone foolish enough to appreciate them with anything other than their eyes.

No other visitors roamed the aisles. The place was as quiet as a . . . museum. As I walked past the artwork, turning my head sideways at yet another confusing *Kama Sutra* drawing, the elevator doors opened and Billy Idol stepped out. Instead of jumping away from the welcome penis as I had, he stood there, admiring it for a moment, before turning his eyes on me.

I rushed directly toward him and stepped into the elevator, ignoring his probing eyes. Down to the first floor I went, past the edible condoms, the candy panties, the ointments, the unguents and the creams, out the door and into the welcome daylight of Joachimstaler Strasse, forgoing the once-in-a-lifetime opportunity to purchase my very own COPY DICK.

Hurrying across the busy street, one eye over my shoulder, the other on the row of idling German automobiles, I found myself walking past the Hotel Hardenburg. What an appropriate name for a hotel positioned directly across the street from the Beate Uhse Erotik Store & Museum. The Hardenburg. Inside one darkened chamber or another, inside closets and bathrooms and on trembling mattresses, I'm sure a number of Hardenburg guests have opened a box from which Tyrone leapt into action.

SNOBS 'R US

◀······················▶

I arrived looking like a pauper.

Having donated most of my clothing to a homeless shelter before departing Miami nearly one year earlier, I'd worn the same four pairs of pants across six continents. Of the T-shirts that survived the journey, most were frayed and faded. My Nikes looked like shredded tires. My socks had grown stiff enough to stand up and walk on their own. What better place than Rome to upgrade a wretched wardrobe? But here, in one of the world's most fashion-conscious capitals, an attractive appearance—or lack thereof—can make shopping a unique experience.

Beneath the handsome fifteenth-century Trinità dei Monti Church that towers above the Spanish Steps and Piazza di Spagna lies a grid of narrow streets. Each is lined with elegant shops that make up a virtual *Who's Who* of Italian clothing design: Giorgio Armani, Salvatore Ferragamo, Ermenegildo Zegna, Dolce & Gabbana, Versace, Fendi, Valentino, Missoni. Dozens of juxtaposed designer shops create a virtual high-fashion theme park, crammed with thousands of well-heeled shoppers.

Dressed in shabby jeans that had recently endured the back roads of India, Ethiopia, and Egypt, I stepped through the glistening glass doors at Salvatore Ferragamo and immediately felt out of place. A squadron of salesmen in dark, stylish suits whirled around and stared at me. Wearing gleaming leather footwear and expensive silk neckties, any one of them could have stepped from the pages of *Gentlemen's Quarterly*. In contrast, I looked as if I'd stepped out of the gutter.

Nevertheless, I had an urge—no—a *need* to shop. I also had, in my wallet, a zero-balance MasterCard with which to do my bidding. But when I saw a shirt I wanted and inquired about a dressing room, the salesman looked at me and raised an eyebrow.

"You want to buy?" he said, in a clipped Italian accent.

"Yes, but I'd like to try on the shirt first."

"You know your size, *sì*?"

"Yes," I said, smiling.

"Then you do not need to try."

In another life I sold men's designer clothing at Bigsby & Kruthers, which, before closing its doors a few years ago, reigned as one of Chicago's finest clothiers. I could therefore understand the salesman's reluctance to unpin an expensive, prefolded dress shirt. Especially for a customer whose appearance seemed inconsistent with the purchase price. But I was willing and able to buy. I tried to make the salesman aware of this fact.

"Look," I said, struggling to maintain a smile. "I really like the shirt. If it fits well, I'm prepared to purchase two or three in different colors."

With brisk, judgmental eyes, the salesman looked me up and down. "I am sorry," he said. "You cannot."

"You don't understand," I said. "I'm not paying *this* much money for a shirt unless I can try it on first."

"I am sorry."

More embarrassed than angry, I handed over the shirt and crept out of the store. Traveling alone for so long, with scant attention given to appearance, I had apparently fallen into a state of disrepair far worse than previously imagined.

During the somber walk back to my hotel, I took note of my surroundings. *Everyone* and *everything* looked good. The salespeople bustling behind the windows at Sisley. The teenagers sporting Guess jeans and wraparound Police sunglasses. The men in crisp white Ermenegildo Zegna shirts and tastefully wrinkled linen Armani slacks. The women strutting along fashionable Via Condotti, sheathed in Valentino dresses and brandishing Prada clutch bags. Giant billboards flaunted beautiful models wearing beautiful clothes in beautiful surroundings. With sleek aerodynamic wind fairings and sculpted seats, even the motor scooters looked sexy.

Alas, I was the odd man out. A walking fashion *faux pas*.

I sat at the magnificently sculpted Trevi Fountain, contemplating the coin toss that is supposed to ensure, or so the legend goes, a return trip to Rome. I wished, instead, for a return to the Australian Outback. In that part of the world, where nobody cares about fashion, Dolce & Gabbana might be confused with some newfangled dessert. Nevertheless, I benefited from advice given by St. Ambrose to St. Augustine nearly two thousand years ago. "When in Rome, live as the Romans do: when elsewhere, live as they live elsewhere."

I returned to my hotel room and regrouped. Donning my only pair of dress pants (made of sturdy black polyester) and the most presentable T-shirt in my repertoire, I headed for Emporio Armani. A salesman named Giuseppe took care of me. He eyed me momentarily, estimating size, build, perhaps purchasing power. With a gentleman's gesture he then led me to the pants rack. He pointed out a variety of styles. Discussed fit and fabric. Stood behind me holding jackets that he slipped onto my frame. Giuseppe had judged correctly. Just about everything I tried on fit perfectly. In the end, he sold me several pairs of pants, a couple of shirts, even a black suit that I could surely use when I returned home and rejoined the real world.

The next day I strutted down Via Condotti, dressed in Armani attire that made me feel human again. There was a bounce to my stride, a fresh feeling to go with a new look. When I strolled into the Salvatore Ferragamo shop and paused to regard the shirt I had originally wanted to try on a day earlier, the very same salesman rushed over to greet me.

"I'm sorry for the day before, *signore*," he said, recognizing me in spite of the new clothing—or perhaps because of it. "Many people were here. It was very busy." He then proffered the folded shirt. "Would you like to try it on, *signore*?"

Admiring the soft cotton fabric, the crisp weave and elegant stitching, I responded in the affirmative. "Why not?" I said. "I'm in Rome."

The salesman led me through a maze of stylish clothing displays and on to the fitting room. Along the way I grabbed two linen shirts, a crocodile-skin belt, an outrageously priced sport jacket, and a couple of fifty-dollar silk ties.

"Ahhh . . . you have good taste, *signore*." The salesman said this no matter which item I selected or how attractive it actually was.

The shirts fit perfectly. As did the jacket. When I stepped from the fitting room and knotted each tie in front of the mirror, the salesman stood behind me, massaging my ego, hoping to increase his commission in the process. "*Elegante*," he said, more than once. "The tie is made for you, *signore*."

I followed the salesman as he carried my selections to the cash register. A dapper cluster of colleagues parted as if I were royalty. The salesman began pulling the tags from the garments and passing them along to the cashier who prepared to ring me up.

I pulled out my credit card. Tapped it absently against the counter. "You know what," I said, flashing back to the humiliating experience of the previous day.

The salesman leaned over the counter. In the soft illumination from the recessed lighting, his jet-black hair looked as if it had been shellacked. "*Sì, signore?* You would like another tie. A pair of slacks, perhaps?"

Before turning to exit through the sparkling doors of Salvatore Ferragamo, I looked at the unwanted merchandise and then into the salesman's puzzled eyes. "On second thought," I said, "I prefer Armani."

HARD NIPPLES, LIMP DICKS

◀┄┄┄┄┄┄┄┄┄┄┄┄┄▶

After spending more than two months in the dusty recesses of Asia and Africa, my propensity for partying held respectfully in check by religious and cultural convention, I was thrilled to reach the debauched island playground that is Mykonos. Not that this tiny Greek enclave is without its own dusty recesses. Virtually no trees exist on the island. The landscape is arid, rocky, and devoid of grass. Even weeds have a difficult time finding a good place to root. But Mykonos had something I hadn't seen since Bali. Good beaches. More than thirty whitish strips of sand, each and every one lapped by cool Mediterranean waters into which I couldn't wait to plunge.

To get to Paradise Beach, the most popular strip of sand on the island, I rode a motor scooter from the whitewashed sprawl of Mykonos Town. I motored downhill, past whitewashed farmhouses and Greek Orthodox chapels that seemed barely larger than phone booths. The winding road, hedged on both sides by an ancient stone fence, led down the hillside and onto the beach.

When I had visited the island a few years earlier, Paradise was merely a strip of sand behind which hid a campsite where backpackers paid peanuts to sleep beneath the stars. Naked bodies sprawled on beach towels and unrolled mats. Crowds were kept to a minimum due to the lack of public transportation. If my memory serves me correctly, there were few if any food vendors, and the only entertainment was a dip in the sea.

But now things were different. Regularly scheduled public buses ran between Mykonos Town and Paradise. Thatch umbrellas sprouted like giant mutant mushrooms in a field of sand. The beach towels and mats had been replaced by rows of cushioned beach chairs. A Greek vendor walked among the rows, collecting from new arrivals and stuffing newly minted euros into a bulging fanny pack. The campsite was still here. Buried behind a couple of sprawling cafeteria-style restaurants where youthful Europeans munched on gyros and Greek salad. The most striking change, however, was the elaborate beach bar perched behind the sand. When I showed up early that afternoon, only a smattering of people sat on the bar stools. But later on, the place became a zoo.

Even with the banana boat operation and the jet skis, Paradise maintains a noncommercial air you won't find at similar beaches throughout the world. A few backpackers ignored the cushioned chairs and the umbrellas, choosing instead to lie on beach towels and bask in the sun. Topless women strolled along beside the sea. Gays reposed among the straight. Beautiful people from all over the world mingled among average Janes and Joes. Greeks sat up in their chairs, slathering sunblock into olive skin and talking at a volume that might make even Americans tone down a bit. The human smorgasbord sizzled beneath a bright white sun that hung in a cloudless blue sky.

As was the case back in Australia, I tried not to stare at topless women. But *trying* not to stare at a woman's naked breasts is like having someone mention purple elephants and then telling you not to think about purple elephants. It's impossible not to do. Especially when two well-endowed Italians happen to stroll along the beach wearing nothing but thong bikini bottoms. They stopped suddenly in front of my beach chair. Lost in the throes of conversation, the two women gesticulated with a ferocity that shook more than the foundations of propriety. Everyone stared. Even the nudists.

Yes, my periodic sidelong glances had revealed a number of buck-naked bodies on the right-hand side of Paradise. Every so often one of these brazen souls would rise from the sand, weave through tufts of reposed sunbathers—most of whom pretended not to look—and then wade in the water for a minute or two before taking the chilly plunge. Moments later they would come sashaying through the crowd, flaunting shaved vaginas and retracted dicks.

Herein lies the difference between male and female nudists. A naked woman emerges from the ice-cold Mediterranean, beads of water dripping from her supple body, nipples glistening and erect. A naked man surfaces from the same chilly waters and his penis becomes as shriveled and defeated as a dying earthworm. This fact will forever prevent me from parting with my swim trunks in public.

At exactly 5:00 P.M. the peace was broken when dance music blasted from the speakers at the Tropicana Bar. Backpackers rolled up their beach mats. The nudists reluctantly put on their clothes. I made my way to the bar with perhaps fifty or sixty revelers and was immediately offered a Kamikaze shot. Three Belgian party people, two guys and a girl, lifted their glasses my way. I nodded gratefully. Raised my glass. We drank. Oh how we drank. Kamikazes. Ouzo. Absolut and Red Bull. Each time I reached for my wallet, one of the Belgians said, "*Non!*"

Tropicana is much more than just a beach bar. It's a mininightclub. A sloping roof—beneath which hangs a track of disco lights—extends above the sand where twentysomethings danced with frenetic abandon. But the real action was on top of the bar. Several bikini-clad girls had climbed on and were moving in wicked, wicked ways. Ignoring my better judgment and encroaching middle age, I leapt from my stool and found myself dancing on the bar with a half-naked girl who was easily half my age.

Hip-hop music pumped viciously, hurling my dance partner toward me in a wicked, wicked way. She wore skimpy black shorts and a matching bikini top that was maybe three sizes too small. Through an Ouzo-Kamikaze haze I watched her remove the long red scarf from around her neck. She tossed it around *my* neck and reeled me in, licking her lips in tune to the music and the moment. I kicked over a napkin holder, a shaker of salt. But the bartender never noticed. He did notice when something much larger fell from the bar, however. Something big and brown-skinned and not quite sober enough to ride his motor scooter back to Mykonos Town.

BARCELONA II:
RETURN OF THE DRIFTER

Fifteen years earlier, back in the days of my first fledgling adventures, when my passport had only a few entry stamps to show for itself, when credit cards and good hotels were luxuries I had yet to experience, I landed at the airport in Barcelona and fell victim to the whim of Murphy's Law. As passengers transferred from the aircraft to the people mover, the gray sky opened and released torrential rains. Wet clothing and a touch of the Asian flu had me stumbling around the train station and onto the wrong train. Unable to speak the language, I rode the rails for hours on a zigzag adventure that ultimately led to Plaza Catalunya, where the hunt for accommodation produced dismal results. An international automobile show had apparently come to town. Every budget hotel room in the city center had been booked. And like I said, I was traveling without a credit card.

With only five dollars remaining in my wallet, and lacking the plastic that would rescue me from similar situations later in life, I dragged my weary butt along the convoluted back lanes of Las Ramblas, looking for a suitable dive in which to lay my head. One hotel clerk after another shook his head, delivering the bad news in Spanish. *"Lo siento, señor. No tengo una habitación."* The rain fell. The search continued. Soggy as a crouton in yesterday's soup, I walked into a decrepit establishment and secured what may have been the last remaining hotel room in Barcelona. It was Saturday afternoon. An old ceramic sink, its faucet dripping at full volume, jutted from a bare wall in my room. The drip, which may have started decades earlier, had eaten away at the white ceramic, leaving a rusted gouge as ugly as a canker sore. I closed the door and fell into a void at the center of a spongy mattress. In spite of the sneezing and the achy head and muscles, I planned to hit the town that night. But first, a nap was in order.

I woke up on Monday morning, almost forty hours later.

During my lengthy flu-ridden siesta, I experienced hot and cold flashes. Weird dreams. Spanish-speaking phantoms called my name, asking if I'd like to try *paella*. Worried that I'd contracted a tropical disease from a recent excursion into the jungles of Thailand, I reached into my bag and swallowed malaria pills that hadn't been consumed since Bangkok. Five limp U.S. dollars occupied a crease in my wallet. I needed cash. I carried an ATM card but had no money in my checking account.

The one smart thing I'd done before departing the States was to leave one thousand dollars in emergency cash with my good friend Cliff Rallins. Having learned a lesson from an Austrian debacle that had me sleeping in an abandoned kitchen, I asked Cliff to wire emergency funds should I find myself in trouble. I was now officially in trouble.

As you probably know by now, I do not speak Spanish. I asked the desk clerk where to find a Western Union office. Unable to understand his response, I stumbled through the narrow streets of Barcelona, craning my neck toward promising storefronts, staring into office windows that bore familiar-looking signs, approaching bewildered locals and asking, "*¿Donde está* Western Union?" I couldn't find the listing in the telephone book. Didn't know how to dial directory assistance and would not have understood the operator's response if someone had dialed the number for me. My fruitless mission led me to the unsmiling face of a clerk at the U.S. Consulate.

From behind a glass window, the clerk told me that Americans who needed emergency money were allowed to call friends or family members in the United States. That person would then wire funds to a Washington address. The wire would be forwarded to the consulate in Spain and collected the next day by the needy traveler.

As Murphy's Law would have it, I couldn't reach Cliff by phone. My mother, father, sister, brother, even two ex-girlfriends could not be reached. Remember, this was two decades earlier. Nobody had a cellular phone. The word "hyperlink" was jargon used only by computer nerds. The Internet was in its infancy. E-mail had yet to grab hold of the soon-to-be techno-savvy masses. All I could do was leave bleak messages on a series of antiquated answering machines. "Help. I'm stranded in Barcelona. Please call the following number when you get this message. I'm out of cash. Can't pay my hotel bill. This is not another joke. I repeat, not another joke."

My multisegment airline tickets had been purchased in advance from Qantas and Air France. The two remaining legs, Barcelona-Paris and Paris–New York, had open dates. From a booth in the hotel lobby, I called Air France to book a flight that afternoon. For some strange reason, the Air France agent said I needed to show up at the city ticket office and make the booking in person. When I showed up at the office near Plaza Catalunya, the agent hit me with bad news. According to her, my flight from Barcelona was scheduled to arrive at Paris Orly. The connecting flight to New York departed from Charles de Gaulle. There wasn't enough time for the connection between airports. I'd need to spend the night in Paris and catch a homebound flight the following day.

Five dollars—that's all I had. Five lousy dollars. Lonely Planet publishes a guidebook called *South America on a Shoestring*. I once heard of *Bali on a Budget*. But *Paris on Five Dollars a Day*? If anyone were silly enough to write such a book, it would be found on bookshelves between *Parisians: Europe's Friendliest Urbanites* and *The French Obsession with Deodorant*. With one swipe of my forearm, I wiped a rivulet of snot from my nose. Coughed into my fist. I blabbered on and on about my financial predicament, my illness, begged the airline representative to make an exception. She shrugged her shoulders; there was nothing she could do.

When all hope had been dashed, I felt a gentle tap on my shoulder. I swung around to meet the smiling face of a young American woman. Dressed in the vintage layers of a Beat-generation poet, she had been waiting patiently for her turn at the counter. Having heard the epic story of my dilemma, she offered a solution. "You can stay at my apartment in Paris if you like."

"Huh?"

"You can stay at my apartment in Paris if you like."

"Are you serious?"

"Sure," she said. "I'm flying to Paris on the same flight as you. We have a sofa you're welcome to sleep on."

I went mute. What do you say to someone who has snatched you from the jaws of despair? "Thank you" sounds woefully inadequate. This would prove to be the first in a serendipitous pattern that would bless my travel life. *You can stay at my apartment in Paris if you like.* Kinder words had never been spoken. Smiling, I waited for my saviour to complete her transaction.

But Murphy's Law was billing overtime. The American woman, an exchange student on holiday, had flown from Paris to Barcelona on a special "Twenty-five and under" one-way fare. Her passport revealed the fact that she was twenty-five years and some three hundred days old. The agent claimed that passengers needed to be *under* the age of twenty-five to qualify for the

"Twenty-five and under" discount. This made no sense. The literal translation of "Twenty-five and under" is anyone up to and including the age of twenty-five. A twenty-five-year-old remains in that age bracket until the day he or she turns twenty-six.

An argument broke out. The American woman claimed that if the airline office in France had issued the discount based on the fact that she was not yet twenty-six, the airline office in Spain was obligated to do the same. The agent disagreed. As is often the case when airline policy is involved—even when it's applied incorrectly—the American woman lost the battle.

"I'm sorry," she said, turning to me after snatching her documents from the counter. "I don't have enough money for the airline ticket. I'll have to take the train." I wasn't sure which one of us was worse off. The blonde, for having to take a twelve-hour train ride to Paris. Or me, for having to sleep at Orly Airport with no money for food. I thanked her profusely and kissed her on the cheek. Then I hobbled back to the hotel and braced myself for the drama that was about to unfold.

With a lump in my throat, I presented myself to the desk clerk and told the whole pathetic story. It came out like Catholic confession: I stood on one side of the glass window, unable to look the desk clerk in the eye. He listened as I whined about the soggy search for a hotel room, the flu, Western Union, the U.S. Consulate, Air France. At the end, I cleared my throat. Told him I had no credit cards. Told him how much money I had in my wallet. He responded in a manner quite unlike a Catholic priest would. He yelled so loudly and so viciously that for one alarming moment the swelling vein in his neck seemed ready to explode.

"Please," I said. "I'll leave you my camera. It's all I've got." Begrudgingly, he accepted. I collected my belongings from the room, turned over my 35mm Minolta to the clerk, and asked for directions to the nearest metro station.

Alas, Señor Murphy's Law delivered a decisive blow. In broken English the clerk told me that a general strike had been called.

City trains and buses were not running today. A twenty-dollar cab ride was the only way to reach the airport. I had five dollars. Five frigging dollars. For the first time in my adult life, I almost cried in public.

Hoping to halt my emotional breakdown, or at least delay it until I left the premises, the desk clerk thrust one hand in his pocket, and pulled out twenty dollars' worth of pesetas. "I promise to mail it back to you," I said. But he shook his head defiantly and motioned for me to leave.

The cab ride to the airport depleted every peseta the desk clerk had given me. After checking my bag at the Air France ticket counter, I spent all five dollars on a Wendy's hamburger, Coke, and fries. Still, the hunger would not go away. What would I do when my plane arrived in Paris? How would I get from Orly Airport to Charles de Gaulle? When and if I got there, would I be allowed to sleep on the floor? Would I end up cruising the International Terminal, begging strangers for money? Would Tad and Buffy turn a new leaf and find happiness in Port Charles?

Above the clatter of voices in the departure lounge, above the public address announcements, the footsteps and my growling stomach, someone shouted what sounded like my name. Knowing I'd heard wrong, I nevertheless glanced over my shoulder at the flood of humanity rushing across the terminal floor. Then it came again. My given name. Three distinct syllables, crisp, clear, launched from what had to have been an American tongue. I spun around. Saw a gesture from the corner of my eye. A glimpse of a familiar face. The face grew closer. A wave. A smile. That's when the bright light of recognition began to flash. Miracle of miracles, it was the American woman from the Air France office. She smiled again and told me *her* story. After the Air France office, she found a travel agent who sold her the appropriate "Twenty-five and under" airline ticket.

Together, we boarded the flight to Paris. Upon landing, we took a series of buses to the apartment she shared with two other women. One roommate happened to be out of town. The other was a correspondent for *U.S. News & World Report*. The three of us sat down to great conversation and a delicious homemade meal. Pasta, if my memory serves me well. After dinner, I was directed to the unoccupied bedroom and drifted off to sleep.

The next morning, my good Samaritan gave me a few French coins, wrote down directions to the Paris Métro, and sent me on my merry way. I followed her directions to the airport and flew home.

Home. A four-letter word with a nice ring to it. Fifteen years after that first disastrous arrival, here I was at the Barcelona airport once again, having cleared immigration and customs, ready to see the city with a fresh pair of eyes and a slightly more agreeable budget, and yet all I could think about was home.

I'd been on the road for a year. More than a year, in fact. I had grown tired of clearing immigration and customs. Tired of jumping into a cab or onto a bus and heading to another hotel. Tired of schlepping my duffel into another nondescript room. Tired of sleeping in a bed that was not mine, communicating with my hands, familiarizing myself with a city map, finding a favorite place to eat alone. I had become tired of making new friends and then leaving them. And yet when I stepped outside customs at the Barcelona airport and saw a familiar face bobbing in a sea of strangers, the fatigue suddenly melted away.

Happy, smiling, and many months pregnant, my one and only sister, Dordie, was here to greet me. It was strange to see her bursting with life, this woman who was once the girl who trailed behind me on the way home from school because I had deemed it uncool to walk neck-and-neck with a younger sibling.

Dordie and I embraced awkwardly, and not just because of her protruding belly. Despite showing up for all the important events during the thirteen years she's lived here (her thirtieth birthday party; the opening of her tiny restaurant; her marriage to David Alcalde, a Catalan veterinarian; and now, the birth of her first child), we hadn't spent much quality time together. With Dordie living in an adopted European country and me flying the friendly skies above the other side of the pond, my sister and I had become intimate strangers, connected only by blood and the telephone. I had no idea what her day-to-day life was like. No real understanding of the person she had become. During the drive to my prearranged apartment in the city, I found out.

"The neighbors are driving me *crazy!*"

I sat in the passenger seat of the Dodge minivan (a Dodge minivan in Spain?), listening to the details of her life.

"What's wrong with your neighbors?" I asked. And then it came. The whole ugly mess of it. The horror. The disbelief.

"It's the noise. The noise is driving me crazy. We moved to Santa Perpetua to get away from the noise of Barcelona, to get some space without having to pay three hundred thousand euros for a tiny flat in a dumpy neighborhood far from the city center. We moved out there to get away from the expense and the noise and all we get is more noise."

"What kind of noise?"

"Mainly, it's the children. I told you we live in a town house community, right? Well, the neighborhood kids, they run up and down the sidewalk in front of our bedroom window until two o'clock in the morning. Screaming. Throwing rocks at the lampposts. I can't sleep. The noise is driving me *crazy!*"

I stared at her swollen belly and wrinkled my brow, knowing she'd catch the drift.

"Oh no, no, no, no," she said, moving her index finger like a windshield wiper as so many Latins seem to do. "*My* child is not going to be running around outside at two o'clock in the morning. That's what I don't understand. Why do their parents let them stay out so late, even on school nights? Because I've complained so much, half the neighbors think I'm a witch."

My sister, the soon-to-be mother and reinvented Spanish witch, drove me to a six-story apartment building that would be my new home for a while. El Born, according to Dordie, had become Barcelona's newest gentrified neighborhood, a three-hundred-year-old *barrio* teeming with new restaurants, bars, and trendy shops. She figured I would like it here. With one major exception, she turned out to be right.

I collected the keys from the apartment manager, kissed my sister good-bye (I would rest a few days before taking the train to the suburbs and dining with her and David), and dragged my huge duffel into a tiny elevator that could barely accommodate the both of us.

I stepped into the studio apartment and immediately felt at home. The six-story edifice, a smaller version of New York's Flat Iron Building, was shaped like a triangle, and so was the tiny apartment. It boasted exposed brick walls. A small, renovated kitchen area. Old wooden beams traversed the low ceiling. It was comfy and cozy and temporarily mine. The glass dining table, wicker chairs, lamps, even the stainless-steel cutlery had been provided by one of two thriving IKEA stores on the outskirts of Barcelona.

I grabbed the remote, turned on the TV, and flopped on the bed. The exact same bed owned by hundreds of thousands of IKEA lovers the world over. But I didn't mind one bit. Watching the international news, most of which I could barely understand, I saw a report the gist of which I managed to get. Through the garble of Castellano I learned that noise levels had been recorded across the globe. Ambient sound had been factored and compared. Trailing only slightly behind Japan in terms of decibel output, Spain was officially the second noisiest country in the world. After that first sleepless night in my cozy apartment in El Born, I concurred with the report.

By day, Carrier Rec, the narrow street upon which I lived, enjoyed only a trickle of traffic. By night, however, the street hissed and clanged like an automobile factory during peak production.

Later that night I was roused from sleep by the hydraulic hiss of a garbage truck. I leapt from an IKEA dream, peering through the window, watching as the truck consumed its load directly in front of my building. As is the case in New York, a city without alleys, trash is left in Dumpsters and plastic bags on city sidewalks. Unlike New York, however, where garbage collection begins at the crack of dawn, the garbage truck in Barcelona rolled by my place shortly before midnight.

I crawled back in bed, drifted off once more, and was snatched from slumbering bliss by the squeal of more high-powered hydraulics. The second truck roared to a halt near the spot vacated by its predecessor. It was half past midnight. A time for sleep, or hard-core partying. Not a time for a hydraulic truck to pick up a load of discarded bottles. A huge plastic Dumpster—into which bottles are tossed by conscientious neighbors at all hours of the day and night—was hoisted high into the air, releasing a payload of beer and wine bottles, soda and mineral water bottles, olive oil bottles, bottles of every shape, every size, every level of thickness and fragility.

The explosion that followed was not unlike the sound of ten pins being struck by a bowling ball. A bowling ball hurled at top speed by an angry Arnold Schwarzenegger. Only worse. Like every other narrow street in El Born, Carrier Rec is lined shoulder-to-shoulder with six-story buildings. The three-hundred-year-old walls of stone face one another from across the narrow pass, creating an echo canyon that magnifies even the most minimal sound. The detonation of breaking bottles actually shook my apartment. Splinters of sound lodged in my head. My brain hemorrhaging, I lay awake, staring at the attractive beamed ceiling, a prisoner to the same urban cacophony that had driven my sister to the Barcelona suburbs. The noise was driving me *crazy*!

The corner of my building had been designated—officially or not—as the drop-off point for discarded items too large for the Dumpsters: broken microwave ovens; busted chairs; old lamps;

sofas; wooden planks—any and every type of oversized refuge you can imagine. After the first two garbage trucks had come and gone, a third truck appeared. Mercifully, this one had no squealing hydraulics. It was a simple flatbed truck from which three spry workers jumped. Nevertheless, heavy wooden planks were tossed angrily into the back of the truck. A chest of drawers crashed suddenly, as if dropped from a fifteen-story window. Glass shattered. Metal clanged. During the process, the three men shouted at one another, hurling directions, bitching about their wives, reliving last night's soccer game perhaps. Their voices echoed maddeningly at two o'clock in the morning, as did the irrepressible racket delivered by their heavy hands.

The next day, I went shopping. Not for clothing or toiletries or food with which to stock the mini-fridge. I went shopping for *tipones* (earplugs). After visiting several well-stocked *farmacías* in the neighborhood, I returned to the apartment with silicone *tipones*, wax *tipones*, two boxes of *tipones* made of sound-resistant foam. When I woke the following morning from an uninterrupted sleep, when sunlight burst through the windows of all four French doors, I stepped out onto the balcony and inhaled the crisp September air of Barcelona.

Gazing at the gauntlet of eighteenth-century buildings that make up Carrier Rec, at the damp clothing hanging like banners from the terraces, the blossomed trees, the patch of blue sky, the man pushing a trolley stacked with orange propane canisters, the motorbike sputtering past him, the elderly couple moving along the narrowest of sidewalks, and the serendipitous pile of dog shit poised to turn their leisurely stroll into an urban adventure, looking at this, vaguely aware of a rising epiphany that suddenly burst into full view, I realized, looking down at *all* this, looking within and not without, that Barcelona was indeed a beautiful place to be.

Epilogue

There's No Place Like Home,
There's No Place Like Home*?*

◄·······················►

It's my first night home in the United States after traveling the world for more than a year. Having long ago given up my Miami Beach apartment, I find myself holed up in a Miami Beach hotel room, eating a double Quarter Pounder with cheese and watching television. The Channel 7 Eyewitness News Team brings me up to speed on all the action I've been missing. Murder. Armed robberies. Drive-by shootings. Health scares. "A deadly disease could be lurking in the classroom . . . is *your* child at risk?"

I've just visited more than fifty destinations in twenty countries and experienced my fair share of mishaps. But after watching thirty minutes of televised pandemonium masquerading as the local news, I feel the first urgent pangs of real danger. Lock the door. Switch on the burglar alarm. Carry a canister of pepper spray on a key chain. Buy a GLOCK 9mm semiautomatic handgun with the "semi–double action" trigger system. It's enough to make me spit out my Happy Meal and *scream!*

At some point during the previous year, while drinking ouzo with Oui Oui in the Australian Outback, gazing at the Taj Mahal, dancing salsa with a Russian girl on an Estonian beach, going "Hollywood" in the Czech Republic, or falling in love with *fútbol* in Argentina—somewhere along the way I was bitten by the travel bug. Not your garden variety travel bug, mind you. Mine was a huge, nefarious, venom-squirting creature that opened its maw and sank fangs the size of elephant tusks into my flesh. My blood is now contaminated. My brain rewired. I'm Dr. Jekyll after that ill-fated sip. Jeff Goldblum in the remake of *The Fly.* Every impulse, every breath, every thought born of a yearning I can neither understand nor hope to control. Instead of turning into a man-sized insect or the homicidal Mr. Hyde, however, I've morphed into a hard-core travel freak.

And yet I sit here, motionless, in a Miami Beach hotel room, staring at the flickering images on a muted television, preparing to rejoin the Real World, wondering if Neo would have been better off if he never unplugged from the Matrix.

An eerie, prophetic voice—a voice frighteningly reminiscent of Dickens's Ghost of Christmas Future—whispers in my ear, previewing a life of consumption and dread:

You're plugged into the Matrix again. Putting on that polyester flight attendant uniform. Happy to earn a paycheck by serving chicken and beef in the not-so-friendly skies. You needed to buy that little black Mazda—even though it set you back five hundred dollars per month for the next five years. You needed that overpriced condo, which you "bought" but will never actually own. You needed high-end furniture, DIRECTV, a new Yamaha RX-V741 digital stereo system to replace the RX-V740 you sold a year ago. So you whipped out those credit cards. Bought a new desktop computer with 768 megabytes of D-RAM and a 120-gigabyte hard drive. Then you logged on to an online dating service, found a compatible mate, and waltzed her straight to the virtual altar. Three years and two rug rats later, you are floundering beneath the sheets, betrothed in lame, ninety-second, Tired Mommy sex that lulls you into a depression that neither therapy nor Xanax can yank you out of. You're eating breakfast at McDonald's. Dinner at KFC. You're gaining weight. Losing confidence. You've joined Jenny Craig, the Catholic Church, switched to the Republican Party. You listen to Tony

Robbins motivational tapes and read books by Dr. Phil. You've stopped drinking, stopped traveling outside the United States, stopped taking your devoted wife for granted. And yet, ever since you took her on that spiritual retreat with the Johnsons, your wife has been sneaking behind your back and fucking both of them. That's right. Tired Mommy somehow found the energy to do threesomes with your best friend and his evangelical wife. They even videotaped the sessions on mini-DVDs and made a bundle selling copies on the Internet. At home with you, inside the sanctity of the matrimonial bedroom, your wife is as passionate as an inflatable doll with a slow leak. But for $29.95 per month, or $4.95 for a three-day limited trial offer, you can watch your lovely spouse get her freak on at www.ScrewMyBrainsOut.com. Divorce? Ha, ha, ha, ha . . . Go ahead, my friend. You've got two kids, a mortgage, a low-paying job, and a mountain of credit card debt. And let's not forget, even though your savings account is depleted and your condo devalued, even though you were penalized for cashing in early on your 401-k, even though your second mortgage is as disastrous as your first marriage, and the closest thing to sex is when you bend over and let the Cablevision Guy or the MetLife Health Care Representative or your friendly Geico Insurance Agent shove another rate hike up your unbuttered butt, your ex-wife will take half of everything!

Nooooooooooooooooooooooooooooooooooooooooooooooooooooooooo oooooooooooo

"Stay single, stay liquid, keep traveling for as long as you can. Stay single, stay liquid, keep traveling for as long as you can." Eyes shut, chest heaving in the aftermath of paralytic horror, I steady my right hand on my bible: *The Lonely Planet Guide to Wherever the Fuck.* The words come as urgently as lyrics to a Lenny Kravitz song. "Stay single, stay liquid, keep traveling for as long as you can. Stay single, stay liquid, keep traveling for as long as you can." It's my new constitution, a mantra that will deliver me from evil—or at least from the clutches of one possible future—and to the sugar-white beaches of the Seychelles, the

Maldives, or maybe the mountains near Marrakech. "Stay single, stay liquid, keep traveling for as long as you can."

Ahhhhhh . . . I feel better already.

With one click of the remote, the Channel 7 Eyewitness News Team is disbanded. That ghostly Dickensian voice is no longer whispering in my ear. I am standing in front of a full-length mirror, wearing a T-shirt, jeans, and a pair of dirty Nikes that bear the warp and whiff of fifty thousand global miles. I close my eyes. Begin the chant. Click my heels together three times just like Dorothy in *The Wizard of Oz*. Except that Dorothy wasn't wearing Nikes. And instead of repeating, "There's no place like Oz, there's no place like Oz," as *I* would have, given the chance for a once-in-a-lifetime Yellow Brick Road adventure, she scooped up precious Toto—America's first designer doggie—and started bitching to the Wizard about wanting to go home.

"Stay single, stay liquid, keep traveling for as long as you can. Stay single, stay liquid, keep traveling for as long as you can." I open my eyes and am no longer in the hotel room, no longer in Miami Beach, in fact. I am lying instead on a pristine stretch of pure white sand. (The sand in Miami Beach is actually dove-gray and was hauled in during the late 1970s by the Army Corps of Engineers, dumped on the eroded shoreline, and packed by heavy equipment, which is why today's manufactured beachfront is as hard as concrete in some places and not a single shrub or palm tree has managed to take root.)

Here in the Seychelles the beach is magical. The indigenous sand is unbelievably soft, the granules pulverized to the fine, white, powdery disposition of confectioner's sugar. This particular strip of white sand on this particular island—one of more than one hundred tropical islands that make up the Seychelles Islands group—curls around the base of a lush green hillside and looks out to the azure Indian Ocean, toward Madagascar, and beyond to the African continent. Palm trees shoot from the sand at dizzying angles. The surf nudges rhythmically against the shore.

I reposition myself on the beach chaise. Take one final sip of another fu-fu la-la cocktail. Then reach down and choose from among a half-dozen guidebooks stuffed in my trusty knapsack. The Maldives. According to the map, the Maldivian archipelago is about fourteen hundred miles away, halfway between here and Sri Lanka. Same ocean, different waves. Apparently, the Maldivians speak Divehi, an Indo-European language similar to Sinhalese. Hmmm. . . . What in the world does Divehi sound like? In which country might you meet up with someone who speaks Sinhalese?

Dreamer, runaway, irresponsible fool—an escape artist of the most deviant persuasion—I pack my duffel, jump into a cab, and head toward Seychelles International Airport. Along the way, I stick my head out the window and let the warm air tickle my smiling face. My passport is tingling in my pocket. The time zones conspire to collapse. Blue skies guarantee a smooth departure, or at the very least a picturesque ascent. As the cab pulls up to the terminal, I feel that familiar quickening of my pulse, the weakening in my knees. Inside my head there's a sudden burst of music—a soundtrack to a way of life so exhilarating, so open to place and possibility, I have to pinch myself to make sure I'm not dreaming. I feel the twinge. Hear the music. Can't stop whistling as I stride to the check-in counter because a big, beautiful, bodacious Boeing is waiting on the tarmac, revving her Pratt & Whitney engines, ready and oh-so-willing to take me for another ride.

Who knows where I'll end up next, or what urge will lead me there? I'm not qualified to answer unimportant questions. Suffice it to say, I'm a continental drifter. A lover of leaving. A nomad with an e-mail address.

AUTHOR'S BIOGRAPHY

Bestselling author Elliott Hester is an award-winning travel writer and former *Salon.com* columnist. His syndicated travel column, "Continental Drifter," appears in more than fifty U.S. newspapers. Elliott owns no furniture and has no permanent address. He travels continually from one foreign destination to the next, writing his column and toting his worldly belongings in a rolling duffel bag.

Follow Elliott's journey at www.elliotthester.com.